D0618671

VALOR'S
MEASURE

BASED ON THE HEROIC CIVIL WAR
CAREER OF JOSHUA L. CHAMBERLAIN

THOMAS WADE OLIVER

Second Edition
Copyright © 2013 Thomas Wade Oliver
All rights reserved.

ISBN: 0615878385
ISBN 13: 9780615878386

Library of Congress Control Number: 2013949334
Substance Press
Los Angeles, CA

BOOKS BY
THOMAS WADE OLIVER

Of Guardians and Angels

To Watch the River

Best Story

"True greatness is not in nor of the single self; it is of that larger personality, that shared and sharing life with others, in which, each giving of his best for their betterment, we are greater than ourselves; and self-surrender for the sake of that greater belonging, is the true nobility."

Joshua Lawrence Chamberlain February 12, 1909

"In great deeds something abides. On great fields something stays. Forms change and pass; bodies disappear; but spirits linger to consecrate the ground for the vision-place of souls."

Joshua Lawrence Chamberlain 1889

ACKNOWLEDGMENTS

I would first like to bestow my gratitude to Willard Wallace, John Pullen, and Alice Trulock for their excellent biographies of Joshua Lawrence Chamberlain. Without their exhaustive research, I would have never been able to bring real truth to this story.

To the various citizens of Bangor, Brewer, and Brunswick, Maine, who displayed such gracious hospitality and kindness during my visits there, I also give you my thanks.

Special recognition goes to the men and woman of the U.S. National Park Service, specifically those who are assigned to the Civil War battlefields of Pennsylvania, Maryland, and Virginia. Your dedication and impressive wealth of knowledge was not only an asset to me, but continues to be a great asset to this country.

And finally, to all those individuals I have spoken to during the course of my research for this book, who either gave me valuable information or pointed me in the right direction, I sincerely offer my thanks. From the Chamberlain House Museum staff {Pejepscot Historical Society}, to my oldest brother, U.S. Army (retired) Lt. Col. Bryan L. Oliver, U.S.M.A. 1974, you will never know how much I appreciate the time and energy you gave me.

INTRODUCTION

The American Civil War is one of the most fascinating periods of our nation's history. Few can realistically imagine how so great a number of Americans could turn on each other with such violent result. The story of the Great Rebellion is so multi-faceted we continue to have piles of literature written about it even today. Fortunately for those seeking the truth, much of the new works have done a great deal toward dispelling the clouded history of the war we were taught from classroom text books when we were children. It is difficult to fathom how such a monumental event in our history could have become so distorted in such a relatively short period of time, the greatest culprit being our public school system.

In grammar school for instance, I remember being taught that the war was simply about slavery. We were even led to believe nearly every Southerner owned slaves when, in fact, only about six percent actually did. In middle school, the slavery issue was reinforced and Abraham Lincoln and the rest of the Union Army were glorified as the saviors of the black man. This may have been so in the eyes of slaves during the 1860's, but freeing them was far from the highest priority of most white Northerners. The fact is; Lincoln didn't formally introduce the idea of freeing slaves until the war was well into its second year, and then, arguably, only did it to keep Europe from siding with the South. The House of Representatives waited even longer, not having passed the 13th Amendment abolishing slavery until January of 1865.

In high school, we started writing book reports and essays on prominent figures in the war. I look back on it now and recall that Robert E. Lee was about the only Confederate leader who wasn't completely demonized. And by the conclusion of my public school education, I had been brainwashed into believing your average Rebel soldier was a white-hooded racist. Remember those William Quantrill stories? If you were raised in Kansas as I was, your example of the Confederate-style of waging war was the infamous raids on defenseless towns like Lawrence, where the Rebels shot everything that moved in the back. There was never any mention of Union soldier atrocities, but that made sense when you considered the entire army consisted of noble abolitionists fighting a war over civil rights. I was also convinced that the war was a fair fight between two evenly numbered and supplied armies, and the North had won because they were the good guys- God was even on their side. The bottom line is that, in my generation and I suppose yours too, the only way we got the truth about the war was to study it on the college level, or have a personal interest in the subject and we studied it on our own.

I grew up in an Army officer's home, and visiting historic battlefields took precedent over amusement parks during summer vacations. I'm not complaining. On the contrary, I wish I would have paid more attention. Of the many things I'm thankful to my father for, one is the profound sense of respect he taught me to have for those who offer their lives to defend this country and its ideals. With that in mind, it should be easy to see why I might find the Civil War era so intriguing.

As a young man I began filling my bookshelves with Civil War novels. I slowly learned the truth about the cause and effect of the war, and discovered some particularly interesting characters along the way. One of those characters was Joshua Lawrence Chamberlain.

Prior to our generation, Chamberlain's heroics were hardly mentioned in anything other than accounts of his deeds during the Battle of Gettysburg in early July of 1863. And when it was mentioned, his name was commonly no more than a blurb during the description of the dramatic performance of his regiment, the 20th Maine, while defending the southern flank of the Union Army. As I write this, he's still not included in the Harper Encyclopedia of Military Biography, and continues to be rarely mentioned in any public school text. During my research for this book, I even discovered his name was misspelled in the Library of Congress's book of Medal of Honor winners.

A movie about the Battle of Gettysburg was released by Turner Pictures in 1986, and Chamberlain's famous bayonet charge at Little Round Top was finally brought to life. Suddenly interest in his story skyrocketed, and thirty-year-old biographies about him were republished to meet the demand. Some good folks up in Brunswick, Maine, even purchased Chamberlain's old neglected house in 1994, and turned it into a nice museum in his honor. Check it out- it's worth the drive.

I think my initial attraction to Chamberlain came in the fact that, though he was extremely well-educated, he was hardly a man you would think had the potential to become a war hero. Born in 1828 and growing up in the tiny rural town of Brewer, Maine, Chamberlain was a farm boy who had an exceptional ability to retain information. When he got older he used that ability to master foreign languages, and over-achieved in just about every academic subject that was taught to him.

I wouldn't go so far as to say he was a genius, but compared to our day and age, his exceptional wealth of knowledge would certainly be considered rare. By the time young Chamberlain was twenty-six, he spoke 8 different tongues, had bachelor's and master's degrees from Bowdoin College, and another degree from the Bangor School of Theology.

His initial ambitions to become a Christian missionary changed when he married and started a family. Instead of doing God's work abroad, he accepted a teaching position at his original alma mater, Bowdoin College, and within a year was given a professorship. There, he languished for several more years until the war began.

By 1861, Chamberlain had grown tired of his job, but there are no real accounts of what alternatives he might have had in mind. What is certain is that he was very concerned about the direction of the war. He was particularly troubled when it eventually became clear that the South was not going to lie down and die as most of the North originally expected.

Chamberlain decided that, as an American male, it was his responsibility to join the fight to save the Union. He had no military skills, lived in the northern most state of the Union, which was hardly threatened by the possibility of invasion by the Confederates, and had two young children at home with a wife who was battling depression. As for his career, joining the Army as a volunteer would mean a dramatic cut in his salary, and the possibility that his job would not be there for him when he returned from battle was very real. Still, his patriotic duty to defend the sanctity of the Constitution was his priority. Against everyone's wishes, Chamberlain joined a new volunteer regiment and was commissioned as a lieutenant colonel. What followed became three years of legendary deeds of heroism and fantastic examples of leadership even the greatest storytellers find hard to believe.

My personal interest in Chamberlain's story is not only bred from his gallant actions in battle. He was also one of the few Union officers present in nearly every major conflict after the summer of 1862. Add to that fact that he was twice thought to have received fatal wounds, had his horse shot out from under him on six different occasions, and once nearly died of malaria and pneumonia, and you have quite a story. To top off the tale is the perfect ending; Chamberlain's most gracious gesture of calling his men to a marching salute as the defeated Confederate Army of Northern Virginia surrendered to him at Appomattox Court House.

My intentions in writing this book are to somehow bring Joshua Lawrence Chamberlain back to life. Several excellent biographies covering his military and political career have been published, and they all basically offer the same accounts of his past. But I personally found something missing in those pages. I wanted to explore his motivations, experience his train of thought, and feel the things he must have felt as he faced such trying times and grew into one of this country's most respected military generals.

Unfortunately, those who write autobiographical material are limited by the parameters of fact and speculation. I concluded that the best way to transform Chamberlain back into a real man we can all relate to, was to challenge those barriers and insert some humanity back into his story. After all, that is what is most remarkable about Chamberlain- his fundamental belief in the strength of the human spirit.

This story of Joshua Lawrence Chamberlain is fact-based, yet a fictional story of his life during the Civil War. I spent several years researching every printed word I could find about Chamberlain, and I quickly discovered there is now a lot of it! Once I believed I had a grasp of his character, I set off to see what his eyes actually saw, including walking the Pennsylvania, Maryland, and Virginia battlefields where he fought, and going so far as to sit in the church pew he shared with his family in Brunswick, Maine. Not until I finally stood on the dusty Richmond-Lynchburg Road at Appomattox Court House, and could clearly sense the spirit of Chamberlain there, did I feel I was prepared to write a single word.

What you will find in these pages are accounts of amazing incidents of tactical genius, bravery, and perseverance that are absolutely true. You will read of Chamberlain's compassion toward his men as well as the enemy, which is also documented fact. The only portions of this book that are fictional, are brief conversations and incidents that I use to reinforce the idea of the kind of man I believe Chamberlain really was, again, based on historic accounts of his real life.

I hope this story captures your imagination whether you enjoy Civil War history or not. And I hope it leaves you with the idea that the greatness of this American hero is worth remembering and talking about. If it does, I also hope it encourages you to change your ideas of the types of people we look up to as role models today. All too often we elevate the likes of professional athletes, entertainers, and millionaire businessmen to idol status, when we have such great patriots in our history who are so much more deserving. With that in mind, I give you the story of my personal favorite hero, Joshua Lawrence Chamberlain- truly, Valor's Measure.

CORPS

APPROXIMATELY 45,000 MEN DIVIDED INTO 3 DIVISIONS

1ST	2ND	3RD
# DIVISION	# DIVISION	# DIVISION
3 BRIGADES	3 BRIGADES	3 BRIGADES
1 ARTILLERY	1 ARTILLERY	1 ARTILLERY

BRIGADE

APPROXIMATELY 5000 MEN DIVIDED INTO 5 REGIMENTS

REGIMENT

CONSISTING OF 5 BATTALIONS

BATTALION

2 COMPANIES

* The composition and strength of these units varied greatly throughout the war as casualties mounted and realignment became necessary to meet particular battle plans.

CHAPTER 1

ANSWERING THE CALL

The day was perfect. A soft spring breeze gently lifted the hair from the young man's brow as he stared into the valley before him. At the bottom of the aspen and pine covered slopes, the Penobscot River wandered steadily southbound to join the Atlantic Ocean less than a day's ride away. Across the river from the tiny town of Brewer, Maine, stood the tall square brick buildings of Bangor, each erected uniformly with the other businesses along the main streets of the booming ship and lumber town. But the young college professor was oblivious to the living portrait he was gazing into. This was the backyard of the home where he had been raised and he'd long ago grown accustomed to the scenic vision. Instead of basking in the newness of the season, he struggled with the thoughts in his head. And he only had a few moments to assemble those thoughts into perfect words. For they would have to be perfect to finally convince his father of his absolute confidence in the endeavor he was about to pursue.

The slamming of a porch door behind him roused thirty-one-year-old Joshua Lawrence Chamberlain from his daydream. His father,

1

and namesake, stepped confidently out of his white two-story farmhouse and paused momentarily on the small wood platform to adjust his britches around his full belly. He then stepped down onto the grass and headed toward his son, who was seated on an old bench the two had made together almost twenty years before. As the elder Joshua Chamberlain grew nearer, his first son, called Lawrence to avoid the confusion of two family members with the same first name, moved to the far right of the bench to make room for his father. Lawrence acknowledged his father when he sat down next to him but didn't speak. He preferred to continue silently gathering his thoughts, paying little attention to the greenish-brown river flowing lazily in the distance toward the New England coast.

Lawrence had called his father to the yard for a private conversation. Out of respect for his adult son, Joshua elected to wait patiently for him to speak first. It wasn't as if he didn't know what was coming. The subject had already dominated the family's late afternoon meal that had just concluded a few minutes earlier.

Lawrence expected his mother's negative reaction to his news, but not the lack of support on his father's behalf. Now he found himself preparing for a debate in which he was not prepared. Even with the list of notable American patriot's names he'd recited during supper who supported his position, Lawrence was still unable to sway his father's view. The only thing left to do was privately plea to his father that it was not only his duty as an American, but also his faith in God that required he join the war. The men continued to sit and imagine each other's thoughts.

The senior Joshua Chamberlain had a great deal of respect for his oldest child. His academic accomplishments and reputable standing in the community had brought nothing but honor to the family. That sense of pride in his son made it that much more difficult to know he was disappointing him. But it was for the best, and his son making this decision poorly could be the greatest error of his life.

Joshua noticed the beads of sweat forming on his son's brow. As each moment passed, he watched as confusion and disappointment grew to anger in his son's face. This didn't need to be a fight, but it would be if Lawrence was given any more time to build the frustration inside him. It was time to get the inevitable confrontation over with. "I disagree with mother," Joshua said as he again adjusted the waistband of his trousers.

Lawrence felt the churning in his nervous stomach suddenly ease. His father had come to his senses and, as was originally expected, was about to give him his blessing. He was himself a retired military man. How could he not?

"I think the mustache is right gentlemanly," his father continued.

Lawrence turned slowly and smiled. It was far from the topic he wanted to address, but the wisdom in the humor was appreciated. Earlier during supper, Lawrence's wife, Fanny, and her mother-in-law, the senior Mrs. Chamberlain, had made very clear their dislike of the new thick patch of hair draped over Lawrence's upper lip.

"I would gladly trade your support for my new appearance, Father, for your understanding in my wanting to join this fight," Lawrence replied.

Joshua leaned back and draped his right arm over the top of the bench. "Son, this is not our war," he said. "Hell, those folks down there are killing for reasons *they* don't even understand."

"It's about maintaining the Union," Lawrence answered firmly.

"It's about politics and egos," his father countered. "Remember, I voted for Lincoln. Thought he'd be the one to put this country back on the path we've strayed from. It wasn't his doing that the Confederacy seceded. They started that before the man was even sworn in. But Lawrence, you cannot tell a man he is free and then march on his home when he decides to act on that freedom. If the South wants to throw a fit like a child because they don't like what our government is asking of them, then I say let them go and do it. Let those spoiled brats run away and spend a few nights in the woods alone. They'll come back. And when they do they'll be humbled, and they'll appreciate and understand the good things they had before they left.

"I frankly don't agree with the President on this," Joshua continued. "I have yet to hear one single word that makes reason out of sending Federal troops and state militia into the South to beat those people into submission. The only result of this great debacle, if we can even win this war, is that we will have lost thousands of Americans over nothing more than a temper tantrum. And the Virginians, Carolinians, and all the rest of them will only hate us that much more when this thing is done."

Lawrence thought carefully for a moment, assembling his rebuttal in an articulate script. It was a method he had taught himself to help overcome the anxiety attacks he suffered when he was a student of Rhetoric and Foreign Languages in college. "This country cannot separate in two," he began carefully, "with the idea that the very freedom we are founded upon grants us the right to do so. This war is not as complicated as some would have it, Father." Lawrence took a deep breath before continuing. "Southern prosperity has been gained almost exclusively on the backs of an enslaved people. What economy can truly succeed on free labor when there is truly no such thing? What more evil practice could a nation be founded upon?"

"I agree," his father answered. "And that is why I believe the South will eventually fold under its own doing."

"But how long are we to wait?" Lawrence pleaded. "How long do we stand by and allow the negro to be driven like oxen, and watch the Rebel bureaucrats continue to convince their people that we are the cause of their every woe?"

"I don't believe everyone in the South believes everything their politicians tell them, Lawrence."

"No, sir, I don't either. But you saw the danger I'm speaking of even with the election last year. The senators and congressmen from the South misled their people with the idea that if President Lincoln was elected he would drain them of every resource for the benefit of the North. There is a certain effect when a mob of ignorant fools gain number, and I fear it is obvious this mob now calls itself the Confederacy."

"And you prefer crushing this mob with blood," Joshua countered, "instead of letting it starve itself on its own misguided argument, in its own land, where the cost will only be theirs to pay?"

Lawrence angrily clasped his hands together and declared, "I would join to dispatch that Rebel force, sir, for nothing more than to save it from its own destructive hand."

The two men locked eyes as two confident adversaries, both studying their opponent and plotting their next move. This was no simple disagreement and whatever the outcome, the two men would never see the other in the same light again.

Lawrence had never challenged his father before, and though it made him uncomfortable, he fought to hold his ground to make clear his stance would be unyielding. Joshua Chamberlain could not help but admire his son's spirited stand. With every word, he was proving how strong a man he had become.

Many years had passed since Lawrence had thought of his father as a stern disciplinarian. The childhood fears of hard punishments for not completing an order or a chore to his father's satisfaction had long subsided. Instead, Lawrence, now a graduate of both the Theological Seminary in Bangor and Bowdoin College in Brunswick, saw his father as a man of great character and integrity, not a parent who ruled his house with a thin pine switch. They might not agree now, but as a man, gaining his father's acceptance of his view and blessing of support was very important to Lawrence. It would become the last stitch needed in the uniform coat of honor Joshua Lawrence Chamberlain would wear gallantly on the field of battle for the next three years.

"You have considered what your absence would do to your family," Joshua asked.

"Fanny will keep the children in Brunswick," Lawrence answered. "Her cousin will stay at the house. Her parents are only around the street corner. When she is not so occupied at home, she will have only a road to cross to get to church." Lawrence's own words flashed a vision in his mind of the white wooden church just outside the Bowdoin College gates where he first saw the preacher's daughter he would later marry.

"And have you discussed with Fanny the possibility you may end your days in a Virginia cotton field with a lead ball in your belly?"

Lawrence was not comfortable addressing the idea he may perish in battle. His reluctance to even entertain the thought also prevented him from discussing it with his wife.

"I am going to join the men who are defending the union of this country, Father," Lawrence said. "Fanny understands the hazards of war. I found it unnecessary to address the specifics of such a black topic. As you could see at supper, my darling wife is not at all happy with my parting in the first place."

That was an understatement. When Lawrence began to discuss his plans to join the Union Army during supper, the usually outspoken Fanny withdrew to another room where her two children, six-year-old Grace, called Daisy by her father, and four-year-old Wyllys, were napping.

"Have you spoken with Tom?"

"Yes," Lawrence answered reluctantly. He knew that his youngest brother, Thomas, had also expressed an interest in joining a volunteer regiment, but Lawrence was unsure if his parents were aware of it.

"Did you know he wants to go, too?"

"Yes, sir."

The elder Chamberlain leaned forward on the bench, put his elbows on his knees and raised his hands to his face. He slowly rubbed his tired eyes and finished with a swipe across his nose. "I should have expected this from you," he said as he looked up again and sat back into the bench. "Thomas, maybe more. He's young and got the sense of a moose crossing iced-over water. But you, Son, you've been thinking too much ever since I could hold you up in one arm. When you were little I'd talk to your mother about how we'd find a way to get you into West Point. Your mother wouldn't have it, though. I loved my days in the old war in Mexico. I can still remember the smell, the sounds, the order. But that was a different time," he reminded his son. "This...rebellion is a different kind of war. I fought foreigners in a foreign land." Joshua Chamberlain looked into his son's eyes and pointed at his chest. "When you get out on that field, don't you ever forget the man you're trying to kill is also an American. And that field you're marching through, and that city you're burning down, it still belongs to Americans."

Lawrence nodded that he understood. He also recognized that he would remember those final words for the rest of his life. For, though they were not the words of encouragement he had hoped for, they were the words of wisdom that signified his father respected his decision. Just then the porch door slammed shut again and two small children barreled out onto the yard. The youngest, Wyllys, stumbling onto the soft green grass several times before reaching his father and "Grandpa."

The mood instantly changed with the distraction of the well-rested children. Daisy climbed up into her father's lap while Wyllys had to be lifted by his grandfather onto the bench. There, the four discussed the different ships docked in the harbor and what great adventures they might be headed toward next.

∽

A little more than 700 miles south of Brewer, in the mud and sludge surrounding a swollen riverbed, 34,000 Union soldiers and 39,000 soldiers of the Confederacy were killing each other in the fields of a place called Seven Pines, Virginia. Nearly 11,000 would become casualties during the two day battle.

∽

Seeking the approval to become a soldier had consumed Lawrence for the past few months. The mere mention of the idea to his wife had caused a great deal of added stress to their marriage. Their life together had already suffered the death of two babies to illnesses. Chamberlain had also recently been deeply depressed over the loss of the closest of his three brothers, Horace, who passed away just before the previous Christmas of a respiratory infection. Beside the recent family tragedies, the news of the war seemed to cast an even darker shadow over everyone's lives. This ominous mood of despair was only lifted by the innocent lively spirits of young Daisy and Wylly, whose playful antics were the temporarily distractive cure for any troubling thoughts.

Fanny was in no manner happy with her husband's decision, and was not about to let him forget it. Had the idea been addressed a year earlier, before the family tragedies and when nearly the entire country believed the war would be over in a single decisive battle, Fanny may have felt differently. But the repeated news of Union defeats, and the subsequent great losses of lives, caused many young spouses to beg for their husbands not to turn to soldiering. Still, Chamberlain would not be swayed. His motives were fueled by something greater than what he considered selfish needs. His country was in harm's way, and he was compelled to defend it as his father had, and even as his great-grandfather had during the Revolutionary War.

Having his loved one's support would prove to be the lesser of the obstacles he would face in joining the Federal Army. The most difficult would be leaving his professorship at Bowdoin College with a commitment from his superiors that his job would still be available to him when he returned.

Lawrence received his first college degree from Bowdoin College in 1851. With his mother's constant prodding he had decided on a career as a missionary. Actually, Chamberlain's mother wanted him to be a church minister, which would have rewarded the family with a great deal of respect and privilege within the community. But Chamberlain didn't care for the idea of being stuck in the same congregation for the rest of his adult life. Instead, he settled on the alternate goal of becoming a missionary, which was gladly accepted by his mother. His decision to try missionary work was rooted in his mastery of foreign languages, and Chamberlain spent the next three years of his life after Bowdoin conveniently attending the Bangor Theological Seminary across the river from his hometown.

By the time he graduated from the school in Bangor, Chamberlain spoke eight different languages, having learned Arabic, Syriac, and Greek during the latter portion of his formal education. Lawrence was able to learn the foreign languages so quickly because of his uncanny ability to adapt to different sentence structure. He quite literally thought like a German when he spoke German, and then with the snap of a finger, could easily be mistaken for a Parisian with his nearly flawless French. His skills were not lost in the college classroom, either. Chamberlain's father often called upon him to translate while conducting business with French Canadian timber men who didn't speak English.

The idea of becoming a missionary failed to materialize. Chamberlain did finish his degree at Bangor, and even received an honorary master's degree back at his alma mater in Brunswick at the same time. But between all of the schoolwork and tutoring younger students to help pay for his tuition, young Lawrence had fallen in love.

Francis Caroline Adams was the preacher's daughter and the First Parish Church's organ player. She was also Chamberlain's first love interest of any kind, as his devotion to his education had superseded any time allotted to pursuing women. He found himself captivated by her, though, as he sat quietly on a hard wooden pew with the rest of the choir, glancing up to the balcony. There, the raven-haired beauty sat alone, patiently waiting for her father's cue to begin accompanying a hymn.

It was easy for Chamberlain to introduce himself to her. He had become the choir director during his junior year at Bowdoin, and much to his advantage, it was only appropriate that he have a working relationship with the organist. Chamberlain slyly began spending more time around her until it was clear his interest was more than that of a colleague. What followed was over five years of courting, even through extended separations while Chamberlain completed his studies in Bangor. Upon his graduation, they were married by her father in the church where they met.

At first, the maturing college student was often skeptical of Fanny's love for him during their dating years, but he was convinced early on in the relationship that he wanted her hand for marriage. It was, therefore, out of the question, once they were finally married, for Chamberlain who had finally completed seven years of higher education while juggling a relationship with his new bride, to suddenly leave her to do missionary work abroad. Chamberlain, instead, applied for a teaching position at Bowdoin, and was quickly hired as an instructor of Logic and Natural Theology in 1855.

He was particularly pleased with the appointment because it had been one of his favorite subjects as a student. His professor at that time had been Calvin Stowe. Professor Stowe would occasionally invite a promising student to his home for dinner, and it was during several of those visits by Chamberlain that he spoke with his teacher's wife, Harriet.

Mrs. Stowe was writing a book- the subject matter was always the main topic of the evening. The book was a story about slavery, and Mrs. Stowe was telling a tale of the abuses and wrongs of what she called, "Our most singular atrocity." Chamberlain was also bothered by the existence of slaves, but he had never heard such vivid detail of their mistreatment. There were no slaves in Maine, and he had only on a few occasions ever even seen a black man.

Chamberlain was easily captivated by the tale being created by Mrs. Stowe, and she enjoyed discussing her project with Lawrence. It was also during those visits to the Stowe residence that Chamberlain learned of the abolitionist movement in the country, and formed his own strong anti-slavery views. Later, Chamberlain would read the story of Uncle Tom's Cabin with thousands of other Americans, and it would even further strengthen his belief that slavery was an abhorrent and sinful practice.

After a year at Bowdoin, Chamberlain was promoted to Professor of Rhetoric and Oratory. It meant more money, and the prestige of a professorship gave the young Chamberlain couple a higher degree of standing among the citizenry of Brunswick. The newlyweds then bought a house across the street from the campus and began having children.

Seven years dragged by and Chamberlain grew bored with his daily work. He had spent his young life absorbing ideas and information, and now he was reviewing the same stale material over and over again with each class, only to start over again with each passing semester. The tedium was wearing on him.

But it was 1862 now, and the Great Rebellion had rekindled his interest in the political affairs of the country. Each afternoon he anxiously scanned the newspapers, following every new development of the war. And with each passing semester, another handful of his students would disappear from class and volunteer their services to one of the new Maine regiments being formed to join the growing Union Army.

Chamberlain never entertained the thought of joining the military when the government initially called for volunteers a year earlier.

He, like most others, believed the fight would be over before most of the men could even be trained properly. *Why else would the President only call for 90 day enlistments*, he thought to himself at the time. But the first battle at Bull Run Creek had changed all that.

Chamberlain would always remember the day he sat behind his oversized oak desk in Brunswick, reading the Harper's Gazette account of the Manassas, Virginia, battle that had resulted in the resounding defeat of the Federal Army. Then came the loss at Wilson Creek, Missouri, and smaller losses in Kentucky and Virginia. When months later, in the first week of April 1862, Chamberlain read of the 13,000 Union casualties at the Battle of Shiloh, in Tennessee, he knew he could no longer stand by in the comforts of his classroom and allow other men to fight for a cause he also believed in.

With the newspaper describing the carnage of the battle still resting on the side of his desk, Chamberlain wrote a letter to Maine's governor, Israel Washburn, volunteering his services. He then wrote another to the Bowdoin College president, Henry Woods, requesting the appropriate leave of absence. The next morning Woods sent his secretary to Chamberlain's classroom and directed him to respond to his employer's office forthwith.

Chamberlain complied and was subsequently subjected to a rather animated tirade by Woods on the topic of how ridiculous it would be to risk such a valuable investment the school had made in him. It was clear President Woods assumed if his young prodigy went to war he may not return. Woods eventually recoiled from his tantrum, and spoke more calmly of his remembrances of Lawrence as a young student.

He reminded his young professor that he had given him a break when, as a student, Chamberlain refused to give the names of some fellow students he had witnessed riding recklessly through town in "Drunken folly." Chamberlain should have faced dismissal for his lack of cooperation, but Woods had recognized that his pupil was only trying to be loyal to his peers. This was especially made point when Woods asked young Lawrence what his father would think if he was expelled. Chamberlain answered that his father would think the more of him for being trustworthy to his friends. Chamberlain could not help but smile at the incident as it was revisited by President Woods.

The meeting ended with a handshake and the conclusion that Chamberlain simply could not leave his post. The matter wasn't over yet, though. Chamberlain was not only a well-educated man in his early thirties now, but he was also intelligent enough to know when it was appropriate to argue, or save his breath. More specifically, he knew better than to burn a bridge with his boss.

Chamberlain resorted to a back-up plan that had already been well-thought-out. As part of his contract with the school, he had been offered the opportunity to take an overseas sabbatical to study cultures abroad that coincided with the languages he spoke. Since the spring semester was about to conclude, it was a perfect time to cash in his trump card. Chamberlain waited a week and then presented his request with the College Board. Woods had already spread the word to other board members that their Professor of Rhetoric wanted to temporarily defect for military service.

When Chamberlain met with the college review council, he ingeniously, and almost under his breath, commented that it would be good to get away for a while. The Bowdoin administrators took the bait, believing if they sent their employee out of the country for a year he would lose his desire to involve himself in the hazardous business of joining the war. His leave of absence was unanimously approved. But instead of getting on a ship for Italy, Chamberlain got on a horse and rode to Augusta to meet with Maine Governor Washburn.

Washburn had already sent several Maine regiments to Washington as requested by Lincoln. But there had been another call for more troops and Washburn was glad to have an educated Mainer willing to join the Army. Most of the previous regiments had been formed in individual townships and counties, affording the men the near certainty of being led by someone they already knew and trusted. Now, the new regiment that was being formed consisted of Maine men from all across the state, and their leader would be a twenty-five-year-old Pennsylvanian, only a year out of West Point.

Washburn originally offered Chamberlain the command of the regiment as a colonel. Chamberlain told the governor that he appreciated his confidence, but explained he was not well-versed in military tactics yet, and would certainly serve better in a lesser role of authority. Governor Washburn thanked Chamberlain for his honesty, and sent him away with the understanding that he would find a position for the professor later when the new regiment was more closely formed.

Chamberlain then returned to Brunswick and waited anxiously for word of his call to arms. In the meantime, he began the campaign of getting his house in order, which included breaking the news of his enlistment to his parent's still in Brewer and asking for their support in taking care of Fanny and the children. It also meant time to console his wife, and convince her into believing what he was doing was honorable and necessary.

On August 8, 1862, Joshua Lawrence Chamberlain received his commission as Lieutenant Colonel of the new 20th Maine Volunteer Infantry Regiment. His first orders were to respond to Camp Mason in Portland as soon as possible.

CHAPTER 2

THE BIRTH OF THE 20TH MAINE

C hamberlain's train pulled into the coastal city of Portland early in the afternoon of August 18. He then boarded a carriage and traveled to Camp Mason just outside the city limit. The small Army post bustled with men in both civilian and clean blue Federal uniforms. There were no walls or fences surrounding the grounds. The actual camp was little more than a large field that had been commandeered by the state and turned into a mustering point for newly formed regiments. The grass was completely worn away, leaving nothing but a giant dirt square, surrounded by a white canvass tent city and supply wagons.

Chamberlain dodged several mounted soldiers as he crossed the camp to a small log building. He stepped up onto the wooden plank porch and read a painted sign indicating this was the camp's headquarters. He walked through the opened threshold and took off his hat.

"You a Twentieth recruit?" a whiskered old veteran sergeant asked from behind a desk.

"Yes, sir," Chamberlain replied nervously. He had no idea what he was in for, but had envisioned the worst during his train ride down from Brunswick.

"Well come on over here then and let me get you signed up."

Chamberlain stepped over to the desk and set his carpetbag on the dust-covered floor.

"Name?" the sergeant growled. He dropped a ledger book down on the table top and prepared to find the name about to be given to him by the new recruit.

"Chamberlain. Joshua Lawrence Chamberlain."

The sergeant flipped back and forth through the pages and shook his head.

Chamberlain assumed he was having trouble finding his name on the list. "From Brunswick. Actually, I'm from Brew..."

"I don't give a God damn where you're from," the sergeant interrupted. "Long as you're from Maine and long as you're on this list, that's all I care about."

"Yes, sir." Chamberlain apologized. A sheepish grin began to pull at the corners of his mouth. He'd suddenly remembered he was a lieutenant colonel- very much this enlisted man's superior.

The Sergeant continued flipping through the pages of the ledger several more times and then looked back up at the narrow-shouldered professor in front of him. He noted his soft pale hands and clean fresh suit.

"You sure you're here to join the Army?"

"I am, Sergeant," Chamberlain replied, now in a more confident tone. He knew he was being sized up and saw great humor in it. His grin turned to a lip parting smile. "Sergeant, it would probably result in your great embarrassment for us to continue on this present course. You are surely a good soldier, and I don't want your frustration to lead you down a path that might alter the good nature of our future relationship. I am Lieutenant Colonel Chamberlain. My commission is in my bag if you would like to see it."

The sergeant's scowl dropped as he scrambled to his feet. "I'm sorry, sir," the sergeant apologized with a salute. "Uh..." he stammered nervously. "No, I don't need your papers. Let me call one of your staff officers over and they can get you set up."

"Thank you, Sergeant," Chamberlain said warmly and returned a casual salute.

The desk chair slid back from the table and the sergeant briskly shuffled to the doorway. "Major Gilmore!" he yelled across the camp. Colonel Chamberlain is here!"

"Thank you, Sergeant!" a voice called back from across the yard.

Chamberlain began to rummage through his bag for his paperwork. The weathered infantryman stepped to his side and stood at attention. Chamberlain rose up and clasped his hands behind his back. It was his first physical attempt at striking what he believed to be the appropriate pose of an officer.

"I apologize, sir, for my tone," the Sergeant said humbly, his eyes fixed straight forward on the wall across the room.

Chamberlain stepped in front of him so their eyes could meet.

"Have you been in the fight, Sergeant?" Chamberlain asked.

"Yes, sir. I was with the Second Maine all last year."

"Did anyone else come over to join the Twentieth with you?"

"Just me and Major Gilmore. We're the only ones who even got a dirty uniform so far."

"How do the new men look?" Chamberlain asked.

"Well, sir...," the sergeant tried to make his comment appropriate yet honest. "They got a ways to go. We' been drillin' 'em with sticks for muskets all last week, and they're comin' along."

"Good."

A stomping of boots on the wood porch redirected Chamberlain's attention.

"Colonel Chamberlain?" the young confident officer dressed in a perfectly fitted dark blue uniform asked with an extended hand. Gold oak leaves adorned his shoulders, identifying him as a major.

"Yes, sir," Chamberlain answered as he firmly took the hand being offered him and shook it.

"Charles Gilmore, at your service, sir. If you had been in uniform, a salute would have been more fitting," the major apologized.

"Well, I think we all may have to give ourselves a pass on today's breaches of etiquette." Chamberlain glanced at the still frozen sergeant standing in the corner and winked.

The sergeant sighed with relief.

"Let me take you to your tent, sir, and we can make arrangements for a uniform." Gilmore took Chamberlain's bag and started for the front door.

"Should I meet the commanding officer first?" Chamberlain asked. He was unsure of military formalities and wanted to make sure he didn't violate any code of conduct himself.

"You're it, Colonel," Gilmore answered. The two men stepped back out into the sunlight and off of the porch. "We don't expect Colonel Ames for another week."

Chamberlain felt strangely out of place as he followed the major across what he later learned was called the parade grounds. He had no idea what he was supposed to do, and he was even more uncomfortable with that fact, knowing he had just stepped into the temporarily role as the senior officer of the entire regiment. His already nervous stomach began to churn with nauseam.

Almost his entire life had been spent in some form of academic institution, so when the opportunity arose for him to transcend from student to teacher, it had gone very smoothly. But other than having spent one year in a military school when he was fourteen, Chamberlain had no idea how to conduct himself as a soldier. He felt completely lost. The wise professor quickly decided it would be best that he avoid making any decisions, and find someone to latch onto who knew what they were doing.

"So, Major Gilmore," Chamberlain began, "the sergeant told me you have some prior experience."

"Yes, sir," Gilmore answered as they turned into an aisle of large empty tents. "I was a captain with the Seventh Maine. When the governor decided to form this regiment, I was provided the opportunity to promote and come here to help get these men trained. It's also a nice rest from the front, if you don't mind me saying so. They let me go home on leave for a week to see my family before I had to be here. The whole arrangement has gone well for me."

The two men stepped into one of the empty tents where the major dropped Chamberlain's bag on a canvass cot.

"Well, sir, this is home for a few weeks at least," Gilmore said. "We're being fed well so I'd enjoy it while it lasts. The officers should continue to get decent rations when we get out in the field, but it won't be anything like what we have now, that's for certain. I'll send a corporal over to take your measurements and we'll get you a uniform. Officers have to pay for their coats. The enlisted men are issued theirs. If you have any questions about the style of coat you want, just ask. That wooden trunk over in the corner has your mess supplies in it. It folds out into a small table top if you want to use it for writing. We get the men up at five-thirty, get some breakfast in them around six, and then we start drill. They don't look too good yet, but I don't suppose they are any worse than any other new regiment. Some big boys-I'd be afraid to see them coming. If you'd prefer, I will continue drill instruction, at your direction of course."

"That would be fine," Chamberlain answered and continued to scan the interior of his new quarters.

"Our colonel is a West Pointer," Gilmore added. "He's young, but they say he made a good name for himself already at Bull Run. He'll probably be tough on these green men. I figure if we can get these boys in order before he gets here we'll all be better off."

"That sounds like a good idea," Chamberlain agreed.

"Is there anything else, sir?" Gilmore asked.

Chamberlain wanted to ask, *What do I do now?*, but he knew better. "Shall we dine together, Major?"

"Yes, sir, it would be my honor. I'll return in an hour and take you on a tour of camp. In the meantime, I'll have the mess officer cook up something special for us."

"Another good idea, sir," Chamberlain told him.

"Thank you, Colonel. Will there be anything else?"

"No. Thank you."

Major Gilmore stood at the opened flap of the tent and waited. Chamberlain rolled onto the cot, believing he was now alone. He closed his eyes for a moment and immediately felt the presence of someone near him. He opened his eyes again and was startled by the figure of Gilmore still in the tent.

"Is there something else, Major?" Chamberlain asked.

"No, sir. Am I dismissed, sir?"

"Yes, Major. You are dismissed."

Gilmore turned and marched out of view. Chamberlain closed his weary eyes and stored the new military procedure away in his head. *They won't go away unless I tell them they're dismissed*, he recited to himself.

That evening the two officers dined inside the major's tent to prevent the camp flies from sharing their meal with them. A cook from Waterville, Maine, prepared a Canadian goose with beets, green beans, and sweet corn biscuits. Both men agreed it was delicious.

It quickly became obvious to Chamberlain that Major Gilmore had field experience. His tent was full and well-organized. A small folding desk with papers and maps on it was placed neatly in one corner. His wooden mess box also served as a night stand, and an oil lamp glowed from the top of it. An extra gray wool blanket and a shiny silver sword scabbard rested at the foot of his bed. Several empty ammunition crates formed the stand for their dining table, which was covered with a clean white table cloth.

Chamberlain confessed to the major that he believed he was in no way prepared to lead a regiment, or even be a part of the command staff for that matter. Gilmore had already experienced the confusion and chaos that ignorant superior officers caused on the battlefield, and was always leery of new officers until they proved themselves capable in the field. He was prepared to grant his new lieutenant colonel a respectable level of confidence though, for no reason other than he was first to admit he had no idea what he was doing.

The two men mostly talked of battle tactics and Gilmore's war experience during the course of the evening. Chamberlain was once again the student, and he opened his mind to all the major could feed him. The two men eventually moved outside and sat together in front of the major's tent, periodically stopping their discussion to listen to the weary men around them. Somewhere in one of the tents a music lesson was being given- a harmonica played a portion of a march, and then a fife would try to echo the tune. Chamberlain himself played the piano and base violin, and his instinct to want to join in the music-playing tugged at his attention. But soon the lesson was ended at the grumbled requests of several men trying to sleep.

Chamberlain also felt it was time to end the evening and rose up from his folding chair. He thanked Gilmore for his hospitality and returned to his own tent. When he stepped inside he discovered his bed had extra blankets on it and the sheets had been turned down. He knew the other soldiers in the camp had figured out who he was simply by the attention he had been given by Major Gilmore. He could only hope that he could actually earn the respect afforded him by his new rank during the next few weeks.

As he lay on his cot after stripping off his shoes, he prayed a short prayer asking God to give him guidance during the next few days. His head then filled with visions of gallant cavalry duels and acts of heroic chivalry. He slowly drifted off to sleep, not once envisioning spilled blood or death in those romantic pictures he painted in his head.

Chamberlain awoke the next morning to the sounds of muffled conversation and footsteps. A faint orange glow filled his tent. He slipped out from beneath his blankets and slung the flap of his tent open to investigate what was happening outside. The dawn was just beginning to appear on the eastern horizon, yet the camp was already alive with awakening men. Chamberlain closed the flap again and dragged his bag to the corner of his bed. He pulled out fresh trousers and a clean shirt and began dressing. He had just begun the thought that he must have slept through the morning's bugle call when it sounded from the center of the parade grounds.

Chamberlain was accustomed to rising early in the morning and was ready to begin his first day as a soldier. By the number of men already shuffling about before the morning's wake up call, it appeared they were also ready to get the day started. But before he was completely dressed, the fear of the unknown returned to him.

Chamberlain rinsed his face with the water from a large tin bowl that had appeared in his tent the night before. The cold water gave him a jolting chill, so he decided to find some warmer water to shave with. A young corporal appeared at the tent and opened the flap after Chamberlain granted his request for entry. The soldier looked to be no more than a teenage boy as he stood erect and recited the morning's breakfast menu. He then asked his superior if he wanted his meal delivered to him, or if he would like to retrieve it himself from the officer's mess wagon. Chamberlain told the young enlisted man he would get his breakfast himself, and then told the soldier he was, "Dismissed."

Less than a minute later Major Gilmore appeared at the tent opening. His appearance was flawless and his manner was as if he had been up for hours. Chamberlain asked if his civilian dress was appropriate. Gilmore told him that whatever attire made him comfortable would be appropriate due to his rank. The two men then walked to breakfast together through a crowd of parting and saluting men. Chamberlain recognized that the salutes were directed at Gilmore, so he returned the gesture with only a nod of acknowledgment. He would wait until he was uniformed before he participated in the customary recognition of authority.

The two men walked to the front of an assembly line of soldiers and were handed tin plates piled with ham, eggs, fried potatoes, and large wedges of bread. Gilmore directed Chamberlain to a long wooden table were several younger officers were already seated. When the two reached the table, the other men stood and waited.

"Gentlemen," Gilmore started, "in case you haven't figured it out yet, this is our lieutenant colonel, Lawrence Chamberlain."

The men at the table extended their hands and welcomed him to the regiment. After the greeting, Chamberlain saw that they were remaining on their feet and assumed it was because of him.

"Please sit, gentlemen," Chamberlain told them. "I don't want to be the cause of your coffee getting cold."

The officers smiled and returned to their breakfast.

Chamberlain was not only uncomfortable with being the only man out of uniform at the table, but was also uneasy with how he should speak and what he should speak about. The men had been engaged in a lively conversation when he and Gilmore walked up to the table, but were now quietly to themselves. Chamberlain knew it was because of his presence.

"How do the men look?" he asked, an attempt to ease the men and start a conversation.

"They're trying," one of the men answered.

"It would help if we had some muskets to drill with, sir," another added.

"What are we waiting for? I'd think we'd be better served by a regiment of straight shooters than straight marchers."

"We have no weapons to issue yet, Colonel."

"When are they supposed to get here?" Chamberlain asked.

"No one knows," Gilmore answered. "I wouldn't be surprised if we weren't issued arms until we get to our next post. I don't believe Washington has much concern with our supplies until we get closer to the fighting."

"Do we know where our first post will be?" Chamberlain enquired.

"Probably Washington," Gilmore answered. "Almost every new regiment is dispatched directly from the Capitol's front lawn."

"Do we march or sail?" a young lieutenant questioned.

"I think we'd all prefer to take a steamer or ship at least half the way," another officer answered.

The lieutenant who asked the question reacted with a worried frown.

"Colonel Chamberlain," a tall soldier sitting next to the young lieutenant began, "you ever met a man from Maine who gets the sailing sickness?" He then pointed to the officer next to him and winked.

The men laughed together as they rocked back and forth on the bench, pretending to be passengers on an unsteady boat. Chamberlain was glad to see there was already camaraderie building among them.

The rest of the morning's banter was of the uncertainty of where the new regiment was going to engage in its first battle. Some believed they would probably get stuck in Washington for several months with the thousands of other units they heard were being stockpiled there. But the more realistic idea was that of quickly joining another large Federal movement that would be marching through Central Virginia, aimed at tracking down the new Confederate Army Commander, Robert E. Lee, and his Army of Northern Virginia.

Major General George McClellen had recently been relieved of his position as the Union Army Commander, and had been replaced by Major General Henry Halleck. The reason, according to some of the young officers, had to be because the President was displeased with the slow, overly cautious movement of the Army commander the officers referred to as "Little Mac." Chamberlain listened intently to his new subordinates. He was unsure of how accurate their forecasts of the regiment's future were, but he was impressed by their apparent zeal to join the fight.

After breakfast Chamberlain returned to his tent where he was fitted for uniforms. He selected a kepi cap from a pile stored in a quartermaster's trunk, and had it sent off with the tailor to have a 20th Maine insignia sewn onto the front of it. He then joined Major Gilmore on the parade grounds. Both men climbed up into a log tower and watched the various company commanders attempting to drill their men. There were already nearly a thousand new soldiers on the field, and a few more were still expected to arrive within the week. Also expected were haversacks, additional uniforms, and hopefully their muskets that were still en route from Washington according to Gilmore.

As the morning grew warmer the air within the camp clouded with brown dust. Chamberlain paid particular attention to the marching commands being given on the field and wrote them down in a notebook he had tucked away in his shirt. He remembered some of the basic movement commands from his days as a military school student, but the orders involving the men's weapons were relatively new to him. As for the commands commonly used to position the men during battle, he'd never heard them before.

Chamberlain appreciated the assistance he was being given by his major. He knew that it would have been easy for Gilmore to be less helpful, especially if his plans were to promote rapidly. What better scenario than to be able to replace one's supervisor due to his incompetence. But instead of gloating in his superior's admitted lack of knowledge, Gilmore pointed out the reasons why such troop movements were necessary, and he coached Chamberlain on how to properly instruct soldiers who were not performing the orders correctly. It was most helpful to the fledgling officer, and his interest in the day's training made it pass rapidly.

The afternoon continued much the same as the morning had. The Maine summer breeze helped keep the men cool in their dark wool uniforms. Still, breaks for water and coffee became more necessary toward the later part of the day.

That evening Chamberlain realized his face and nose had been badly sunburned. After another filling supper with Gilmore in his tent, Chamberlain returned to his quarters to nurse his hot skin with a cold cloth. The major had loaned him an Army manual on field infantry procedures, and Chamberlain studied its pages as he dabbed the heat from his pores.

The routine of meals, drill, another meal, and then more drill consumed the next three days. Chamberlain received his new uniforms and was now more comfortable in involving himself with the men. He enjoyed the respect displayed to him, but the fact that he was much more college professor than soldier made him reluctant to exercise his new authority. He often politely excused gestures of service or respect by the enlisted men when he didn't think they were necessary. He polished his own boots, retrieved his own water, and kept his own coffee pot full.

Chamberlain's youngest brother, Thomas, arrived a few days later and was appointed the rank of sergeant. Thomas was only twenty-one-years-old, tall and scrawny, and not near the level of maturity as his oldest brother. He'd worked as a store clerk for the past six years and was still living under the guidance of his parents. Thomas was actually the first to express interest in joining the Army, but had been given a resounding, "Absolutely not!" by his mother. Then, when older brother, Lawrence, decided he was going to join with or without his parent's blessing, Thomas gained the strength to do the same.

The situation of having two brothers in the same regiment with such a wide gap in their rank was rarely a problem with the Chamberlain boys. Lawrence had his hands full with the duties of a regiment commander and had little time to socialize with his little brother. Once in a while their eyes would meet and the two would smile at each other, but both understood more pressing matters were at hand during those first days of training. When they did have opportunities to speak briefly, the elder of the two would frequently have to remind his sibling that he should not be addressed as, "Lawrence," in front of the men. As hard as he tried, the sometimes unbridled spirit of the youngest Chamberlain son continued to result in many a slip throughout the rest of the war.

On August 22, Colonel Adelbert Ames arrived at the gate of the camp on horseback. Gilmore and Chamberlain saw the dashing figure coming into the parade grounds and scurried down the observation tower to greet him. They reached their new regiment commander as he climbed off of his horse at the front of the headquarters cabin. Gilmore and Chamberlain stood at attention and saluted him. When the gesture was returned, Gilmore took the horse's reigns from the colonel and secured them around a hitching post. Ames told his two officers to follow him inside, and when they did, the old sergeant seated behind the desk waiting for new recruits, was dismissed by the senior officer. Ames dropped his forage cap on the table and walked over to a window facing the drilling men outside. He leaned on the windowsill and scanned the parade grounds.

"How do they look?" he asked- his voice deep with command presence.

Chamberlain glanced at Gilmore and realized, since he was second-in-command now, it was his position to answer. "Sir, I believe they are coming along quite nicely."

"A year ago I marched on Manassas with a regiment of nicely trained men, Colonel Chamberlain." Ames rose up from the window and looked at his subordinate. "And those that were the most nicely trained abandoned the field and ran like cowards all the way back to Washington."

Chamberlain wisely chose not to clarify himself.

"Sir, if I may?" Gilmore started, and continued when Ames nodded that he should proceed. "We have no experienced men in this new regiment. Only one enlisted sergeant from the Second Maine has joined us. It took a number of days for us to train the company commanders before they could even begin drilling their own men."

"And what is your progress?"

"Well, sir, Colonel Chamberlain arrived a few days ago, and with his assistance we've improved a great deal."

Chamberlain silently appreciated the unearned recognition.

"Then assemble the men and let me have a look. Regiment formation on the tower," Ames ordered. "I want to see one circle around the field and then run them through the arms commands."

"Yes, sir," Chamberlain and Gilmore replied in unison.

"You are dismissed."

Salutes were exchanged and the two subordinate officers hurried out of the tiny headquarters building.

The camp soon filled with echoed commands of assembly. The result was a calamity of scrambling men trying to quickly gather their equipment and assemble in regimental mass in front of the log observation tower. Each soldier was armed only with a long wooden stick, some having been ornately carved while the men passed the evening's boredom. Colonel Ames stepped out onto the porch and adjusted the wide-brimmed hat on his head. He dramatically scanned the yard and then headed toward the tower. There, he was joined by Chamberlain. Gilmore was already on the field, positioned in front of the now assembled regiment.

The two senior officers climbed the narrow ladder up to the observation deck. Chamberlain stood to the right and just behind the colonel.

"Why are these men not armed, Colonel Chamberlain?!" Ames queried angrily.

"Their muskets have not yet arrived, sir."

"Dear God," Ames mumbled to himself. "Am I to take this regiment into Virginia with tree branches for arms!" He then turned to the rows of blue below him. Ames paused for a moment to settle his anger and then addressed the men.

"Soldiers of the Twentieth Maine!" Ames began. "I am your regiment commander, Colonel Adelbert Ames! I have been sent here to lead you into battle! Every day history is being written of this rebellion! And I will see to it that the Twentieth Maine is among those honorable chapters!"

A great cheer filled the parade ground.

"All I ask of you is that from this moment forward, you commit yourselves to the task at hand! You must trust your officers, as their orders come directly from me! When the call for battle sounds, you must be prepared to go bravely into that great fire! I should never need question if you are with me, only if I can hold you back! Are you with me Mainers!"

Again, a cheer arose from the ranks.

"Major Gilmore!" Ames continued. "Take command of this regiment and proceed as ordered!

Gilmore saluted Ames and spun around to face the invigorated 20th Maine.

"Regiment!"

A chain of echoed commands followed.

"Right...Face!"

A dust cloud rolled up from the feet of the pivoting infantrymen.

"Forward!"

The command was repeated by each company commander.

"March!"

The regiment shifted forward like a ship being separated from its dock.

Chamberlain was relieved to see the men were sufficiently keeping in step with the small drum corps at the front of the long blue mass, many of whose members were fresh-faced boys. But he was unable to see the colonel's reaction from behind his back, and there were no comments made of his approval or disappointment.

The blue columns turned to their right and then made another right turn, following the perimeter of the parade grounds. With each re-direction, a few of the men would step out of cadence and their heads would pop up from the ranks when they skipped to regain their step. From the observation tower the break in uniformity was even clearer as each turn produced more soldiers who began to march out of step. After the final turn, Major Gilmore halted the regiment in front of the tower and returned them to facing their colonel.

Gilmore then ordered the men through a series of rifle movements and carry positions. Again, there were noticeable errors within the ranks. Ames raised his chin and scratched his throat. Gilmore completed his last command and turned to face the tower.

"Major! Let me see them simulate loading their arms!" Ames ordered.

A chill of terror ran through Chamberlain's chest and he nervously stepped forward to the colonel's side. "Sir, we only began to instruct that subject a few days ago," he said, "and the men are not yet well-trained in that procedure."

"What?" Ames asked for clarification.

"Sir, when I arrived last week and saw the men were being trained with sticks for weapons, I notified the quartermaster immediately. I was subsequently informed that no arms would be shipped to us and we would receive them at our first duty station. We delayed instructing the men on the loading orders until they were competent at the march, sir. They only recently met that level of competency. I can assure you that this is only because we have had no actual muskets to train with."

Ames slowly turned to face his second-in-command. "Well, Colonel Chamberlain, how many of your fellow statesmen down there have ever fired a musket before?"

"I'm sure all of them have, sir."

"And do you also assume that they loaded that musket before they fired it?" Ames added with a bight of sarcasm.

"Yes, sir," Chamberlain answered. He knew he had opened the door for this scolding.

"Then why should it take more than a few days to teach these men how to load by the count. You said they've had the training for several days. How long does it take to teach a man something you admit he already should know how to do?"

Chamberlain and his commander knew it was not that simple, but the point had been made. Ames turned to Gilmore and ordered him to proceed.

Gilmore spun around to the formation again and began the nine commands for loading the muskets they did not yet possess. The first two commands were self explanatory, but the drill quickly became a free-for-all. The men knew how to load their weapons, but they had only just received the instruction on how to do it by the numbers. Having to simulate the loading procedure with a stick made the drill even more confusing. Chamberlain couldn't bear to watch the confusion anymore and looked down at his boots.

"This is one hell of a regiment," Ames declared in disgust, then climbed down the tower ladder before the exercise was even completed.

Gilmore finished the last command and had to gather his courage before turning back to face the colonel. He was sure to be the target of a tongue-lashing. But when he cautiously turned again to the tower, the regiment's new commander was gone. Chamberlain gestured to his left and Gilmore followed his signal. There, Colonel Ames was already on the ground, stomping off to his tent. Gilmore quickly ordered the battalion commanders to dismiss the men and then joined Chamberlain for an impromptu debriefing with the officer staff.

Chamberlain calmly reassured his subordinates that the exercise had gone much better than what they all clearly perceived. But there was room for improvement, and now that Ames was in camp they would have to get better quickly before their new colonel thought it necessary to start punishing the regiment. Chamberlain then told the battalion majors and the company commanders to get their men in smaller groups and go over the loading drill. He suggested that they find some sergeants who knew what they were doing, and have those men instruct the others into the evening. Chamberlain told the officers to allow their men to drill in casual dress after supper, and he didn't want any groups over ten. His idea was that the men might learn faster if they were more relaxed and not being barked at. The sight of the men apparently training on their own might also sit well with their new colonel. Chamberlain then dismissed the small cadre and walked off alone to face Ames.

The colonel had already gathered a group of soldiers to unload his supplies into his tent. He was standing by giving direction with a cigar in his mouth when he was joined by his lieutenant colonel.

"Sir, is there something you would have me do?" Chamberlain asked.

"Yes," Ames answered through a cloud of smoke. "Tell our cook to prepare dinner for seven o'clock tonight. I want our table set in the headquarters cabin, and I want our staff present with the battalion and company commanders."

"Do you have any preferences for our meal, Colonel? I'm sure the mess officer will ask."

"Poultry of some kind. We shall have enough meat and pork while on the march."

"It is done, sir," Chamberlain replied. Anything else, sir?"

"No. You're dismissed."

Chamberlain walked away and headed for the mess wagons. He was relieved that he was no longer the regiment's senior officer, but he was not so sure he was happy with the stern young colonel who was now his boss. He was such a young man, yet he carried himself with a great deal of character. Chamberlain decided he would do everything he could to not interpret criticism by his new superior as a personal attack. It would be difficult though, as he was not accustomed to being so rudely challenged, or having to take orders from someone much younger than himself. Still, he understood that the Army could not function without discipline and rank structure, and he was simply thankful he was closer to the top of that chain of command than the bottom.

The officer's cook would have preferred the opportunity to have impressed his new colonel with a turkey for supper, but he had not been advised of the special menu request early enough in the day to prepare one. He did cook three delicious geese for the officers, which were plentiful in that area of the country, yet still considered a specialty.

During the course of the staff dinner the young officers sat straight up in their chairs and listened to Ames rattle off his memorized list of expectations. Chamberlain listened intently as he repeatedly swiped at the bottom of his mustache to clear it of drink and crumbs. He wanted to make sure his colonel didn't think him a slob. His whiskers now hung over his entire mouth and the thick corners surrounded his chin. But Chamberlain enjoyed his new mustache, and the minor inconveniences of wearing it were just that.

The men moved out to the porch following dinner to smoked cigars and sip various selections of liquor. Chamberlain stayed close to Ames, believing his position as second-in-command meant he should act as his superior's most direct assistant. As the evening wore on, the colonel grew more personable and told stories of West Point and the battles he had already been a part of. Chamberlain noted the difference in Ames personality when he was not in the presence of enlisted men. He could see that his colonel's stern demeanor was more of conscious command style than that of ego.

The other men eventually filtered back to their tents, but Chamberlain stayed at the colonel's side. As the table was being cleared behind them, Chamberlain took the opportunity to speak candidly with his commander, who was now seated on the top porch step.

"Are you aware of my background, Colonel Ames?"

"Well, I assume, due to your lack of input during supper, you don't really have any. In the military sense, I mean." Ames clarified. "I know you're a professor and not a politician. I'm not sure either qualifies you to lead soldiers. Would I be incorrect to assume you have an association with someone of society? Or possibly your family has accumulated some elevated degree of financial prosperity?"

Chamberlain smiled and shook his head. He admired the honesty. It was true most men who received such high commissions with no military background usually fit into one of those categories. But Chamberlain certainly didn't.

Ames noted the reaction. "I am wrong then?"

"Yes, sir, with all due respect, you couldn't be more wrong," Chamberlain answered. "My father is a veteran, but now is a farmer. I make a decent salary as a professor at Bowdoin, but I often have to teach foreign languages on my own time just to pay my debts."

"Parlez-vous Française?" Ames asked.

Chamberlain smiled and answered, "Oui, monsieur. Deutsche?

"German?"

"Ya."

Anything else?

También hablo poquito Español.

"Spanish?"

"Bueno." Chamberlain playfully chided with him. "Uh eh Italiano, Greek, Syrian, Hebrew, and Arabic."

"Surely you jest," Ames replied.

Chamberlain then uttered something completely baffling to Ames. "What was that?" he asked in response.

"I just told you in Greek that I am humbled by your military achievements, as much as you are amazed I can speak in the language of Zeus."

"Very good, Colonel," Ames laughed. "You will have to teach me some of your skills before this war is over."

Well, sir, actually I was hoping for a rather expedient lesson in *your* skills," Chamberlain said. "I am ill-prepared for my position in the regiment, but I am most eager to learn."

"I think I can help you with that, Chamberlain," Ames answered. "I have several books of tactics I carry with me in the field. I will loan them to you if you wish."

"That would be greatly appreciated, sir."

"And since it is you who is helping me to steer this disorganized herd of malcontents, I would be foolish not to give you some private lesson. I need a man who knows what he is doing. Stick by me and at the end of this war you will have received a course of study even the great halls of West Point could not administer."

"That is my wish, sir," Chamberlain said.

"Good then." Ames stood up and stretched. "What a beautiful night. Look at it, man. We are so very small when compared to the heavens."

Chamberlain gazed up into the clear northern sky and drew a deep breath. He thought of Fanny and his children. They seemed less distant under the same stars.

"I say we call it a day, Colonel," Ames told him.

"I agree, sir."

"Have the men on the field ready to drill at six. Make it known we will not break for lunch until we have learned to load our muskets. Understood?"

"Yes, sir." Chamberlain stood at attention and waited.

"Let's turn these men into soldiers, Chamberlain. If we don't, those gray bastards of the Confederacy will send them to their graves."

"Yes, sir."

Ames paused for a moment to make sure his lieutenant colonel comprehended his words.

"Dismissed."

∞

The rest of August proved to be much different from the previous days Chamberlain spent at Camp Mason. Colonel Ames was not at all pleased with his new regiment and grew more frustrated with each passing day. The men who made up the 20th were mostly loggers and boatmen, and none were accustomed to having orders shouted at them by such a youthful leader. Ames often appeared pompous and arrogant to the men, who saw his physical demeanor as that of someone who looked as if he was always posing for a photograph. Chamberlain's manner was quite the opposite. His lack of command presence and posturing was seen by the men as a symbol of him being more like them- a man who had joined the Army to fight, not put on airs.

Still, it was clear to everyone, including Chamberlain himself, that he was uncomfortable with his new authority. The new lieutenant colonel had yet to settle into his own style of leadership, and often mimicked the other officers who appeared to know what they were doing. About the only thing that made him look like an officer, other than the coat he wore, was his habit of walking with his hands clasped behind his back, only drawing them to his side when the colonel was near. It wasn't a natural pose born of character and leadership skills. It was a conscious effort by Chamberlain to conceal his nervous and often trembling hands.

Ames was privately doing everything he could to teach Chamberlain how to behave like an officer. Initially, he had chastised his lieutenant colonel for not showing more command demeanor, and would then privately proceed to give him a lesson in how to bark out an order with authority. Chamberlain was coming along though, much faster than the rest of the 20th Maine, and Ames began to treat him more as a protégé than assistant.

The two men spent every evening in the colonel's tent, reviewing West Point war manuals and historic battle plans. Chamberlain was able to quickly grasp the strategy of using natural landscape and coordinated attacks, which had been one of the Federal Army's weaknesses thus far in the war. Ames' confidence steadily grew in Chamberlain and he began to not only respect him, but also like him.

In the early afternoon of September 2, a slapping on the canvass of Chamberlain's tent turned him away from a letter he was writing to Fanny. He had not been separated from her for any length of time since their marriage and he missed her deeply. Especially since the death of his close brother, Horace, Fanny had also become his closest friend. In the rare moments he had to himself, he was either thinking of her or expressing his love for her in poetic script.

"What is it?" Chamberlain asked, and then blew the ink dry on the nearly finished letter.

"Sir," the voice from outside huffed. The messenger was out of breath and had to gulp for air before he could continue. "Colonel Ames wants to see you immediately at his tent. We got our orders."

"Tell the colonel I am on my way."

The private turned and ran back to return the message.

Chamberlain pulled his jacket over his shoulders and fumbled with the buttons on his double-breasted coat. He then placed his cap squarely on his head and checked its alignment with a small mirror he carried in his breast pocket. When he reached for the bill of the cap to straighten it, he caught the image of his trembling hand. He held the other out in front of him and confirmed both were just slightly quivering. Chamberlain rubbed them together and examined his hands again. It was no use. Yet these tremors gave him little concern, for the uncontrollable shaking wasn't born of fear. It was the result of his excitement that he would finally be going to war.

Chamberlain stepped away from his tent and brushed the dust from his trousers. He made every attempt to compose his jubilation during his short walk to meet his superior, fearing an outward display of glee would appear unprofessional. When he arrived at his commander's tent he found Ames sitting in his chair with a document in his hands.

"Come in," Ames said with a grin.

It was the first time Chamberlain had seen an expression of joy on the colonel's face, and it was every bit that of an excited young boy.

"We've been assigned to the Third Brigade of the First Division of the Fifth Corps. The Army of the Potomac. Butterfield's Light Brigade!"

Chamberlain joined Ames in a broad smile, finally releasing the bottled emotions inside him. "When do we leave, sir?" he had to know.

"Tomorrow morning." Ames looked back at the document and synopsized its content for Chamberlain. "We assemble the regiment at the train depot at seven a.m. We'll be transported to Boston and then by ship to the capital in Washington. It will take a few days so make sure the men have plenty of rations."

"Yes, sir."

"Are they ready, Chamberlain?" The colonel was suddenly solemn with concern.

"It appears, sir, we will soon find out." It wasn't the type of answer he would have given three weeks earlier, but Chamberlain knew better now than to give his opinion that the men were ready. How would he know? He had never experienced battle before. On the other hand, he didn't want to spoil the moment by questioning the regiment's competence.

"Yes," Ames said to himself. "We surely will."

The mood in the tent changed as the young colonel stared into the official document. The idea that the regiment might not be prepared for duty was suddenly very sobering.

Chamberlain could tell his commander was lost in his thoughts. "Is that all, sir?"

"Yes," Ames answered as he broke from his spell. "Assemble the men and I will brief them. You may inform them of the particulars when I am finished. You are dismissed."

"Yes, sir."

"Oh, one more thing, Chamberlain." The colonel caught him just before he left the tent. "Tell the men to leave their sticks here."

"Yes, sir," Chamberlain replied gladly. He then saluted his superior and hurried back to his staff.

The news of their movement had quickly spread among the men, well before the formal call to assembly. But it was the confirming notice by Colonel Ames from atop the parade ground tower that resulted in the eruption of cheers from the ranks. The men were tired of the monotony of drilling and they believed they were ready to do what they had signed up to do- *fight!*

The rest of the day filled with last minute instructions and the preparation for a long week of travel. The men filled their new haversacks with extra hardtack biscuits and an extra allotment of salt pork and coffee. Some had been given dried fish from loved ones who frequently visited the camp in the evenings. Those that had it packed away as much as they could, knowing there would be little time for fishing while fighting Rebels.

Late in the afternoon Chamberlain was called to the camp's headquarters to receive a package. Fanny's letters had been arriving less frequently and her lack of correspondence had begun to worry him. Chamberlain hurried to the small log building, assuming his delivery was a group of letters that had been delayed and had finally arrived. As he anxiously jogged up the dusty wooden steps to the opened front door he couldn't help but notice the beautiful, stone gray stallion tethered to the hitching post outside. He thought the horse had to belong to a high-ranking officer of some kind, so he straightened his uniform before walking inside.

Much to his surprise, the only man inside the headquarters building was the sergeant who had originally signed him in the first day he arrived at the camp. Chamberlain now knew him by name, as he had frequent dealings with the gruff old veteran when it came to matters of administration.

"At ease, Sergeant Miller," Chamberlain said before the man could reach his feet. "Do you have something for me?"

"I sure do, Colonel," he answered. His lips parted in an uncharacteristic smile, exposing his near toothless gums.

"Then, let's have it," Chamberlain insisted impatiently.

"Miller handed his colonel a single small envelope, not the stack Chamberlain had hoped for or expected. Chamberlain smelled it first and was even more disappointed it did not emit the sweet perfume his wife included on her letters. He then peeled it open and unfolded the handwritten note inside.

GOOD LUCK LIEUTENANT COLONEL CHAMBERLAIN. GOD'S SPEED, AND BLESSINGS ON YOU AND THE 20TH MAINE.

FROM YOUR FRIENDS IN BRUNSWICK

Chamberlain forced a grin at the kind words but couldn't hide his disappointment. Miller read his face and realized Chamberlain didn't have any idea what was happening.

"They must really like you upstate to do you like they're doin'," Miller said.

"I don't quite follow you, Sergeant," Chamberlain answered.

"The gift. I don't believe I've ever seen anything like it 'cept in pictures."

"Is there a package with this?"

"Why sure. It ain't in here, sir. It's outside."

"What do you mean?"

"That horse out there just got delivered and the name on it's yours."

Miller showed Chamberlain a shipping invoice and point-ed to a line that indicated the horse was to be delivered to *Lt. Col. J.L.Chamberlain, Camp Mason, Portland, Maine.*

The two men walked back outside and studied the majestic ani-mal waiting patiently for a rider.

"That saddle came with the horse, too," Miller said.

Chamberlain tried to picture himself taking such a beautiful horse into enemy fire. What a waste it would be to destroy such a marvelous creature.

"He's a beauty ain't he?" Miller commented.

"Yes, he is," Chamberlain answered hesitantly. He stepped down off the porch and examined the finest mount he had ever seen.

"It'd be a hell of a thing to have him all shot up."

Chamberlain glared at Miller's comment, though he was thinking the same thing.

"I mean, sir, that animal is almost too perfect to be runned around on a battlefield."

"Well, I'll agree with that, Sergeant." Chamberlain told him. "Does he have a name?"

"Nothing in the papers, Colonel."

Chamberlain stepped back and studied the broad shoulders and haunches of his new horse. "I believe I shall call you...Prince."

"That's a fine name, sir," Miller said. "Matter of fact, I don't think a horse like that could be named anything other."

Chamberlain scratched Prince's white mane and talked softly to him for a few moments before he climbed onto his back. The stallion was calm and only shifted slightly when Chamberlain swung himself into the saddle. He then led Prince around the parade ground, trotting among the men who were still preparing for the next day's departure. Many a head turned along the way to see who the proud young officer was mounted on the handsome white steed. Chamberlain was embarrassed of the attention at first, but soon pictured how gallant a sight he would be leading men onto the field on such a spectacular horse.

It was a perfect gift and it made him all the more anxious to find a Rebel fight.

The 20th Maine's last night in camp was more celebration than last minute preparation. Alcohol was not permitted in the camp, yet several bottles of whiskey and beer found their way into the men's hands. Some of the men even paid off a quartermaster's aide and borrowed a supply wagon to ride into town for one last visit to a Portland whorehouse.

Chamberlain reluctantly left Prince in the hands of the stable master and then walked among the tents in his customary form, occasionally stopping to chat with the groups of soldiers seated around their campfires. Most of the talk was of "Killing Rebs," and, "Showing old Jeff Davis what a Maine man could do." There was little reflection of home or the discussion of the hazards of war. Chamberlain was glad to see the men's spirits were so high. He found the suddenly boosted morale infectious, and knew it would certainly increase the colonel's confidence in the regiment.

ᔕ

The train ride to Boston went smoothly. The men passed the time playing cards and swapping lies. Ames and his staff sat together, privately reviewing tactics and military procedure. When they disembarked in Boston, the 20th Maine began a march through the old New England streets toward the historic wharf. The sidewalks filled with woman and old men cheering the green regiment on to battle.

"Where you boy's from!" a snaggle-toothed man leaning on a cane yelled out.

"The land of spruce gum and buckwheat cakes!" was the reply from the center of the regiment.

Chamberlain and Ames, from horseback at the front of the column, looked at each other and smiled.

"Then three cheers for the Old Pine State!" the old man called out and waved his hat over his head.

The air came alive with synchronized cheers, the men proudly marching through it as if they'd already conquered many a foe.

The huge steamer Merrimac sat waiting for them at the pier when they arrived. The soldiers marveled at its size as they marched passed it toward a nearby bivouac area where tents were already set up. The regiment filed into the temporary campsite and then the men were given last minute instructions before they were dismissed. It had been a long day, and since the men were forbidden to leave the camp area, they had nothing to do but sit around in small groups near campfire light and wonder out loud what their future entailed.

The rumors of another battle having occurred at Manassas, Virginia, were confirmed while the men were in the city. Ames and his staff were issued copies of several of the field reports from the battle and they told a disheartening tale. The second battle at Bull Run Creek had been even more tragic than the first. A Confederate general named Thomas Jackson had nearly decimated the Federal force there under John Pope. The reports were estimating Union casualties as high as 13,800, compared to some 8,300 estimated Confederate casualties. The door was now open for the Rebels to march on Washington, which was only a long day's march east of the Manassas battlefield. The men of the 20th Maine immediately assumed they weren't going to the capital to be routinely dispersed to the South, anymore. Now, they were going to their nation's headquarter to defend it. With the unexpected news of another defeat, the evening was far from the party the men had indulged in the night before.

Early the next morning the men were given time to eat and then provided a last few minutes to relieve themselves and fill canteens from a well before assembling on board the Merrimac. The ship was spacious and the men spread out in the ample sleeping quarters. But the rhythm of drum beats and the shuffling of mass footsteps slowly grew from outside the ship. Soon, the 1,200 strong 32nd Massachusetts Volunteers were also preparing to board. The Maine men scrambled to gather their belongings and make room for their new shipmates. The two groups mingled cordially, and the following four day voyage was only made comfortable by the friendships that were formed by the new comrades.

The final leg of the trip found the Merrimac passing the Mount Vernon home of George Washington. Both regiments crowded the deck and removed their caps in respect for the man they knew as the father of their country. A few hours later, the men arrived at the port in Alexandria, Virginia, where they again moved to a bivouac area already prepared for them.

The relief of being back on steady ground was short lived, though. The small port was also receiving hospital ships carrying casualties from the second battle at Bull Run. Men from both regiments watched in silent horror as war ravaged bodies were carried down the wooden planks on canvass stretchers.

Chamberlain noticed the attention being given the activity on the pier and quickly called for the regiment to assemble. He then spontaneously ordered his company commanders to review musket maintenance procedures- a feeble attempt to distract the already tainted men.

The 20th Maine was still without rifles, but Chamberlain insisted they continue to train as if the men were armed. This was particularly important since the general assumption was that they would soon be engaging with the enemy.

The two regiments marched to Washington the next morning, their first stop being the weapons arsenal. The men were relieved to find the capital safe, and were even more relieved to finally being issued weapons. The 20th men were each given an Enfield musket and 40 paper cartridges, each containing powder and a 58 caliber minié ball. The weight of the added equipment made the men finally feel complete and there were no complaints.

The regiment was then marched onto the Army's assembly grounds in front of the giant new Capitol building. There was no sense in trying to keep the men in step, as few of the Mainers had ever seen so many people in one place before. Their heads swung from side to side in amazement of the thousands of other soldiers milling about the Capitol's yard.

It was far from a beautiful sight. The ground was muddy and rutted from horseshoe prints and wagon wheel scars. The stench of sewage and horse manure and men being massed together permeated the autumn breeze. Even the scaffolding on the unfinished Capitol dome gave it the ugly appearance of having been recently bombarded.

Ames sent one of his captains to find a suitable area to place the regiment for the night, preferably up-wind if possible. A few minutes later young Ellis Spears returned with news of a spot among some dogwood trees at the west end of the giant sea of men. The regiment quickly scrambled to the spot at the route step before it could be claimed by another unit. They then made camp on the yard that would later hold the Abraham Lincoln Memorial.

The next morning the 20th Maine crossed over the Potomac River via the Long Bridge and marched seven miles to Fort Craig, Virginia. This was their first real march, and the men discovered the added weight of their new equipment and carrying full rations was rather uncomfortable to say the least. Even their new Endfield rifles, that were so welcomed the previous day, had become a burden to shoulder during the march. To make matters even worse, the tired fife and drum unit performed so poorly that Colonel Ames eventually ordered them to, "Cease that racket!"

By the time the 20th arrived at Fort Craig exhausted and hungry, Colonel Ames was livid with his men's performance. Some of them had fallen over a mile behind the rest of the regiment and heavy pieces of equipment had been sporadically discarded along the road. Ames knew that the men would soon be ordered to march three times the distance with much less in their stomachs and on little sleep. If the regiment couldn't weather such a short march already, they were in no way prepared for what lay ahead.

Ames had Major Gilmore take charge of the regiment and then he and Chamberlain rode off to inform their brigade commander, Colonel T.B.W. Stockton, that they had arrived.

Stockton had recently replaced General Dan Butterfield as the 3rd Brigade's commander, and he was convinced the entire 5th Corp would soon be moving out. He shared his expectations with Ames and told him to make sure his men got plenty of rest, because a long march was probably in their near future.

Already in camp were five other regiments from New York, Pennsylvania, and Michigan. They were made up of Bull Run veterans who were glad to see they were being reinforced. But the new

20th Maine still had to prove itself worthy of the respect of the more seasoned 3rd Brigade regiments. After all, they had yet little more than sweat having soiled their uniforms.

Ames and Chamberlain returned to the scattered men who were either sitting or lying on a knoll adjacent to the road. Ames assembled his staff and gave them a list of chores to be performed before the day's end. He then returned to the brigade headquarters to investigate how his regiment might be used in the next few days.

The men were led to a clearing where they ate and discarded some of their gear. After an hour's rest they were ordered back on their feet and positioned in a battle line facing a thick wooded area. Chamberlain and Gilmore then stood by with the rest of the officer staff and supervised the drill of loading and firing the new muskets. The last minute exercise proved to be a wise idea- a few of the new rifles were inoperable and needed to be exchanged. Five volleys were eventually fired and then Chamberlain ended the training to avoid the waste of ammunition.

Ames called the regiment's drummers and fife players to his tent later in the evening. As the rest of the officer staff stood behind him, Ames declared that he would never be associated with such embarrassment again. "If you can't do any better than you did today, you'd better all desert and go home!" he scolded. He then sent them away to practice until they, "Got it right!"

On September 12, 1862, the entire 1st Division began a long march toward Frederick, Maryland. Two grueling days of marching at the route step followed, each day covering over twenty miles. On the second day of the march the men's spirits were lifted when they learned that the well-liked General George McClellan was again the commander of the Federal Army.

The regiment set up camp on the banks of the Monocacy River that night, where the men soaked their aching feet in the cold clear water. Many had developed blisters and they picked them open to release the fluid, believing it would allow the wounds to scab and heal faster. It was a blunder typical of inexperienced soldiers. Marching with open sores on their feet only exposed them to much more severe infections.

Though the late afternoon sky was clear, the rumble of distant thunder filled the sky.

"Cannon?" Sergeant Thomas Chamberlain asked another soldier who was seated next to him at the river's edge. Both men had their feet innocently dangling in the water.

"Yep," was the confident answer. "Somewhere out there is the war we been itchin' to fight. I suppose it's too late to turn around now."

"Yah," the youngest Chamberlain agreed. "I guess we're gonna be in it tomorrow."

"I'd guess you're right, Sergeant."

Both men sat silently, staring into the shallow river bottom until dark.

The next day the 20th Maine marched through the town of Frederick, Maryland, surrounded by a throng of Union supporters who cheered and waved handkerchiefs in the air. The regiment camped with the entire 1st Division later that night, among hundreds of campfires glowing in the northeast Maryland countryside.

Early the morning of September 16th, the 20th Maine began its march into what could only be called a valley of death. Strewn items of discarded equipment littered the roadside- an eerie sign they were not the first legion to travel the road. Burned and crumbling farmhouses

sat alone on trampled and gutted farmland. The homes had been reduced to nothing more than abandoned piles of wasted debris. Dead
and bloated wagon horses then appeared and the rancid odor of rotting
flesh grew stronger with each step forward. Swarms of hungry flies
buzzed around the sweating men.

When the regiment entered Turner's Gap, a pathway through
South Mountain, Chamberlain could see small dark mounds scattered
around a stone wall that ran adjacent to a country road. From atop his
mount the figures of those lifeless piles gradually came into focus, and
Chamberlain's spine chilled at the sight. The morbid piles where the
Confederate victims of Union General John Gibbon's Black Hat Brigade.

Two days earlier they had taken the stone wall after a bloody stand
by the outnumbered Rebels defending it. The Union casualties had
been tended to, but the dead enemy soldiers had been left to rot. The
soldiers of the 20th Maine covered their noses with their sleeves and
swatted the flies away with their free hand. The grizzly deformities
of disfigured limbs and brain matter spilling from open head wounds
caused many to break rank and cough up their breakfast on the road-
side. No man of the new regiment had prepared himself for such a
sight, and they were anxious to pass through the tragic scene.

Chamberlain spotted a disarmed Rebel soldier sitting up against
a tree, and rode out to offer him aide as his regiment watched from
the road. But when he approached the beaten warrior, he discovered
he was already dead and, sadly, no more than a teenage boy. His tattered gray Confederate uniform was stained with his own dried blood.
A tiny New Testament bible lay in his opened right palm. Tears rolled
into Chamberlain's thick blonde whiskers as he prayed for his enemy's
soul. It would become a memory he chose never to forget.

The 20th Maine marched on to Boonsboro and then Keedysville, Maryland, where their division joined the rest of McClellan's army, and the 5th Corps. Along the way the deep booming of cannon fire in the west was a constant reminder the men were moving closer to battle. Then the crackling sound of distant musket fire and bugle calls began to fill the air.

There was no time or space to set up shelters for the night. The enemy was close by and the 20th's current position could very well become a battlefield at any moment. The 1st Division's commander, Major General George W. Morrel, wanted all of his units ready to move within minutes if called to do so. Ames relayed the order to his staff and it was filtered down to the men.

The waiting resulted in a long almost sleepless night. To add to the tension, a steady drizzle turned to rain by midnight, and the Union Army of 75,000 that had assembled just beyond Sharpsburg, Maryland, was drenched as they tried to sleep in the open.

Chamberlain managed to drift off to sleep under his rubber blanket, but was rattled from his slumber at dawn by the sudden rumblings of artillery fire. The rain had ended sometime during the night, and the hazy morning fog was clearing. The distant booms separated as an opposing battery began to return fire. Chamberlain quickly rinsed his mouth with canteen water, relieved himself behind a tree, and reported to the command post tent where Ames had slept. The colonel was already awake and dressed. He spotted his second-in-command and waved him in.

"This is it, Chamberlain," he said anxiously. "We've got the whole Army of Northern Virginia trapped out there. I wouldn't be surprised if Bobby Lee was right up in the middle with them."

"Do we have orders, sir?" Chamberlain asked.

"Not yet, but we will soon. Get the men up and fed. It's going to be a long day so make sure they're ready. There will be a few who got their powder wet last night. Have them all check for damaged ammunition and make replacements immediately. A man who can't fire a cartridge is no use to me."

"Understood, sir."

Ames walked over to Chamberlain and uncharacteristically put his arm around his back. "Lawrence, you will learn more today of battle than anything I have taught you. Remember, the key to success is in our command. Lead with valor and your men will follow." He patted Chamberlain on his chest and stepped away from him. "Go on now and get the regiment ready."

"Yes, sir."

Chamberlain walked back among the 20th men and called for his company commanders. He told them to get the men up and have them check their ammunition for water damage. As soon as their equipment was checked the officers were to get the men fed and ready to march. Chamberlain then walked back to his bedroll and assembled his own gear.

The enlisted men had already started small fires only large enough to heat water for coffee. Chamberlain joined one of the cold huddled groups and added a portion of his own coffee ration to their pot. The men wanted to know what was happening, but their lieutenant colonel had no idea. It was obvious an assault had begun, but by whom and how many, that was anyone's guess.

Chamberlain took reports of illness and requests for equipment replacements throughout the rest of the morning while the sounds of war raged across the Antietam Creek. He assumed many of the men had just gotten sick by having to sleep in the rain the night before. There was no call for anyone to receive lighter duty. He had himself developed a mild fever and his stomach churned with nervous anxiety.

Chamberlain finished his menial duties and decided to join a few of the other 1st Division officers who were riding out to a Union battery post to see what was happening down below. From the observation point among the Federal cannons, the small group of men watched two armies battling through a wide open cornfield. The Union force was General Joseph Hooker's I Corps, and his men were being pummeled by a line of Confederate cannons placed in the yard of a small white church.

Chamberlain watched intently as the Federal line would gather momentum in the field, only to fall back under a fusillade of shrapnel and musket lead. The retreat would be pursued by a line of gray Rebel infantry, but then they would fold under the same rain of destruction by Union cannons. The pattern repeated itself for three hours until the field was covered with fallen corpses. The site of distant battle was surreal to Chamberlain, and the idea that so many Federal soldiers were being held in reserve while others were being slaughtered angered him. A bugle suddenly sounded nearby and Chamberlain recognized his regiment was finally being called to move.

The brigade was marched approximately two miles south to reinforce another division, but was then later turned around to return to their original post. As the sun slowly dropped behind the western horizon, the sounds of war silenced and the Battle of Antietam was done.

On this single bloodiest day of the war, places called The Cornfield and The Bloody Lane would find their way into the pages of American history. Yet the 20th Maine would not be a part of that tale, as they stood in reserve on September 17, 1862. Joshua Lawrence Chamberlain would only listen and watch on that day as Federal soldiers sacrificed their lives for the Union. And even though he watched the slaughter safely from the high ground of a ridge far above it all, Chamberlain was suddenly afraid.

CHAPTER 3

FIRST BLOODING

The day after the Battle of Antietam, the men of the 20th Maine loitered about the camp impatiently waiting for orders to begin the pursuit of the retreating Confederates. General McClellan declared the battle a resounding victory and promptly sent his self-congratulatory report to President Lincoln. But while the cautious Army commander patted himself on the back for the next few days, the Army of Northern Virginia slipped, unopposed, back across the Potomac River into Virginia, having inflicted some 2000 more casualties on the Union Army than it had lost. And this from a Rebel force half the size of the Federal Army amassed at Antietam.

Chamberlain and Ames learned that there had been at least two opportunities for their regiment to have been called to service during the battle, and each incident would have likely saved countless Union lives. The first instance was clear to Ames and Chamberlain. They had personally watched the furious fighting in the initial assault on the cornfield, and saw how, for hours, two enemy divisions attacked and counterattacked in senseless slaughter. Had another Union regiment been sent into the fight, the Rebels would have been repelled much sooner.

The second opportunity had come during the fighting over a sunken road, where two Union divisions had been held back by a Rebel division entrenched in the lane. The 20th Maine had been moved forward by that time in the day, and was less than a mile away when that part of the offensive took place.

Ames shared his view with his subordinate officer that their regiment could have easily been used to flank the enemy position. In hindsight, though, Ames was relieved that the inexperienced 20th had not been called to the front. In his opinion, they were far from battle ready. Chamberlain didn't share that opinion, yet kept his view to himself. He believed the men needed a good fight and the sooner they got into one the better.

On September 20, the regiment was finally ordered with the rest of the 5th Corps to begin the pursuit of the Rebel force. At Shepherdstown Ford, just north of the nearly abandoned town of Harpers Ferry, the regiment was one of many ordered to cross the Potomac River into Virginia. When the long blue convoy ahead of them began crossing the shallow, rock bottom river, cannon fire and musket balls suddenly poured from the surrounding ridge tops. At first the Federal troops lumbered forward in a mad scramble to the cover of the Virginia side of the bank. But the Rebels concealed in the hills soon found their marks and Yankee infantrymen began to fall lifelessly into the cold rapids.

Ames called the 20th Maine to the river's edge and ordered his men into the cold clear water just as responding Union artillery began to answer the Rebel cannons. Chamberlain and Ames, both on horseback, then waded into the water with sabers in hand, pushing their men forward.

The *fizz* and *zip* sound of Confederate minié' balls flying through the air drove many of the men to stop and hunch down behind fallen trees and large boulders for cover. Within minutes the wide rocky ford was a mass of disarray. Soldiers having nearly crossed the river retreated without command. The injured that were unable to support themselves cried out for help as they were swept down river.

Ames realized the congestion of panicked men was making them too easy targets. He yelled out to his lieutenant colonel, "Get these men across! We can't defend ourselves in this water!"

Chamberlain wheeled his horse around to face the men still behind him. "Come on Twentieth Maine!" he yelled. "There's a Rebel for each of you on the other side!"

With his sword swinging above his head, Chamberlain repeated commands of "Forward!" and "Come on boys!"

The trudging mass slowly moved forward, the 20th Maine passing through their fellow retreating regiments toward Virginian soil. Soon the shallows allowed the men better footing, and they began to jog to a dirt embankment lining the river. But the Confederate artillery of General A.P. Hill had already established concentrated fire marks on the river bank and the shoreline erupted with flying lead and mud. Those still in the water watched as men from the 118th Pennsylvania, the first to reach the enemy's side of the riverbank, were suddenly caught in a murderous crossfire of Rebel guns. The Union men still in the river answered by senselessly firing into the hills without acquiring targets. The Rebels were clearly at too great an advantage. Only a few minutes after the first Union infantrymen reached the other side, bugle calls sounded from the Federal position behind them. Retreat!

Ames and his officers yelled out the command in echoed chorus and the 20th Maine dove back into the frigid Potomac. The Confederate artillery followed them and great plumes of white water splashed into the air with each deadly blast. Chamberlain rode out to the center of the river and stopped his horse. There, he stood erect in his saddle, waving the men back to the place they had started.

A Confederate sharpshooter spotted the careless Union officer and placed his sights on the Yankee prize. Chamberlain heard the *zip* and a thud sound below him, but didn't realize his horse had just been shot until the borrowed mare stumbled and dropped down to a knee. Chamberlain jumped into the water and continued his duty from the side of the dying horse as she rolled onto her side.

When the last group passed him, he studied the shallow rapids one last time to locate any injured men he could save. There were none. The only soldiers still in the water were dead and being swept down river along with discarded packs and blankets that had been weighing down the soldiers frantically attempting to make the crossing.

Ames assembled the regiment in an open meadow and took a count. Only three men had been wounded. None were dead. The 118th had lost over one-third of their men. Ames couldn't help but feel relief at knowing his regiment had survived the debacle with so few casualties. He even found humor in the condition of his soaked lieutenant colonel when he first came upon him. His blonde hair was matted to his head and his drooping whiskers were still draining onto his chin.

Chamberlain didn't find any humor in his condition, though, and his eyes were piercing like those of an eagle. This had been his first real taste of leading men into enemy fire, and he was as equally terrified of what he had just been through, as he was proud of his performance. A burgeoning new confidence in his abilities had been born.

Ames' initial instinct was to comment on the appearance of his drenched pupil, but the look on Chamberlain's face made comment inappropriate. He had stood fearlessly in harm's way and had kept the regiment intact. It was the performance Ames needed to see, and now he was confident in the spirit of his new regiment.

The men were moved away to safety and then after a short rest were marched back to a camp area near Antietam Ford.

All the next week the 20th Maine helped dig graves and bury dead soldiers from the great battle on the 17th. The men eventually grew morbidly accustomed to the site of the grotesque wounds inflicted on the bodies, but they could never develop immunity to the stench of the rotting flesh.

Chamberlain spent his time visiting the wounded that were still holding onto their lives. Several farmhouses and a small white church that had once been a Confederate artillery position had been converted into field hospitals. Chamberlain spent much of his time there, though there was little he could do except offer encouraging words and assist with letter writing.

On the 24th, Chamberlain had finally grown tired of watching the piles of amputated limps accumulating outside of one of the hospitals and he voiced his displeasure of the display with a supervising field surgeon. When the frustrated doctor sarcastically told Chamberlain he had no concern with what went on outside of the building, Chamberlain demanded he follow him outside for a private conversation. The doctor reluctantly agreed and followed Chamberlain out the back door where a mound of arms and legs was being photographed by a reporter.

"I appreciate your services, sir," Chamberlain told him. "I have personally watched you save many men these past few days. But the men have come to believe you are quick with the saw. How am I to argue in your defense when you insist on turning the yard of your hospital into the scene of a cattle butchery?"

"I need every man assigned to me caring for wounded, Colonel," the doctor responded. "I haven't the resources to detail men to appropriately discard these limbs. But, sir, if you for a moment believe I find some satisfaction in this, you are mistaken."

"Then I shall dispatch a company to you this evening and we will resolve this issue."

"I'll be here."

Chamberlain extended his hand in an attempt to show he was sorry if he'd been disrespectful to the surgeon. The doctor accepted the gesture, but showed the lieutenant colonel his blood-soaked hand was in no condition for shaking. Chamberlain disregarded its condition and grasped the surgeon's hand, holding it firmly. The two men then parted as gentlemen and Chamberlain returned to his regiment's campsite.

The weary lieutenant colonel and Ames were now sharing a tent, and there he found his superior reading a Maryland newspaper.

Ames laid the paper out on his cot and pointed at it. "There it is," he said to Chamberlain.

"What is that, sir?"

"Take a look for yourself," Ames told him. "By God, I almost don't believe it," he continued.

Chamberlain took the paper to his bed, sat down, and scanned the front page. It was an article about an official *Proclamation* that Lincoln was going to enact on the first day of the new year. He read further and it became clear that the *Emancipation Proclamation* was a notice that slavery was going to be formally abolished. Chamberlain lowered the paper and looked at Ames, not sure what his point of view on the subject was.

"Did you read it?" Ames asked.

"Enough of it, yes, sir," Chamberlain answered.

"Do you know what this means?"

"I assume it means that we will soon be liberating a great deal of slaves," Chamberlain surmised.

Ames sat down next to his naive pupil. "It means this war is now *about* slavery. Correct?"

"I can see that, yes, sir," Chamberlain agreed.

"Why do you suppose Lincoln decided to write this order now, and not at the end of the war? Do you think the men will fight harder?"

Chamberlain had to think for a moment about that question.

Ames didn't wait for his answer. "Do you think now suddenly those who have not joined our fight will run to take up arms with us for the purpose of liberating slaves?"

"There might be a signi..." Chamberlain tried to answer.

"Lawrence, think," Ames interrupted. "The only way the South is going to win this war, is if they get assistance from someone across the Atlantic. You're a man who has studied the cultures of the world. What European government is going to support an army fighting to maintain slavery? The French? The British?"

"No one," Chamberlain answered confidently. "At least no one who can truly affect us."

"Precisely." Ames looked at Chamberlain, waiting for the strategy of the proclamation to sink in.

Chamberlain was still puzzled. "You think the President did this just to keep Britain out of the war?"

"Ah, my favorite student," Ames congratulated him. "He did it *now*, just to keep Britain out of the war. Genius- absolutely genius. "

"To some of us," Chamberlain said, "this war is already about slavery."

"But wouldn't you agree it is more about preserving the Union?" Ames asked.

"Certainly."

"So why would President Lincoln suddenly decide to drastically alter the subject of the war, unless it meant a great advantage in our favor?"

"I don't think he has changed the subject of the war," Chamberlain answered. "He has only formally addressed one of the reasons we are fighting."

"My dear Professor, you have just made my point," Ames declared. "You and I, and everyone else in this great army know, when we win this war, slavery will be abolished. Our President Lincoln has only taken that fact and written it in bold letters for all those who might interfere in our cause to see. On your own admission there is not a threatening power left in the world that will come to the Confederacy's aide now."

Slowly Chamberlain was able to recognize the politics behind the announcement of the proclamation. He accepted Ames' conclusion that it was not a dishonest ploy, but a tactical maneuver to end the war more promptly without the fear of European influence. Personally, Chamberlain was pleased that the question of his government's dedication to the anti-slavery movement had finally been clarified. It made him that much more confident that his involvement in the war was the right thing to do.

On October 1st, the camp came alive with rumors that President Lincoln was present to review the condition of his army. The talk was confirmed when the entire 5th Corps was called to inspection. Chamberlain and Ames, both on horseback, proudly stood before the 20th Maine. When Lincoln's entourage passed them, the President stopped and said a few words to McClellan about the beautiful white horse the Maine lieutenant colonel was mounted on. Chamberlain was proud of the recognition, even if it was only directed toward his horse, Prince.

Chamberlain studied the tall wrinkled face of his commander in chief as he passed by. He could see the weight of the war in his tired eyes. The President, in his characteristic stove top hat and black suit, seemed incapable of a smile. And even with his staff surrounding him he appeared very much alone. Chamberlain felt sorry for Lincoln, and wanted to somehow break rank and bestow his support for the man. It was only a thought though, and Chamberlain remained in place during the remainder of the ceremony.

The President left McClellan's headquarters the next day and the camp fell back into its usual routines. Ames drilled the regiment relentlessly and became more despised by the men with each passing day. Sergeant Thomas Chamberlain became so concerned for his colonel's welfare that he wrote a note to his big brother, requesting an urgent informal meeting to discuss it. When the elder Chamberlain read the note requesting his private audience, he immediately summoned his brother, believing the subject was news from home. The meeting was set for after supper when the two could slip away unnoticed. They met at the foot of a tall willow tree that both recognized as a distinct out of the way landmark

"So, Tom, how are you?" Chamberlain asked, not as a casual greeting, but sincerely wanting to know how his brother was doing.

"I'm fine, Colonel," Thomas answered uncomfortably. "Lawrence, do I really have to call you Colonel right now?"

"No, Tom," Chamberlain told him. "We're just two brothers talking. No one else is around and I assume this is family business. You can call me Lawrence if you want."

"Well, here's the problem, Lawrence, and I'm sorry but it's not family business. It's about Colonel Ames." Thomas took a deep breath, gathered his wits, and continued. "Now I know you and the colonel are getting pretty close these days. And I'm sure he's a much nicer fella when just you two are sittin' around thinkin' up things for us to do. But his ways with the regiment are making a lot of the men pretty mad and there's been talk they're about at the end of the rope."

"You mean desertion?"

"Hell no," Thomas responded with a frown. "Those men want to kill Rebels so bad they can hardly sleep at night without dreamin' about it. I'm talking about gettin' rid of the colonel."

"And how are they going to do that?"

The young sergeant paused for a moment and began nervously picking the bark off a fallen tree limb. "If those boys find out I told you this, Lawrence, they'll string me up."

"I'll keep it in confidence. Now out with it."

"There's been talk that the next time we get in the mix, someone's gonna make sure the colonel takes a musket ball."

Chamberlain bit at his lip and imagined the consequences of the conspiracy his brother had just shared with him.

Thomas continued. "It's not just one or two of them that feel this way, Lawrence, otherwise I wouldn't tell. But there's a whole mess of them who want him gone. He's just too mean."

"Don't the men understand that the sooner they master their drill, the sooner the colonel will ease his demands on them?"

"That's the problem. We' been gettin' better and he just gets meaner. A more ornery man I've never known."

The two siblings sat silently together while Chamberlain thought about what he should do. Having troops dislike their officers because of the endless commands and often groundless tongue lashings was simply a reality of soldiering. Chamberlain knew the men who made up the 20th Maine were no more accustomed to taking orders than any of the other volunteers. But those men had learned to adjust to the system of obeying a chain of command, so why couldn't the Mainers do the same. Chamberlain told his little brother that he would see what he could do, though he had no idea what that was at the time. Then the two men parted.

Chamberlain walked to an officer's mess wagon to get a cup of coffee and then drank alone as he tried to find a way to settle his disgruntled regiment. He quickly decided the first thing he needed to do was find a way to separate Ames from the men.

Later that night after returning to his tent, Chamberlain offered to conduct the following day's drills so Ames could use the day to himself to catch up on letter writing and other administrative duties. The colonel liked the idea, and told Chamberlain he would probably ride into town with some fellow West Point alumni and pick up some gifts to send home to his family.

The next morning Chamberlain formed the regiment as far away from the other members of the 3rd Brigade as he could so he wouldn't be overheard. He then informed the men that Colonel Ames had been so pleased with their recent progress, he had decided that he need not be present for that day's training. Chamberlain added that he overheard the colonel make a comment to an officer from another regiment that he had the toughest lot in the entire 5th Corps, and that he treated his men like hell because they would prove to be the devils of the entire Army of the Potomac. Chamberlain watched each man in the formation subtly straighten his shoulders and proudly raise his chest. He then looked down at his brother, who stood grinning at the front of B Company. There would be no more talk of the assassination of Colonel Adelbert Ames.

Chamberlain and the 20th Maine remained in place at the camp outside of Sharpsburg for the rest of October and early November 1862. The stagnant army was now suffering the consequences of having thousands of men living together in such close quarter. The cold wet autumn, coupled with poor sanitary conditions, caused disease to spread among the ranks. Diarrhea became a particular problem and the men were shedding pounds rapidly. The tents and crude shelters the men called home kept much of the rain out, but couldn't protect them from the cold and growing rodent infestation. And once the grass had been trampled and the camp turned to mud, it was impossible to keep anything clean.

Chamberlain and Ames rigged a small fireplace in their quarters to keep warm and heat coffee with. Unfortunately, they were unable to design a proper ventilation system that would keep the smoke from filling the tent when the heavy rains caused a downward draft. Eventually, after repeated attempts at rectifying the exhaust problem, the college professor and West Point graduated succumbed to the idea that they simply couldn't devise a way to remedy their problem. Chamberlain ended the ordeal by declaring, "Well, sir. It's either outside to be soaked, or inside to be smoked."

Though the hardships of disease, cold weather, and boredom were all around, Chamberlain remained upbeat about his new life as a soldier. He convinced himself not to dwell on the bad, with the hopes that soon the 5th Corps would be moving out. On October 30, they finally received orders. The 20th Maine would be leaving camp with less than 550 healthy men- less than half of its original size.

South again across the Potomac River into Virginia, the regiment moved unchallenged. They stopped at the old armory town of Harpers Ferry made famous by the abolitionist John Brown, and then to Snicker's Gap, a name found to be quite amusing to the Union infantrymen.

News arrived on November 7 that General McClellan had been replaced again, now by Major General Ambrose Burnside. The

President had grown tired of McClellan's unreasonable restraint from advancing on the South. He was subsequently being replaced to send a clear message to all of Lincoln's commanders that he wanted a more aggressive campaign.

McClellan remained well-liked by the rank and file though, especially with those who had joined the Army at the beginning of the war. They believed his caution was rooted in his concern for them, and had nothing to do with being a timid leader. The men of the 20th Maine took his replacement in stride. They were still new to the war and McClellan had only kept them from the fight they so desperately wanted to be a part of.

The area around Snicker's Gap was grazing land and livestock was plentiful. Unfortunately, the citizen's of the area were mostly Rebel sympathizers and they didn't much care for the presence of the invading Federal Army. Attempts to lawfully purchase their cattle and chickens were rejected by the angry Virginians, but that wouldn't sway the hardtack-tired Yankees. The common result of such a snubbing usually resulted in the nighttime disappearance of the very animals that had been the subject of attempted legal acquisition earlier in the day. In the next morning's light, those same animals could be found tied to a Union wagon or already being butchered. Chamberlain didn't mind the idea of the looting of food items from enemy sympathizers to feed his own men. As far as he was concerned, if his men didn't take it, the Confederates would.

The regiment continued south through a bitter cold snowstorm, the air so freezing that the water solidified in the men's canteens. The march continued for three days until the 5th Corps reached Warrenton, Virginia, where it stopped to rest for several days. Illness and severe frostbite weakened the ranks, but Federal Army Commander Burnside believed he couldn't wait for spring to make his move.

General Burnside never wanted the position as head of the entire Army. He had been offered the job before, but turned it down to continue as a corps commander. Himself a West Point graduate and in his late thirties, Burnside now found himself under a great deal of pressure to win a quick and decisive battle. To do so, he first realigned the Army of the Potomac into three *Grand Divisions*, each consisting of two corps. The 20th Maine and the rest of the 5th Corps was assigned to the Center Grand Division, under the command of Major General 'Fighting' Joe Hooker, previous commander of the 1st Corps. With a new battle plan and President Lincoln's cautious approval, the Army followed the Rappahannock River to Falmouth, Virginia. Across the icy waters lay the cobblestone streets and red brick buildings of Confederate held Fredericksburg.

The 20th Maine camped on a pine covered knoll outside of Falmouth on November 25th, only a few miles from Fredericksburg. The men were issued tents and new overcoats for the winter, but for some reason food rations had been interrupted. This was a particular problem, because the men had been promised that their food supply would be replenished when they reached Falmouth. With that in mind, the enlisted men had gorged all that was left of their rations the day before. Added to the discomfort of the initial lack of food at their new camp was the freezing wind chill. Ames felt that his integrity had been compromised by not providing his regiment with the rations he had promised, so to make up for it he made sure the 20th Maine was passed over for picket duty the first evening they spent on the bluffs looking over Fredericksburg.

Fortunately, supply wagons arrived the next morning and the 20th Maine loaded its haversacks with several days' rations- a pound of salt pork, a small loaf of bread, two scoops of ground coffee beans, and 27 hardtack biscuits. The pork and soft bread would be the first to go. Then the average soldier survived on the large rocklike flour and water biscuits until he was re-supplied.

Simply eating hardtack became an art form. The men who never took the time, or made an effort to indulge in the various hardtack recipes, often paid a price for their lack of initiative. Corps surgeons had to double as dentists to treat the broken teeth of men who impatiently bit into pieces of bland hardtack without softening them first with water. It was also not at all uncommon to see a soldier splintering a biscuit with the butt of his rifle just to break it into more chewable portions. Still, the thin cracker-shaped biscuits were the staple of the enlisted men's diets and they looked forward to having their supplies replenished.

The regiment stayed on the hill through the first week of December. On the 6th, a blizzard swept through the Union camp and continued through the next day. Two soldiers of the 20th, who were already sick with dysentery were discovered frozen to death. Another died from the gangrene he'd developed from infected blisters on his feet.

On the 10th, the men were given picket duty and had to leave the shelter of their tents for the night. The Mainers were used to cold winters, but their bodies weren't accustomed to the germs that tens of thousands of men spread when they were bunched together without adequate sanitary conditions. A fever passed quickly among them and more men began to die. Then, just as morale was about to reach its worst, the 1ˢᵗ Division was given its orders. The men were to march into Falmouth with three days' rations. It could mean only one thing; a battle was finally on the horizon.

CHAPTER 4

THE ASSAULT ON MARYE'S HEIGHTS, FREDERICKSBURG

The 20th Maine marched through the morning fog toward the sounds of laboring men and distant sporadic musket fire. Although they could not yet see the construction, a contingent of Union engineers were trying to piece together a group of pontoon bridges across the Rappahannock River, leading to the banks of Fredericksburg. The engineers were receiving Rebel sniper fire from the buildings along the river front and it was hampering the otherwise routine bridge assembly. When the dawn's mist sufficiently cleared, Union artillery began to pound the small city in an attempt to clear it of the enemy riflemen from a Mississippi regiment.

Colonel Ames stopped the 20th Maine far behind the Union line and called Chamberlain to join him while he scouted the Rebel positions. The two officers could see a long fortified Confederate line west of the city from the bluffs above the frigid river. A wide grassy clearing separated the enemy position from the outskirts of the city, creating a vast open killing field for the Federal infantry to cross. The Rebel force had taken the perfectly defensive high ground and was well-prepared for the Union attack.

Ames had been left in the dark as most of the other regimental commanders had regarding their objective. It was clear now that while they sat for nearly two weeks on the east side of the river freezing to death, the Confederate Army had been reinforcing its position in Fredericksburg. Freshly dug earthworks and a long stone wall were now inhabited by some 75,000 Rebel soldiers.

"Damn him!" Ames growled to himself.

Chamberlain knew he was cursing General Burnside for placing his army at such obvious risk.

"Shall I return to the regiment, sir?" Chamberlain asked.

"No," Ames answered sharply. "I want you to study this. I want you to know exactly what we're in for."

Chamberlain looked back down to the middle pontoon bridge, one of three being constructed. The engineers were easy targets for the snipers in the mostly abandoned merchant buildings along the river's edge. The bridge builders were repeatedly retreating to the safety of the Federal side of the bank, only to regroup and go back out onto the exposed portion that was already assembled. As engineer casualties mounted, they were replaced by infantrymen who volunteered to join the construction. The entire scene was turning into a humiliating embarrassment for the Union side, as their massive force of over 100,000 was being pinned down by a small cadre of Rebel sharpshooters.

Finally men from Massachusetts, New York, and Michigan regiments had seen enough. They volunteered to take the city themselves if they had to, and Burnside gave them his blessing. Thus, the attempt to finish the bridge construction was replaced by those brave infantry soldiers who loaded into the pontoon boats and paddled to the Fredericksburg side. The men then scattered into town where each building was summarily cleared with minié ball and bayonet.

Into the afternoon and evening Ames and Chamberlain watched more boatloads of infantrymen paddling themselves across the river to join the street fighting in the city. All the while the Confederates amassed behind the city stood patiently quiet. With the enemy snipers cleared, the pontoon bridges were completed by nightfall.

Burnside ordered his initial forces across the river the next morning, holding the 5th Corps with the 20th Maine in reserve. The Union soldiers who crossed the bridges discovered the town had been abandoned, and took to ransacking it in mob-like fashion. Pointless vandalism and looting continued throughout the day. From the hillside just west of the city the Rebels watched the senseless destruction with a growing anger. It would make the killing that was sure to come that much easier.

Chamberlain also watched the city's ravaging from afar with his colonel at his side. Only nightfall temporarily halted the gutting of Fredericksburg, and only then because the Yankees knew they needed to rest. For it was clear to every man on both sides of the rebellion that the morning would bring with it a great fight.

The soldiers of the 5th Corps assembled themselves at dawn to watch the impending battle on the other side of the river. Again, a thick fog covered the field and troop movement was masked from view. Then, at 8:30 a.m., the crackling of musket fire to the south broke the morning calm. Rumbling cannon fire joined in and the battle had begun. The actual fight was too far away for Chamberlain to see, though great plumes of smoke appeared on the horizon. The distant sound of battle continued through the morning, but was so far away, none of the men of the 20th Maine even needed to raise his voice to be heard.

The Union batteries still positioned on the east side of the river opened up with a thunderous roar just before noon. Patches of dirt and smoke flew up from the grassy field in front of the Confederate line a mile away. Columns of blue infantry divisions stepped out of the city and formed on the field. Bugle calls and drumming accompanied the deafening booms of the heavy Federal guns. Regimental flags were carried to the front of the lines and flapped wildly in the winter breeze. Chamberlain marveled at the glorious sight. This was the valiant picture of war he had always dreamed of.

A whooping cheer from the Rebel line sounded, followed by a barrage of Confederate cannon fire. The explosions within the Union lines caused gaping holes in their formations. The Federal officers on the field quickly filled the gaps and ordered their men forward. Steadily, the long blue columns moved onto the open ground, their bayonets glistening in the sunlight. The Rebel cannons sprayed the field with deadly lead ball, but still the Union soldiers pressed on. A hundred yards from the stone wall, and suddenly the front of the Union offensive was cut down by a hail of musket fire. Entire lines fell as men still marching with rifles shouldered, collapsed to the ground. Another synchronized shower of lead poured into the Union ranks before they were themselves ordered to return fire.

Chamberlain watched in horror as the men in blue were cut down on the open field. Wave after wave of Union infantry marched out of the city toward the Confederate line, and each new line met the same deadly result.

The assault on the high ground known as Marye's Heights, unfolded before the entire 5th Corps, who watched angrily from their safe position still in reserve.

"Send us in! Put us in the fight!" the men began to yell. They couldn't stand by any longer watching their brothers slaughtered.

The order finally arrived at 3 p.m., and the 20th Maine marched across the Rappahannock with the rest of their corps. They assembled in town and waited for instructions, their view of the battlefield now obscured by the bombarded buildings. Colonel Ames left Chamberlain in charge of the regiment and rode off to get orders. He returned a few minutes later and led the 20th Maine down a narrow cobblestone alleyway toward the front. The end of the alley opened onto the battlefield, exposing a wall of smoke and explosions.

The officers dismounted their horses when they reached the rear of the Union line. They then ordered their men to prepare to advance on the enemy position. Those that were frightened prayed to themselves and squeezed trinkets of good luck. The men that were still seething with anger at having been held back for so long, snarled impatiently at the Rebel fortifications like rabid wolves waiting to be released on their prey.

Ames had to yell his directions to be heard over the noise. Smoke swirled across their column and choked the men who failed to prepare for the cloud of sulfurous fumes. Quickly, the 20th Maine filtered out of the tiny roadway and hurried into three battle lines.

The chaos of ear-piercing percussion, men screaming in agony, and thousands of soldiers wandering around the field, temporarily hypnotized Chamberlain. "God help us now!" woke him from his spell. It was Colonel Ames.

"Take the right wing!" Ames ordered. "I'll lead from here!"

Chamberlain reached across his belt and ripped his saber from its scabbard in one dramatic sweep. He then stepped to the right side of the line and nodded to Ames that he was ready.

"On to victory Great Sons of Maine!" Ames called out to the regiment. The ranks answered with waving caps and cheers.

"Follow me to Richmond boys! Forward...March!"

The 20th Maine lurched forward to the beat of their drummers. Through retreating men and over fallen casualties, they entered the great field of destruction. Ames ordered their weapons to the ready, and after a hundred yard march he stopped the men far short of the enemy wall. There was no use trying to storm the well-fortified barrier. The men stood a better chance taking the time to aim their deadly accurate muskets and inflicting casualties before reaching the stone entrenchment. The line was prepared to fire.

"Find a target, lads!" Chamberlain yelled down the line. Don't waste your rounds!"

Ames swept his saber downward signaling the command to fire. KaBoom!

Fire and sparks flew from the Enfield muzzles.

"Prepare to reload!" Ames commanded.

The regiment was then given the loading commands and again, "Fire!"

"Let's move them forward and to your right! " Ames shouted to Chamberlain after the volley. "I want to get us closer to that ridge!"

"Yes, sir!" Chamberlain answered and turned to the line standing next to him. "At the right angle! Double time... March!"

The men jogged forward and to the right. Chamberlain stopped them twenty yards later, behind a slight rolling knoll that would only provide cover to a man lying prone in the dead grass. The line was formed again and another volley was fired. Now the Confederates were directing their guns at Chamberlain's men and the Mainers began to drop from the ranks. In the panic and commotion of battle, the 20th Maine had passed the regiments that had entered the field before them. It was suddenly clear- they were now the most forward regiment.

"Get them into that ditch!" Ames shouted as his soldiers continued to fall around him.

Chamberlain frantically ordered the men to take cover behind the natural rise in the landscape. The men then returned fire from their bellies, shooting blindly into a fortified enemy position that allowed their adversaries almost complete control of the field. For the next hour and until darkness began to fall, the two forces fought to a stalemate.

The Rebels had withstood a continuous assault for several hours and still held the high ground. Their ranks were exhausted, but overwhelmingly still intact. On the field in front of them, thousands of Federal dead and dying lay in piles on the cold hardening ground. Among them, the trapped soldiers of the 20th Maine.

As the smoke cleared and the sky turned red, the horrific sounds of dying men crying out in agony filled the air. Both sides silenced their guns. The Rebel commanders were far too wise to counterattack from the security of their position. The Federals were in complete disarray and knew continued advance in the darkness would be futile.

As the field settled and the evening cold arrived, acts of compassion escaped from the rage that had earlier driven the two armies to acts of murderous slaughter. A Confederate infantrymen climbed over the stone wall and fed a dying Union soldier water when his anguished cries became too much to bear. The Yankees still pinned down on the field raised their caps and muskets and cheered the enemy rifleman they would later name the Angel of Marye's Heights.

An old woman stepped out of a small shell-battered home and began feeding water to the injured on both sides of the line. Seemingly oblivious to the danger, she made trip after trip, back-and-forth from the well in her yard. None of the men from either side matched her bravery. Instead, they continued to watch each other cautiously as darkness fell over the field of death. Moans and calls for help continued to rise up from the ravaged grounds, but the 20th Maine dared not leave the cover of the knoll.

The air turned freezing and the men huddled together to keep warm. Their blankets and new winter coats had been left with the quartermaster in Fredericksburg to lighten their load before the fruitless attack. Night dragged on, and Chamberlain winced helplessly at the sound of each shrill of agony ahead of him. He peered around the embankment, praying to see a white flag of temporary truce rising above the stone wall. *Too many men are bleeding to death, surely on both sides of the long Rebel line,* he thought to himself. But there was no flag of mercy.

Chamberlain scanned the field for men close enough to be dragged to safety. There, a ghostly picture emerged as the steam off the wounded bodies drifted up like souls being released to the heavens in the cold moonlit night. Chamberlain found peace in the apparition, and convinced himself God's will was being done.

He found himself again separated from Colonel Ames, and assumed the regiment was to maintain its forward position for a resumed attack in the morning. Chamberlain resigned to curling himself in a fetal position to keep warm for the rest of the night as his own officer's coat was no match for the bite of winter. But after only a few minutes he realized his own body heat would not keep him from freezing to death. Chamberlain would not allow himself to perish on the field of battle because of the cold. Even if it meant surviving the night only to be shot in the morning, he would do whatever it took to awaken to see the next day's fight. With new determination he slid himself away from the knoll and grabbed the back collar of a dead soldier, dragging the body back to the embankment next to another fallen comrade. He then placed himself between the two dead corpses and placed his head on a third. The macabre shelter would provide him the warmth to survive the night, but not to sleep.

Hours passed, then near midnight the sound of footsteps behind him alerted Chamberlain.

The regiment's adjutant, Lieutenant John Marshal Brown, knelt down and tapped on Chamberlain's shoulder.

"Colonel Chamberlain, sir."

Chamberlain rolled onto his side. Brown was a familiar face, having only recently graduated from Bowdoin College. Chamberlain had even been one of his professors.

"What is it, Mr. Brown?"

"I can't take anymore of this crying out, sir. Can't we do something?"

Chamberlain sat up and studied the enemy wall at Marye's Heights. Only a few Confederate men were at their posts, and they didn't seem at all interested with the Union ambulance wagons and the men tending the injured closer to town. He thought for a moment and then pulled his coat off. He then stripped one of the coats off of one of the dead enlisted men he was using for shelter and put his arms through its sleeves. Chamberlain then gathered his courage, believing his next move might be his last. With a final deep breath, he stood up from the safety of the dirt mound and faced the enemy. His act of defiance was unanswered.

Lieutenant Brown straightened his stance and stood with his fearful lieutenant colonel, but the Confederate sentries did not fire. Chamberlain gulped at the terror in his throat and turned to Brown.

"Get rid of that coat and find one that doesn't identify you as an officer. Let's keep the regiment down, and you and I can go see what we can do."

"Yes, sir," Brown answered softly.

Chamberlain took the canteens from the three dead bodies at his feet and slung their straps across his shoulder. The moon was now covered by thick dark clouds and the temperature sank with each gust of stinging wind. Chamberlain moved from body to body, offering water and religious words of solace. Seeing the gruesome opened flesh and shattered broken bones sickened him. It was only more heart-wrenching when the trauma had been survived. Chamberlain was asked several times to end the agony with a round from his pistol. He declined with words of encouragement and then moved on to the next fallen soldier.

There were few bandages and the men who could have been saved with tourniquets had already bled to death. Still, Chamberlain ordered the ambulance crews forward after having to convince them of his actual rank. He had wisely donned the less senior man's jacket to avoid becoming the prize of a Rebel who understood his value to the

Yankees trapped in front of the wall. With the arrival of added as-sistance, Brown and Chamberlain continued offering what little aide they could render until both men reached exhaustion. Believing an even bigger fight was approaching with daylight, the two men re-turned to their positions among the rest of the 20th Maine.

Chamberlain closed his eyes and focused his senses on a loose window shudder that was slamming back and forth in the wind. Its rhythm seemed to speak to him, "Never...Forever...Never...Forever." Chamberlain drifted off to sleep repeating the words in his head.

The next morning he awoke to a glistening blanket of frost over the entire battlefield. His body ached from shivering all night and his head throbbed with a growing migraine.

The Union soldiers at the front- the 16th Michigan, the 83rd Pennsylvania, and the 20th Maine- carefully poured water on hardtack biscuits and ate the soggy crackers while lying on their sides. The Confederates, on the other hand, were clanging pots and shuffling about enjoying their breakfast. Their casual manner was if they had no idea an enemy brigade was concealed in the gentle mounds of earth right in front of them. The Mainers were close enough to smell the cooking pork and boiling coffee of their enemy, and considered their rival's much superior breakfast a personal insult.

"God-damned bastards," an angry corporal declared as he waited for the water to absorb into a piece of hardtack.

Chamberlain whirled around and admonished the man with a scowl.

"Colonel, excuse me, sir, but those Reb boys are up there eatin' like kings, and we're down here gnawin' on bread harder'n a rock."

"Keep it to yourself, Corporal," Chamberlain ordered.

"Hey, why don't one uh you boys throw us a piece uh that you're cookin'!" A Pennsylvanian yelled up the hill.

"Why don't you come on up and get it, Yankee!" was the answer from behind the wall.

Several minutes of taunting continued with an almost gentlemanly tone, something Chamberlain found disturbing considering the men were about to resume killing each other at any moment. But the context of the banter also reminded him of something his father told him several months earlier while they sat together watching the Penobscot River- *Always remember, that man you're trying to kill is also an American.*

The hate for his enemy that had been building inside him as he walked among the hellish field the night before subsided. Chamberlain reflected upon the fact that the Confederate men were fighting for what they believed in and the battle had moved to their soil. If the point of the invasion was to bring them back to the Union, there was no room for hate. Chamberlain decided he would do his best to only think of the Confederate force as a group of misled men who were mostly uneducated, and therefore, didn't understand exactly what they were fighting for.

The men of the 20th Maine were so far forward, they couldn't be safely reached to be re-supplied with ammunition. Ames wisely ordered his regiment not to return fire to save what ammunition was left, unless the Rebels advanced from behind their cover. The result was a long morning of three regiments lying against the side of the embankment waiting for a decision to be made by their generals.

Later in the afternoon over a hundred Confederates were spotted moving into a wooded area on the regiment's left flank. Ames dispatched a group of sharpshooters from the 20th to join the Michigan and Pennsylvania regiments in defending their exposed side. The rest of the men frantically dug small trenches in the frozen ground with their bayonets, and piled corpses around their makeshift earthworks for additional cover.

Musket fire soon erupted from the Rebel position now on their left, and the 20th Maine nestled behind the cover of their fallen comrades. A young regiment drummer cradling his instrument in terror, became so sickened by the sound of enemy rounds thumping into the dead bodies, he lurched forward and spat up the doughy contents of his stomach. The gruesome necessity of having to take shelter behind their dead brothers was never before imagined by the inexperienced soldiers of the 20th Maine.

Chamberlain kept the men down and placed his faith in the other two regiments defending their position. If they failed to hold, the 20th would be facing a second front of enemy fire that no one would survive. Even a retreat would mean certain death. His men would simply be cut down from behind as they attempted to flee back to the protection of the city.

Cannonade from both sides sporadically challenged each army throughout the morning and into the afternoon. Beneath the shelling, the 20th Maine remained pinned to their position as if they'd been forgotten by the Rebels above them on the hill. They barely posed a threat. If they chose to advance, the Confederates would simply fill their cannons with canister and mow them down in one mass slaughter.

After a long day of cowering defenselessly in the foremost position of the Union Army attack on Marye's Heights, the sun began to set and again the battlefield fell relatively silent. There were few new 20th Maine casualties, and the fear of the great battle that was assumed to have occurred that day, ended.

With the evening's darkness came orders that the 20th Maine was being replaced. A fresh brigade then appeared on the field and the Maine men were allowed to straggle back into Fredericksburg. Remarkably, the Confederates on the hill above them simply watched the transition of men.

Ames assembled the exhausted regiment once safely behind the city's walls and congratulated the men for their bravery and courage. Only a few had been killed, and though some of the casualties were serious, those men were at least still alive. The men realized their superior officers had saved them. To have continued their assault on the Confederate position would have decimated their ranks. To wisely hold and patiently await reinforcements allowed them to regroup and fight another day when they held the advantage.

A burial team was formed and headboards were carved from wooden debris. Chamberlain put his rarely used background in religious service to use, and said a few words and blessed the souls of the dead soldiers being returned to the city. The bodies were then laid to rest in shallow graves dug in the mud. The men slept in bombed-out buildings later that night, but were awakened several times by the report of erratic musket fire. Even with complete exhaustion, none were able to sleep deeply.

The next morning they were assigned to a section of town where vandalism and artillery damage had made it uninhabitable. Late in the afternoon they were again moved, this time just outside the city where the men assumed they would remain the rest of the evening.

But around midnight the regiment was roused from their slumber and ordered to march back toward the front.

The 20th's brigade commander had fallen ill, and had been replaced by Colonel Strong Vincent, previously the 83rd Pennsylvania Commander. Vincent was ordered to lead the 3rd Brigade back onto the ground before Marye's Heights, nearly the same part of the field the 20th Maine had fought desperately for two days earlier.

Drizzle turned to snow flurries as the men marched back onto the frozen and mangled field. Ames led the men through a dip in the rolling landscape, trying to use the natural source of cover to conceal his approaching regiment. The fluorescent blue moonlight illuminated a line of Federal troops that the Maine men surmised they were about to relieve. But when the line of prone bodies was reached, it was clear they were all dead, a morbid ruse to lead the Rebels into believing the area was heavily defended.

The 20th was assigned to a small area where the ground began to gently rise and dip, affording the men a greater degree of safety than their last position. The storm grew to a blizzard as the men desperately attempted to dig small mounds of earth for cover. Ames walked among his men and encouraged them to keep moving. He then waved Chamberlain to his side.

"Colonel Vincent has ordered me to command the center of the line," Ames said as he held his cap down onto his head to keep it from blowing away. "You have the regiment now. Hold this ground at all hazards, Lawrence, and to the last. Do you understand?"

"Yes, sir," Chamberlain answered instinctively. *Last of what? Does that mean there is no option for retreat?*

Ames walked away and disappeared in the falling snow. Chamberlain watched him go and reviewed the orders in his head. It was clear to him now- the entire regiment would either live or perish at his command. The weight of his assignment terrified him. He decided to calm his nerves by joining the men and getting them prepared.

"Dig deep and keep your heads down," he reminded them as he walked among their positions. "Make every bullet count, boys. Find your targets and keep steady. We've got them outnumbered now."

With the men cowering to stay warm and their faces wrapped to prevent frostbite, Chamberlain found himself walking among men he didn't recognize. He'd also had no time to prepare himself for taking command of the regiment, and he was unsure of the distance between his flanks. The darkness and blinding snowfall made it impossible to see the usual landmarks. As Chamberlain continued to wander across his position, he heard some voices through the howling wind and headed back in their direction. He walked up on a figure standing in a shallow rifle pit, still slinging loose dirt out of his hole. Chamberlain was puzzled at first, convinced he was facing the Rebel line, yet the soldier was constructing a wall of dirt on the wrong side of his earthworks.

"Throw to the other side, my man," Chamberlain told him quietly. "That's where the danger is."

"Golly," the soldier responded without even looking up, "Don't you s'pose I know where them Bluebellies be!"

Chamberlain yanked his sidearm from its holster and stepped away from the Confederate who had no idea a Federal lieutenant colonel had mistakenly come upon him.

"You dig away then," Chamberlain answered. "But keep a right sharp lookout."

Realizing he was standing before a Rebel picket line, Chamberlain chose not to shoot the man, but separate himself from the threat as fast as he could in the opposite direction.

When he reached the 20th Maine line only a few yards away, Chamberlain quietly informed the men of the nearby Confederate pickets. Absolute silence was then ordered.

The storm began to break by 3 a.m., and a lone lieutenant trotted up to the isolated Mainers.

"Who is your commanding officer?!" he yelled down to the men, oblivious to the danger only a few yards away.

The men pointed to Chamberlain, who waved the man over to his side.

"Get yourselves out of this as quick as God will let you!" the young staff officer warned.

Chamberlain held an index finger over his lips, gesturing for the messenger to lower his voice. It was to no avail-the messenger was too excited and frightened.

"Sir, you are alone here!" the young office clarified in a panic. "The entire Army has crossed back over the river!"

All of the Maine men heard it, as well as the Rebel pickets nearby.

"Steady in your places men!" Chamberlain ordered over the field. He made sure he was also heard by the Confederates. "Arrest this stampeder! This is a ruse by the enemy! We'll give it to them in the morning boys!"

Chamberlain reached up and furiously pulled the lieutenant off of his saddle onto the snow. When the startled soldier gathered his balance, Chamberlain pulled him close to his face. "Do you want to get us all killed, sir?" Chamberlain growled.

"But, sir, I..."

"We're close enough to the Rebel line to hear each other breathe, Lieutenant. And you just announced to all of them we're alone and without support! Are you mad?!"

"I didn't know, sir. I've been looking for you for nearly an hour and I had no idea your position."

Chamberlain glared at the man and released him.

"I'm very sorry, sir," the messenger apologized again, "but you have to move your men back to the city."

"Have you located Colonel Ames?" Chamberlain asked.

"No, sir."

"He's the regiment's commander. He should be on our left flank with the Eighty-Third Pennsylvania. Advise him of our condition and return to me with orders."

"Yes, sir," the staff officer replied. He got one foot in the stirrup before Chamberlain pulled him back to the ground again.

"Do you not understand, man?!" Chamberlain scolded him again. "At least a hundred Rebels are out there waiting for you to climb back onto that horse. I'll hold your mount until we are ready to retreat. Now do as you're told."

The young lieutenant saluted his superior and ran behind the line of men toward the center of the brigade. A few minutes later Colonel Ames appeared from the darkness.

"They've got us in a jam again, Chamberlain," Ames told him. "We've got to get this regiment out of here now. Have the men count off in twos. We'll retreat half the men at a time in short intervals. I'll form the new lines and you send them back to my mark. We must keep them quiet, Colonel," Ames warned. "If the Rebels discover what we're doing, we won't make it back."

"Understood, sir," Chamberlain answered.

The regiment was whispered its orders and the men separated themselves by the numbers one and two. At the command, half of the men slowly crawled back a hundred feet from the line and then stopped. The men still at the front then crawled back to form a new line. The process was repeated until the regiment had been safely removed from the field.

The young staff officer had been correct. Fredericksburg was an eerie ghost town. The 3rd Brigade formed loose columns and marched through the desolate city, their eyes fixated on the Federal corpses that were piled along the roadway. Chamberlain himself couldn't help but be drawn to their ghoulish expressions, some with eyes wide open-frozen in time.

The 20th Maine would be the last to cross back over the Rappahannock River to Falmouth. Their weary departure concluded as sunrise awakened much of the rest of the defeated Army that had slept through the night. The outcome of the battle at Fredericksburg could never be disguised as a victory as Antietam had. The city had been laid to waste, but the Union objective was to defeat the Rebel force defending it, not simply turn the city to rubble. There was no way to conceal the hundreds of dead bodies or the hordes of maimed and bloodied. And there was no way to disguise the fact that they were almost all Federal soldiers.

Chamberlain stood alone and leaned against a pine tree while the other men rested on the side of the road. He rubbed his hands together and folded his arms across his chest to warm himself as he watched the depression sink into his men. Even an inexperienced officer like Chamberlain knew that the fault of the defeat was in the higher command. *If only the 5ᵀᴴ Corps had not been held in reserve for so long.* Tears swelled in his eyes when he envisioned the dead they would be leaving behind.

An older officer on horseback slowly trotted up the road and slowed when he passed the exhausted men of the 20th Maine. The rider saw Chamberlain leaning against the tree and turned his horse to approach him. It was Center Grand Division Commander General Joseph Hooker. He was also the man responsible for holding the 5th Corps in reserve for so long during the first day of the battle.

"You've had a hard chance, Colonel," Hooker said as a father would console a son. "I am glad to see you out of it."

"It was chance, General," Chamberlain answered. Not much intelligent design there."

Hooker stood up in his saddle, alarmed at the insinuation of incompetence. "God knows I did not put you in, sir," he replied.

"That was the trouble, General. You should have put us in. We were handed in piecemeal on toasting forks."

Hooker glared at the young officer who dared speak so candidly.

Chamberlain looked away, submitting to his authority. The old general saw that several of the 20th's men were listening to the exchange and decided to move on without furthering the debate.

"Good for you, Colonel," one of the enlisted men offered.

"Yah, you tell'em, Professor," came another response.

Chamberlain didn't acknowledge his supporters. Instead, he looked back down into the ravaged city of Fredericksburg and the war-torn battlefield beyond it. All of his naive visions of chivalry without consequence would be left behind there in the blood-soaked ground beneath the stone walls of Marye's Heights.

CHAPTER 5

WINTER CAMP AND SMALL POX

The 20th Maine set up temporary winter quarters at Stoneman's Switch, not far from Burnside's headquarters in Falmouth. The battered Army replaced their weapons with axes and shovels and quickly constructed wind-proof shelters for the season ahead.

Ames had expressed his pleasure in the regiment's performance under fire and was particularly proud of the manner in which Chamberlain led from the front of the battle line. This was also Ames' style of leading men. A popular rumor was that he was the only regimental commander who advanced his columns while standing before them during the assault at the Battle of Fredericksburg. This test of leadership proved career-ending for some of the lower ranking officers in the regiment. Ames asked for the resignations of several of those he saw standing behind the men during the fight.

December passed with little drill due to the extreme cold and snow. Chamberlain formed a study group consisting of less senior West Point graduates and inexperienced commanders who wanted to learn more of the business of war. While the enlisted men sat around playing cards, letter writing, and whittling on sticks, Chamberlain and a few others completed their crash course in military tactics.

On Christmas Day, General George Meade became the new 5th Corps Commander. Three days later the entire 1st Division marched out to Richards Ford on the Rappahannock River. Because they were moving in such great number, the men assumed a Rebel force had been spotted and they were positioning themselves for a fight. But after two nights of sleeping among skeletal oak and cottonwood trees that offered little shelter from the sleet and wind, the division turned around and marched back to camp.

Deaths from disease and sickness began to match the number of men who continued to perish from their wounds sustained during the battle a few weeks before. New hand-carved headstones appeared on the hillside every day.

On January 20, 1863, the Army of the Potomac was again assembled and moved along the Rappahannock River to the north of Fredericksburg. The day began dry and crisp, but gradually the clouds darkened and rain began to pelt the men around noon. Instead of the usual frozen solid earth, the rain turned the thick red Virginia soil to muck. Supply wagons and artillery pieces sank in the pasty goo. Burnside had also ordered the cumbersome pontoons that were used to cross into Fredericksburg earlier to be transported with the Army. They could then be used to cross the river again north of town. But the additional equipment only caused added delays. As the Army trudged on through the torrential showers, the ground began to swallow them.

The march continued and the storm stayed right with them like a curse of bad luck. When the horses started to drop from exhaustion, teams of men had to be formed to pull the caissons and cannons with ropes. The rest of the infantry slowly separated from the bogged-down wagons, leaving them exposed to enemy attack. Subsequently, on the fourth day of the grueling march, the men's food ran out. They had inadvertently out-marched their rations, which were still miles behind them stuck in the mud.

Frustrated soldiers lashed out at each other and fist fights broke out between the regiments. Another group from Maine, the 2nd Volunteers, was one of those motley disorganized units. The tall strong Bangor men enjoyed a good fight and their donnybrooks were only halted after a full cylinder of pistol was fired over their heads.

To add to the anger and tension growing among the ranks was the occasional appearance of taunting handwritten signs posted on the side of the road. *Need a hand with that cannon Yank?* and, *This way to Richmond,* were a few of the antagonistic Rebel messages left behind.

Burnside had given little thought to attempting to conceal his troop movement and was marching his force along the river in full view of Confederate scouts and pickets. Though no skirmishes took place, it was perfectly clear the Union Army was being closely monitored during their infamous Mud March.

To Chamberlain's great relief, the legion of Federal troops was turned around on the 24th, and they sauntered back to their winter camp in embarrassment and disgust. When news of the latest Burnside fiasco reached Washington, Lincoln promptly fired him. His replacement was the same general officer Chamberlain had so rudely addressed not two months earlier- Joseph T. Hooker.

Chamberlain never spoke to Ames of his altercation with the new Army of the Potomac commander. Ames was, therefore, never able to understand why his second-in-command made such great efforts to avoid being near their new leader. It was Chamberlain's plan to simply lose himself in the crowd of the other less senior officers if he could find a way to manage it. After all, one of the first orders of business General Hooker had made clear was the replacement of inferior staff. Chamberlain was able to finally breathe a sigh of relief when he was dismissed from the field and permitted to travel back to Maine for a short leave.

His separation from the unit wasn't a vacation. His first matter of business was to report to Augusta to meet with the new governor, Abner Coburn. When Ames successfully obtained the resignations of some of his regimental officers following the Battle of Fredericksburg, positions had been opened for some new company commanders. Chamberlain met with the governor on the behalf of Ames who preferred to stay in Virginia. Chamberlain provided Governor Coburn with a list of men Ames wanted to promote, and then added his own faithful support of those recommendations. One of those on the list was Sergeant Thomas Chamberlain of C Company. After the meeting Chamberlain got on a train and rode back to Brunswick, where Fanny and his little boy and girl were waiting for him at the depot.

Chamberlain had always been more affectionate toward Fanny than she had ever been toward him. She even thought it improper to hold her husband's hand in public. But at the site of her now bearded husband stepping off of the railroad car, Fanny broke from the small crowd waiting on the platform and raced to him. Chamberlain reached out to her expecting to only take her hand and gently kiss it in formal greeting. Much to his surprise, Fanny wrapped her arms around him and squeezed the breath from his lungs.

"Oh my!" Chamberlain exclaimed with loving amazement.

"We've missed you so, Lawrence." she exclaimed.

Two sets of tiny arms latched onto his legs.

"Hello, you lovely little angels!" Chamberlain told Daisy and Wyllys.

"We missed you, Daddy," Daisy said.

"And I missed you, Buttercup."

Chamberlain relished in the welcome home for a moment and then tried to pry his children from his limbs. When he discovered his efforts were meeting great resistance, he warmly teased that presents would not be delivered if the children did not release him. The result was immediate freedom. Fanny then gathered herself and the two kids and the young Chamberlain family walked off to a waiting carriage.

Well-wishers stopped by the house on Potter Street throughout the afternoon and early evening. Fanny had alerted many of their friends to Chamberlain's short leave, but had not expected the frequent interruptions to her limited time with him. She wanted to sit with her husband alone and hear his reassuring words that he would soon be home for good. Unfortunately she was hearing just the opposite. With late evening the guests dwindled and the children were put to bed. Chamberlain and Fanny talked for another hour of notable events that had occurred during their separation, and then retired to their bedroom.

The cold February night was still and peaceful, only the popping of burning logs in the fireplace disturbed the quiet. Fanny gently warmed the sheets with a copper bed warmer and then returned it to the side of the fireplace. The couple then slid between their blankets, dressed in loose-fitting nightgowns that would help keep them warm.

It was their normal custom to conclude their day with a simple kiss and then go to sleep. Fanny's excusable melancholy at having lost two young children to illness, coupled with the stresses of raising two others, had all but eliminated any intimacy between them. But in this quiet moment alone, Fanny wanted to talk.

She had listened to her husband earlier in the evening, skirting around the subject of the war with their enquiring friends like a politician running for office. Now she was ready to hear the truth. "When will this be over, Lawrence?" she asked.

Chamberlain stroked his mustache and leaned back against the headboard. "I'm afraid it will be a bloody summer, dear. Those Rebels are fighting with a conviction I have yet to see in our men."

"Are we going to win?"

"Both sides will continue to win battles. We are no longer two great opposing forces that will inevitably find each other on the same field and end this thing in one glorious encounter. We are instead thousands of men in separate units, spread across the countryside from the Atlantic to west beyond the Mississippi. It is as if we've been reduced to very large parties of hunters of men. We chase, hide, retreat, and all the while we are only trying to kill a beast before it kills us. As far as who will stand victorious at the end of this war, it will be a sad and humbling day for both sides."

"But we will win?" Fanny demanded to know.

"Yes," Chamberlain assured her. "God is with us."

Fanny nestled into her husband's chest and they stared together into the firelight.

"If God is on our side, why is he calling for so many of our men to die?" Fanny thought out loud.

"The Lord's greatest lessons are taught through our greatest sacrifices," Chamberlain answered. "I had no idea what an honor it would be to fight in his name for such a cause."

"Then you plan to see this through until it is done?"

"My dear Fanny, I am more sure of my role now than I was when I first volunteered. I know those aren't words you want to hear. But even if I fall, you should find some degree of comfort in knowing that I thought of you constantly. And you were, surely, the last image in my mind."

Chamberlain's eloquence was far from reassuring to his wife. Fanny became ill whenever news came back to Brunswick that Maine regiments had engaged with Confederate forces. Her sickness remained until the list of casualties was printed a few days later and she was able to confirm that her husband was not among them. This talk of his possible demise while at war was the least thing she wanted to discuss.

The two sat quietly, Chamberlain fearing anymore discussion of the war would upset his wife. Fanny was deep in the thought that this might well be the last time she saw her husband alive.

Chamberlain was still very much attracted to Fanny, and he frequently dreamed of her while they were separated. Yet he was also accepting of the reasons for her lack of interest in lovemaking, and vowed never to place her in a position in which she felt obligated to yield to his desire for her. But now Chamberlain yearned for her with the same passion he had when they were newly married. It was as if the hardship and terror of war had somehow awakened the virility in him, and he had become eager to once again share a bed with his wife. Chamberlain embraced Fanny and held her tightly, hoping her mere touch would satisfy his need for her.

In her husband's absence Fanny had also developed a yearning for her spouse's touch. She missed his unwavering compassion and comfort during her darkest days. While he was gone she eventually came to realize her selfishness in not understanding he was also suffering from the losses of their children. And for him to leave the comforts of his post at the college and subject himself to the horrors of war to help save the country was a sacrifice only a man of great character would make. As much as she initially hated him for his decision to leave her, she came to love him more than ever as a result of it. Chamberlain wasn't a simple college professor to her, anymore. He was a brave American soldier.

Fanny slowly raised her head and pulled her husband to her. She then kissed him deeply and raised his long cotton nightshirt over his head, discarding it to the floor. She then sat up and removed her gown. The two then tangled together in a desperate embrace, their warm bodies coming together in a passionate union of two lovers reunited. This was far from the calculated lovemaking in their past- the kind almost solely reserved for the purpose of child conception. This was the reaffirmation of the love between a man and a woman once both so full of despair that they rarely even spoke to one another.

With their bodies satisfied, Chamberlain lowered himself onto Fanny's chest and rested his head below her chin. Fanny gently ran her fingers through his hair. Both lay quietly, afraid that the wrong words would spoil the moment. And soon, Chamberlain slowly drifted off to sleep against his lover's breasts.

The leave was only scheduled for a week and with the travel time and trip to Augusta included within those days, Chamberlain had to make his visit home brief. The next evening was spent at his in-law's house where Chamberlain chose to amuse himself with his children and their two visiting cousins. Woman and children were seldom seen in the field, and Chamberlain's faith in humanity was rekindled by their presence. The next morning he climbed back on the train with renewed strength and much higher spirits.

∽

February and March brought great change to the Army of the Potomac. General Hooker restored the corps system and discarded Burnside's Grand Army configuration. He also made sure camp conditions were made more tolerable with better sanitary and supply systems. Spring-like weather also came early, allowing the men to come out of their hibernation. Card games and socializing was moved outside into the fresh air between routine drilling and work assignments.

Another of Hooker's changes was having new emblems designed for each corps. It was supposed to help the men recognize the different units and to also boost morale. Once the new designs were approved, the men were given a patch depicting their new corps insignia that was worn on the top of their hat. The officers also attached the new patch to their hat, or wore it on the front of their coat. With the emblems came corresponding new battle flags, the 5th Corps' being a Maltese cross.

The President and his wife appeared at the camp in early April, and a day of parades and inspections ensued. The visit by the Lincolns was the final piece to Hooker's new plan. With the vote of confidence by the country's leader and the restored morale of his men, the new commander of the Union Army was ready to move.

But instead of healing like the rest of the Army, soldiers of the 20th Maine were getting sick. In mid-April, after two men suddenly died, Ames ordered a surgeon to his regiment to examine all of them.

"You've got trouble here, sir," the surgeon reported to Ames and Chamberlain as they sat in their tent. "I count about eighty of them that look like they've got small pox."

"All in the Twentieth Maine?" Ames asked with disbelief.

"They're all yours, Colonel. I'm guessing it has to do with that government vaccine Washington sent us. Half the time it's either poison or little more than water."

"Well, what am I supposed to do with them?"

"The first thing you have to do is get the whole lot away from the rest of this Army. If those boys spread small pox around here, we won't have any men left to fight."

"You mean quarantine the entire regiment?" Chamberlain interrupted.

"The whole regiment, yes, sir," the surgeon answered. "This is not a good situation, gentlemen. You'll lose a few more before this illness runs its course."

"Are you sure, Doctor?" Ames pleaded, making one last attempt at saving his future.

"It's clear as day, Colonel. You need to move your camp up over those hills behind you as soon as possible."

"Thank you, sir," Chamberlain told the doctor as he walked out of the tent. Chamberlain then sat down on his cot across from his superior.

"I cannot believe this!" Ames growled, slamming his fist down onto their table.

"Shall I assemble the men?" Chamberlain asked.

Ames rubbed his forehead and calmed himself. After a deep breath he gave his orders. "Send Major Gilmore to General Meade's headquarters and have him inform the general of our status. Have him tell the general I'll respond later with a full report. Then get the men packed and ready to move. I'll join you in an hour and we'll march them to their new home."

"I'm sorry, sir," Chamberlain sympathized with his ambitious boss.

"No, sir, I'm sorry," Ames replied. "Lawrence, I can't sit here with a bunch of sick men while the rest of the Army breaks camp and marches to Richmond. In my report to General Meade I'm going to offer my services to his staff and suggest you remain here as the regiment's commander." Ames reached over and put his hand on Chamberlain's knee. "I'm sorry Lawrence, but I must be on the battlefield."

Chamberlain looked down at his feet while Ames waited for some reaction. Chamberlain knew it was a waste of leadership talent to leave Ames behind, only to babysit sick men. He had witnessed firsthand how great a commander the young colonel was in battle. He also knew that every time he was left in charge of the regiment it was a vote of confidence. Still, the idea of remaining in camp in command of what he envisioned to be nothing more than a leper colony was a great disappointment.

"You're a good man, Chamberlain," Ames said breaking the silence. "You'll get your chance."

Chamberlain looked up and nodded that he understood. "Yes, sir. Will that be all, Colonel?"

"Yes. You're dismissed."

Ames watched his best officer step out of the tent and wondered if he had damaged the bond that had grown between them. He would later find that his spontaneous decision to separate from the regiment would also place Joshua Lawrence Chamberlain in a position to one day cement his name in the annals of American history.

∽

On April 27, 1863, the Army of the Potomac left their winter quarters to begin another season of attacks on the Confederate Army of North Virginia. Colonel Ames had been successful in gaining a position on General Meade's staff. Chamberlain and the 20th Maine were left behind in a new camp they dubbed Quarantine Hill. But as soon as the rest of the Army moved out, the 20th Maine repositioned themselves closer to their original campsite in case they were called to duty. Eight men had already died from the small pox epidemic. Dozens more remained bedridden.

On May 1st, distant cannonade could be heard from the unplowed fields beyond Fredericksburg. The Union Army had again crossed the Rappahannock River, this time far north of the city. Chamberlain moved the men up the river in preparation of being called to cross and join the rest of the 5th Corps. The next day even more artillery thundered from the west and the faint crackling sound of musket fire signaled the two great armies had engaged once more.

The 20th Maine waited impatiently for the order to advance, but it never came. Chamberlain reasoned that his regiment may have been forgotten, so he rode into Hooker's headquarters to see why they hadn't been called to rejoin the 3rd Brigade. He found a staff colonel and offered his regiment's services. The colonel knew the 20th Maine was quarantined and assumed they would be of little help, so he told Chamberlain to go back to his unit and await orders.

Chamberlain believed his offer of support was being callously discarded. He pleaded, "Colonel, I beg you, put us in the fight."

"Colonel, I do not need a regiment of sick men on the field!" The impatient officer answered.

"Sir, if we couldn't do anything else, at least we could give them the small pox!" Chamberlain couldn't believe the desperate response that had escaped his lips.

"Damn you, Colonel Chamberlain! Get back to your regiment!"

Chamberlain wheeled around and stomped back to his horse.

Upon return to the regiment he informed the men crowded around him that their offer of service had been refused. Dejected and unable to actually see the battle across the river, the men returned to card playing and loitering around the camp. And there they remained until the sun set in the west, and the sounds of the battle subsided.

Chamberlain was now certain that the 20th Maine would be left behind if they didn't quickly overcome the illness that was passing through the ranks. Though the nights were still near freezing, he slept on his rubber blanket beneath the stars believing the exposure to fresh air would prevent him from contracting the small pox virus.

At midnight he was rousted from his sleep by one of General Butterfield's messengers. The 20th Maine was ordered to be ready to cross the river at dawn, and begin patrolling the telegraph lines that were being cut by the Confederate pickets during nightfall. Chamberlain got a few more hours of sleep and then spent the next morning assembling his regiment at the Banks and the United States Fords.

The distance between the two narrow river crossings was nearly five miles and Chamberlain's orders were to spread his regiment dangerously thin between the two crossings. The battle that had already raged for two days was another five miles west of Fredericksburg in Chancellorsville, which was still well to the south and west of them. Chamberlain hoped the Rebel scouts, who were surely aware of his position, would misinterpret his long line as a force much larger than it actually was. If they fell for the subterfuge, he assumed his men would be much less likely the subject of attack. With that in mind, Chamberlain spent the day and night riding back and forth placing his men strategically along the telegraph lines.

Still in the saddle on May 4, and having securely posted all of his men, Chamberlain successfully volunteered his services to his division commander, Brigadier General Charles Griffin. Griffin was preparing an assault on Confederate General J.E.B. Stuart, who was entrenched and well supported by artillery. Though the eventual offensive was repulsed, Griffin was impressed with Chamberlain's gallant attempts to rally retreating soldiers. Chamberlain made it out unscathed, but for the second time a horse was shot out from under him. This time it was his beautiful white stallion, Prince.

Chamberlain had no knowledge of the status of the battle in Chancellorsville when he returned to the 20th Maine's position. But it didn't take long to figure out that the Federal Army had again been defeated. Unorganized crowds of tattered Union infantrymen began to form at the pontoons that had been left in position after the initial crossing of the Army a few days before. Chamberlain knew his men were still fresh, and volunteered to guard the rear of the line to protect the retreating Army from a Confederate counterattack. The attack never came.

Once again Robert E. Lee and his trusted General Thomas 'Stonewall' Jackson had skillfully defeated an army twice its size, inflicting 18,000 Federal casualties. Yet the Confederacy would pay a heavy price for their victory. There casualties were some 12,800. The greatest loss would be the impending death of General Jackson, who had been shot by his own men by mistake. He would have his left arm amputated and then perish eight days later of pneumonia.

The Union Army made its way back to its camp near Falmouth, a position it had maintained since Burnside's disaster at Fredericksburg the previous November. The injured were treated and the dead that had been carried back with the retreating force were buried. The 20th Maine was banished again to their lonely outpost beyond a hill, until the middle of the month when they finally received a clean bill of health.

On May 20, Ames was promoted to brigadier general and assigned to a brigade in the 11th Corps. With his old colonel's recommendation, and the added recommendation of 1st Division Commander General Griffin, Chamberlain was promoted to full colonel and Commander of the 20th Maine. Thomas Chamberlain was promoted to lieutenant and became his big brother's adjutant. Major Gilmore, the officer who had done so much to get Chamberlain started when he first arrived at Camp Mason, would fill Chamberlain's spot as lieutenant colonel and second-in-command. Their first order of business; a company of 2nd Maine men had been arrested and the 20th Maine was assigned to be their keepers.

Chamberlain was enquiring about horses for his new officers when a detachment of 118th Pennsylvanians with fixed bayonets appeared with the rowdy group. A captain assigned to the detail introduced himself and handed Chamberlain his orders. Chamberlain scanned the document signed by 5th Corps Commander General Meade.

Apparently the 2nd Maine men had been under the impression that the entire regiment signed up together for a two year enlistment, which had just ended. Unbeknownst to many of them, a large group had actually signed three year enlistment contracts by mistake and the Army was going to hold them to it. In retaliation the men refused to obey orders. To make matters even worse, they had been held under guard for several days without rations. Hungry and extremely upset that they hadn't been relieved to go home with the rest of the regiment, the remainder of the 2nd Maine snarled at the new colonel who was to decide their fate.

"General Meade says you can shoot them if they don't do what you tell them, Colonel," the Pennsylvania captain said.

Chamberlain looked up from the orders and scanned the angry mob. "I don't think that will be necessary, Captain. You are dismissed."

"Yes, sir," the officer answered and marched his detail back to their regiment.

Chamberlain had no time to deal with such a large disciplinary problem. The 5th Corps was about to move out and he still had to commandeer some horses.

"Gentlemen, please relax and sit down." Chamberlain waited for the group to sit before continuing. "I am Colonel Chamberlain, the Commander of the 20th Maine. I understand you have some grievances and in all fairness you have a right to have them addressed. But the entire corps is about to move out and there is no time today for me to hear your concerns. Let me promise you as a fellow Mainer, I will do everything I can to resolve your legitimate complaints. Unfortunately it simply cannot be done today."

"What about food?" one of the men asked. "We haven't been fed in two days."

Chamberlain turned to his second-in-command. "Colonel Gilmore, get these men something warm to eat. I know it's a little late for it, but I'm sure we can put something together." Chamberlain looked at his adjutant. "Lieutenant, issue these men the same rations as everyone else and get them blankets. They're still on the rolls as soldiers and they will be treated as such." Chamberlain's staff scattered to complete his orders.

"You men will have to cooperate with me for a few days before I can sit down to hear your complaints," Chamberlain continued. "In the meantime, elect a spokesman and assemble your thoughts. As long as you are in my charge you will be treated with respect. If at any time you wish to join our ranks, I will make sure you are properly armed and assigned to a company." Chamberlain nodded to the group and dismissed himself.

Chamberlain then walked over to the cook's wagon where Gilmore was arguing with a white-bearded veteran sergeant. "Is there a problem here?" Chamberlain asked.

"Sir," the cook began after saluting his commanding officer, "Colonel Gilmore wants me to make somethin' hot for a bunch of deserters, and I just put out my fires. I got to get packed up, Colonel, or this wagon ain't gonna be ready to go with the rest of the other wagons."

The cook had been loaned to the 20th Maine from the 44th New York, and didn't feel obligated to do any special favors for his new regiment.

"Sergeant, you will prepare a complete meal for those men and you will include a substantially hot portion," Chamberlain demanded. "And you will do it now."

"But Colone..."

"Sergeant!" Chamberlain shouted over the rebuttal. "If you cannot follow this simple instruction I shall release those starving men upon your blessed wagon and then arrest you for disobeying an order! Do you understand, Sergeant?!"

"Yes, sir," the humbled cook apologized.

Chamberlain took Gilmore by the arm and led him to the side.

"You alright, Colonel?" Gilmore asked. He had never witnessed such an angry outburst by Chamberlain.

"I'm fine, Charles. I need you to do something for me."

"Anything, sir," Gilmore answered.

"After you get those Second men fed I want you to split them up. Put a few in each company, preferably with some men from their same hometowns. I don't want them stewing over their problems together. Understood?"

"Yes, sir."

"Good," Chamberlain said under his breath, believing the temporary handling of the matter with the 2nd Maine was done.

༄

The 3rd Brigade, now consisting of the 16th Michigan, the 44th New York, the 83rd Pennsylvania, and the 20th Maine, spent early June guarding various river fords. Their new brigade commander, Colonel Strong Vincent, had been permanently promoted from the command staff of the 83rd. On the 13th of June, Vincent pointed his men north to Maryland, and they joined with the rest of the 5th Corps on the next day. The hot summer air was thick with humidity and the entire corps marching together stirred up a brown cloud of dust that consumed the long weaving columns.

The enlisted men were only told that they could expect to be on the move every day. None had any idea how long those days would be. The only thing that was certain was that the accelerated pace meant the Army of the Potomac was in pursuit. But even the desire to engage again with the enemy could not prevent men from fainting with exhaustion during the daily twenty mile marches. On June 17, four men in the 1st Division alone died of sun stroke.

Chamberlain did everything he could to keep his men full of water and rested. He gave them frequent breaks and would often walk with the men, instead of riding his horse as the other officers did. At the end of the day he would send his brother and another staff officer forward to scout a bivouac area for the regiment. It gave Chamberlain the ability to march his men in the most direct route to their evening campsite, and prevented them from having to maneuver around the rest of the corps, which invariably added time and distance to their march. His efforts were appreciated by the soldiers of the 20th, and they grew to be even fonder of their commander. Chamberlain's efforts were also appreciated by the detainees of the 2nd Maine, and twelve of the fifteen original mutineers wisely decided to join the 20th, instead of continuing with their futile grievance.

Unfortunately, Chamberlain's determination to lead his men by example got the better of him one afternoon during another long troop movement. He began to stagger slightly and Gilmore begged him to get back on his horse. Chamberlain wouldn't have it, but answered Gilmore's concerns by pouring a stream of canteen water over the back of his neck. He then resumed his pace only to wake up surrounded by concerned faces a few minutes later. Chamberlain had fallen victim to heat exhaustion and would have to spend the next two days recovering from dizziness and chills.

On the second day of his convalescence Chamberlain's brother, John, appeared at his side. The second oldest son of the Brewer Chamberlain's had volunteered his services as a delegate of the Christian Commission- a non-profit group that assisted in the hospitals and also provided religious support to the Federal Army. John had joined the Army on June 5th, and had already worked among the wounded for several days before catching up to the 20th Maine.

Lawrence was glad to see his brother and the two sat in his tent talking of their parent's health and life back on the farm. During their brief reunion, a young officer mounted on horseback stopped in front of the opened canvass shelter and slid off of his saddle onto the ground with a thud.

"Well off with my britches!" Thomas Chamberlain said when he recognized his brother, John. "Does momma know you're here?"

John stood up and shook his little brother's hand with a hearty grasp. "Why, she's the one who sent me," he answered with a smile. John stepped back and marveled at his baby brother's officer's coat. "Dear Lord, I'm finished for I have seen it all!" he declared.

Thomas looked into the tent at Lawrence. Sir, may I enter?"

Come on in, Tom," he answered.

John frowned, taken aback at the formality. "Do I need to call you sir, too?"

"He calls me 'sir' because I'm his boss," Lawrence answered.

"Well that can't be so bad, Tom," John told his little brother. "As I recall, you used to be a sergeant. I see things have improved. Might that have something to do with having a big brother as your superior?"

"He earned those bars," Lawrence said. "Our little baby has grown up."

"I do believe he has," John agreed.

All military etiquette was abandoned as the brothers sat together the rest of the evening talking of the old days slaving on their father's farm. John then returned to his unit's encampment, but not before he was able to have himself temporarily assigned to his brothers' regiment.

On June 26th, a light rain fell on the men as they crossed the Potomac River on pontoon bridges back into Maryland. Two days later the Union Army made camp near Frederick. It was there that Hooker received the order from President Lincoln to step down and give his command to General George Gordon Meade.

The bureaucracy of such a high level command change and the previous week of daily twenty mile marches brought the Army to a standstill on June 28. The thankful men spent the day loading up on rations and tending to sore damaged feet. It also gave time for rumors to spread among the enlisted ranks, the most popular being the Rebels had invaded the North and were headed toward Washington. The attitude of the Union force again began to change. If the war had been pushed back to Northern soil by Robert E. Lee, now the Federal Army would have to protect its own land. For the first time in many of the soldiers' minds, the prospect of actually losing the war was a reality.

Chamberlain continued his habit of walking among the men at night and briefly visiting with them as they sat around their campfires. When the talk was of the advancing enemy, Chamberlain would drop an occasional thought of instigation to the already building rage in the conversation.

"Can you imagine what our women must be thinking?" Chamberlain would interject into the pool of discussion. The men would chew on the thought with vulgar threats and words of Rebel hatred. When that subject grew tired, Chamberlain would offer another. "What about our homes and our towns. Remember what Fredericksburg looked like?"

The 20th Maine had been the last to march through the rubble of that city, and could easily envision the same destruction of Portland, or Bangor, or even the capital in Augusta. The men would then stew over that idea while Chamberlain moved on to another group.

None of the men realized the irony of Chamberlain's use of Fredericksburg as an example of Rebel destruction, but Chamberlain saw it. The damage to Fredericksburg had been inflicted at the hands of the Federals, not the Confederacy. If Washington was to fall, it would only incur the same damage the Union Army had inflicted on Fredericksburg, and hoped to impose on the Confederate capital in Richmond.

Chamberlain would continue from campfire to campfire, doing everything he could to raise the men's spirits. If that meant getting their blood to boil a little, then so be it. He would need his men to be motivated for the days before them that would not only be a test of endurance, but a test of their will to fight.

Unknown to Chamberlain and the rest of the Federal Army, just to the north of their camp another army of 75,000 was stepping from behind the cover of South Mountain, Pennsylvania, and really was marching east toward the Union capital. In its path was a tiny town of 2,400, built around the intersection of ten farm roads, each leading out to the rolling countryside. In less than a week's passing the wheat fields and orchards surrounding the quiet unassuming town of Gettysburg, Pennsylvania, would become the sight of the greatest battle ever fought on American soil.

CHAPTER 6

LITTLE ROUND TOP, GETTYSBURG

On June 29th, the 5th Corps marched northward through Frederick, Maryland. Morale was even further boosted with the cheering reception from citizens who lined the streets and applauded their passage through town. Eighteen miles of dry dusty road was covered that day, and another long twenty-three miles on the 30th. Having learned that the Confederate Army of North Virginia was somewhere ahead of them, Meade's replacement at the helm of the 5th Corps, Major General George Sykes, cautiously scouted the area ahead of his columns with skirmishers and picket lines.

During the early afternoon of July 1st, the 5th Corps marched into Pennsylvania. The 83rd was back on their own soil and they rejoiced in their return home with singing and waving their caps. The excitement spread through the ranks and soon the air filled with a festive cacophony of fife and drum. The jubilant display continued for several miles until the men grew weary and settled back into the pace of their march. When the drum rhythms faded, the distinguishable sound of distant cannon fire could be heard rumbling from the west.

The corps moved sluggishly onward to the small town of Hanover, still some sixteen miles east of Gettysburg. Sunlight faded and General Sykes decided to stop for the night. With the threat of the enemy lurking somewhere near, he wanted to make sure he didn't accidentally stumble on them ill-prepared and in the darkness. It had also been another long march, and the men were ready to make camp and eat.

Signs of a brief cavalry battle were all around the thirty-five infantry regiments and five artillery batteries that made up the 5th Corps. Dead horses, a few scattered bodies, and discarded equipment lay among the broken fence rails that lined the road. Just as the men had grown comfortable with their shoes off their feet and haversacks off of their backs, a messenger from Meade's staff galloped into the camp. He bailed from his horse in front of General Sykes and handed him a piece of paper. Sykes read the note and immediately called his division, brigade, and regiment commanders to his side.

The note was orders from Meade to proceed at all haste to Gettysburg. The 1st and 11th Corps had been engaged with the enemy all day and had been pushed back to high ground just south of the city. The fighting had grown so fierce that the 1st Corps commander, Major General John F. Reynolds, had even been killed. If Robert E. Lee's main Confederate force had finally been located, Meade wanted his entire army assembled together. Bugle calls and the shouting of orders stirred the men to their feet. The already fatigued 5th Corps then slung their equipment back over their shoulders and reformed into a mile-and-a-half long column.

Each regiment commander explained to his men that a great fight was ahead and two corps were already battling with Lee's army. The news came as a source of rejuvenation. The men were desperate to join the battle believing their honor was at stake. And again the atmosphere turned festive with fifes and drums and singing. Even the night with its calming cool breeze and full moon watching over the glorious Union ranks seemed to give the men confidence. It was far too peaceful to believe such great hazard was only a few miles away.

Word spread that General McClellan was back in charge of the Army and the men gave three cheers in his honor. The rumor was false. Another story was told that the ghost of George Washington had been seen on a tall white stallion galloping across the battlefield. Chamberlain knew this was also a hoax, but the fairytale imagery filled even his skeptic mind with added vigor.

The 5th Corps continued until after midnight when it grew obvious they could not continue without rest. Sykes stopped the men a few miles south of town and let them sleep on the side of the road for three hours. Then he called them back to their feet just before dawn and led them the additional three miles to the rear of the Union line established by the 1st and 11th Corps. The rest of the 5th Corps arrived at daybreak and was positioned to the rear of the Army's right flank, at a spot called Wolf Hill. Chamberlain left the 20th Maine and rode with Gilmore into Meade's headquarters for instructions.

Chamberlain and his second-in-command found the Army's headquarters a confusing swarm of shuffling Federal officers. Dispatches were going out as fast as they could be written. Frantic staff messengers had to barge their way through the crowd just to get their next assignment. The whole chaotic scene proved what the two men now saw as the inevitable- a great battle was about to begin.

Chamberlain and Gilmore walked away from the madness to examine the wide open countryside. They could see most of the huge Union line that had taken a defensive position the night before. Wisely, they had made their stand against the attacking Rebels on the crest of a gently sloping ridge south of Gettysburg, affording them high ground.

The space to the west of the line was mostly cornfields separated by a small farm road leading into town. The sprawling blue legion curved around a hill on their north side, and then straightened itself along another narrow road that ran south to a sparsely wooded area. In the middle of those woods was a steep rocky rise, and then a taller cone-shaped hill just beyond it. Chamberlain was sure the Union line stretched into those hills, but he couldn't see it.

Only the 6th Corps had yet to arrive and they were on their way. It gave both Chamberlain and Gilmore a great deal of confidence seeing such a massive buildup of blue uniforms. And there was added comfort in knowing that an additional corps was also en route.

Across from the Federal position was another gradual slope upward about a mile away. The crest of that ridgeline was sheltered with trees, but Chamberlain could still make out what was underneath them. Thousands of Confederate infantrymen were doing the same thing he was- staring back across the fertile South Pennsylvania landscape and anxiously anticipating the day ahead.

Chamberlain found his brigade commander, twenty-six-year-old Colonel Strong Vincent, and anxiously asked for his orders.

"General Meade is keeping the Fifth Corp in reserve," Vincent told him.

"All of us?" Chamberlain shot back in astonishment. It was his belief that this business of holding entire corps in reserve was the cause of the Fredericksburg defeat and the near defeat at Antietam.

"Colonel, I shared your initial response to the order," Vincent responded, "but then I looked out on that Confederate Army and realized something." Vincent paused for a moment and then directed Chamberlain and Gilmore to follow him.

The three men mounted their horses and Chamberlain and his major followed their commander to the top of a grassy rise behind their line.

"Look out there," Vincent said, and pointed toward the seemingly quiet town of Gettysburg. "That was ours yesterday. Now it belongs to Bobby Lee." Vincent turned and pointed slightly west of town. "Now look at that tower down there."

Chamberlain spotted a tall white bell tower, surrounded by smaller brick buildings about a mile away.

"That's a seminary, about where this whole thing started yesterday," Vincent continued. "Now take your eyes over on those trees."

Chamberlain squinted to focus on the enemy line he had already seen.

"That's the heart of the entire Army of North Virginia, Colonel Chamberlain," Vincent told him. "We can only see a division or two from here, but let there be no question about it. Beyond that tree line is everything Lee thought it would take to ride into Washington."

"So why keep us in reserve, sir?" Chamberlain asked.

"Dear Colonel, I am trying to show you rather than explain. This is it! The Confederacy is here to take our capital! General Meade cannot let this day pass without crushing their entire army. We will only be held back until those Rebels make their move. As soon as Lee plays his hand, we will react and smash him. And you and I will be right in the thick of it, Colonel. I assure you."

Chamberlain nodded that he understood and the three men rode back to the 5th Corps command post. They then parted and Chamberlain and Gilmore returned to their regiment. There, Chamberlain and Gilmore described what they'd seen to the rest of the 20th Maine's officers and ordered them to get the men rested. Most were already fast asleep. Those that weren't wanted to know what their role would be in the fight they knew was coming. Chamberlain advised them that they were again going to be held in reserve, but immediately followed with the same interpretation of the assignment that Vincent had given him. Chamberlain then tried to take a short nap, but couldn't sleep. The foreboding sense that the battle would erupt at any moment would not let him.

At midmorning, still without an advance by either side, Chamberlain was ordered to move his men south toward the middle of the Union line. A few hours later he was ordered further south, which required crossing a road called the Baltimore Pike and a shallow stream called the Rock Creek. Noon passed and still no engagement with the Rebel Army had begun.

The regiment was now alert, sweating in the blistering heat yet anxious to fight. Suddenly, around 4 p.m., a roar of Confederate cannons boomed from just beyond the southern end of the Federal line.

Smoke began to billow up from the woods as the enemy offensive was answered by a Union artillery barrage.

Robert E. Lee had made his move and the target was the 3rd Corps under Major General Daniel E. Sickles. Sickles had taken it upon himself to advance his corps west of the Union line beyond the protection of his flanks. Though at his left was a large mound of boulders and rocks, the middle of his line and right flank was in open farmland consisting of a small wheat field and a peach orchard. Meade rushed orders to the 5th Corps to move west to support Sickles.

General Sykes crossed his corps across the Taneytown Road and sent his 3rd Brigade from his 2nd Division forward into the fight. The popping of musket fire and deep booming of artillery filled the air. Messengers from different commands rushed back and forth with updates and orders. Bugle calls signaled for more reinforcements. Chamberlain sat nervously on horseback next to his adjutant, waiting for the word to attack. A short time later a staff officer rode into the assembled mass and stopped in front of Chamberlain's brigade commander.

"Sir, I need to speak with General Barnes," the aide said. "Can you direct me to him?"

"He's not here, Lieutenant," Vincent answered. "Do you have orders?"

"Yes, sir. I'm supposed to give them to General Barnes."

"What are your orders?" Vincent asked.

"I'm supposed to give them to General Barnes, sir," the young officer explained.

"Give me your orders, Lieutenant!" Vincent demanded.

"General Sykes wants him to send a brigade up to that hill yonder." The aide turned around and pointed to the smaller of the two hills at the end of the Union Army's right flank.

"Tell General Sykes you could not find General Barnes and the order was given to Colonel Vincent. I will take full responsibility."

Vincent wheeled around on his horse and yelled for his officers. "Get the men up that hill!" he ordered, and pointed back to the Little Round Top behind them.

Bugle calls and clanging equipment followed the brigade as the different regiments began their move at the double quick. Chamberlain and his brother, Thomas, rode together at the front of the 20th Maine. John Chamberlain heard the bugle commands and rode out to join his two brothers and their regiment. Minié balls began to wiz through the jogging formations as the three siblings came together at the front of the Maine volunteer infantry.

The terrain became sloped and rocky, and the three slowed their horses to maneuver around the trees and boulders that dotted the small hill. In the middle of the hurried panic a musket ball buzzed across the front of the three Chamberlains' faces. John stiffened with the shock of knowing he had almost been killed.

"Boys, I don't like this!" Lawrence said as he steadied his mount. "Another such shot might make it hard for mother! Tom, go to the rear of the regiment and see that it is well closed up! John, pass up ahead and look out for a place for our wounded!"

Without argument, both brothers kicked their horses and sped off in opposite directions.

Chamberlain found a clear pathway through the trees and continued up the hill. The loose uneven ground caused his horse to slip and buckle during the short climb. When it was obvious his mount had become a burden, Chamberlain dropped to his feet and climbed the hill with the rest of his scrambling troops.

A rain of artillery fire began to pour into the men. The tall thin spruce trees that formed a canopy over the hill cracked and splintered with each violent explosion. The 20th was the last of the four regiments to assemble and prepare for orders. Vincent placed his regiments as they arrived, directing the 44th New York to the right flank, which attached the brigade to the rest of the Union line. The 16th Michigan followed by the 83rd Pennsylvania held the center of the hill, and the 20th Maine stood alone on the left flank. Chamberlain was putting his men into position when the breathless Vincent jogged up to him.

"Colonel," Vincent began. "This is the left of the entire Union line. Do you understand?"

"Yes, sir," Chamberlain answered, not yet fully comprehending the significance.

"You are to hold this ground at all costs."

"Yes, sir," he answered confidently.

Vincent turned and hurried back to the center of the line.

Chamberlain, alone now with the fate of his regiment in his hands, studied the rugged slope before him. Directly in front of the 20th Maine was a low clearing and then the steep incline of the north side of the larger hill, Big Round Top. Chamberlain knew that if he was attacked from the front, he definitely had the high ground and good cover from some large rocks and trees. To his right was the 83rd, a hard charging brigade fighting in their home state. They would hold without question. But to his left was nothing but an open drop into a brush-covered field. If an enemy attack came from his open left, they would swallow his regiment. To make matters worse, if a well-timed frontal assault on the other regiments occurred at the same time, the brigade would be surrounded and decimated in the crossfire.

Chamberlain decided a hidden company secreted in the woods to his left could block a flanking attack if it came, long enough for the rest of the unit to reposition and then join the defensive. He called for his B Company Commander, Captain Walter G. Morrill. Morrill was a trusted aggressive officer who had proven himself able to think on his own.

"Captain, I want you to take your men down into those trees and conceal yourselves there in support of the regiment," Chamberlain ordered.

"Yes, sir," Morrill answered.

"Sergeant Tozier!" Chamberlain called out to his flag bearer.

The infantryman entrusted with the regiment's colors sprinted to his colonel's side.

"I need you right in the middle of the line."

"Yes, sir."

"If the line waivers, you move with it," Chamberlain said. "I must be able to see you at all times so I can determine the middle of our line."

"Yes, sir!" Tozier answered confidently.

The Confederate artillery gradually silenced and for a moment the southern end of the Union line was quiet. Then the sound of crackling branches and underbrush crept up to the bottom of the hill. The 3rd Brigade braced itself for the wave of enemy troops building before it.

"Steady men!" Vincent yelled down the line.

Chamberlain couldn't see any movement in front of the 20th Maine. The attack was centered on the other regiments.

"For Alabama!" a distant voice called from the mound of boulders across from the Union position. A mad frightening shrill followed from the woods. Chamberlain shuddered at the sound of the infamous Rebel yell signaling an impending attack.

"On Texans!" came another yell, followed by an even more terrific cheer from the army forming below.

Chamberlain ran to the left of his line to see if the enemy was in sight yet. There was nothing. The 20th had been positioned well below the crest of Little Round Top, and he had to climb to the top of the hill to get an open view of the other regiments. He scrambled up to a high point where the back of the 83rd Pennsylvania was poised for the attack. A hundred yards beyond them, three advancing regiments of Confederate infantry were swarming like hornets.

A Rebel officer swung his saber to the ground and a wall of lead smashed into the Union line. The 83rd men didn't waiver, but answered with their own volley, tearing through the Rebel assault.

Chamberlain ran back to his own men, who had yet to come under fire. The Mainers were glued to their own front, waiting for an enemy mass to appear before them.

"Here they come, boys!" Gilmore yelled down the column from the right flank.

Chamberlain was in the center of the line and couldn't see the approaching gray infantry. He yelled back across the woods to his second-in-command. "Give it to them, Colonel!"

Gilmore stepped up to the men of the three companies that made the regiment's right flank.

"Come to the ready!" He ordered. "Take aim!"

The first line of Rebels sprang out of the woods and charged the waiting 20th.

"Fire!"

A crash of musket fire like clapping thunder ripped through the trees. Nearly the entire first rank of Confederate soldiers was cut to the ground.

"Reload!" Gilmore shouted as a cloud of sulfur drifted over him.

The casualties of the first volley slowed the enemy advance up the hill, but it hadn't delayed the rest of the Rebel force from taking its position in front of the other 20th Maine companies. Chamberlain couldn't yet see the enemy attackers, but he could hear tree branches cracking from in front of the center of his line. The Rebel commander was squaring off on his adversary.

"Come to the ready!" Chamberlain ordered.

The figures of hundreds of Rebel soldiers were taking shape, scattered in a motley mass instead of organized battle lines. It was a wise approach that would reduce the high number of casualties that almost always occurred when advancing in organized ranks on high ground held by an enemy.

"Make them count boys!" Chamberlain yelled across his line.

The enemy force had come down out of the base of Big Round Top and was twice the size of the 20th Maine. Chamberlain wasn't going to wait for them to get close to his men. Even a successful first and second volley wouldn't prevent his position from being overrun if he delayed any longer.

Chamberlain climbed to the top of a boulder so his men could hear him clearly. "Take aim!"

The 20th Maine's guns leveled on the Rebels below.

The Confederates were close enough to see Chamberlain and hear the Union colonel's command. Not fully aware they had marched into the face of a prepared regiment, the front of the advancing Rebel force stopped for a moment in panicked hesitation.

"Fire!" Chamberlain roared.

A scattering of enemy soldiers dropped to the ground as a wave of lead and tree splinters crashed through them.

Several Rebel officers ran to the front of their shocked line and began rallying their men. Before the 20th could reload, the Confederates had reassembled and renewed their attack.

"Fire!" Chamberlain roared again.

The second barrage sent even more of the enemy to their graves.

Chamberlain knew chaos was about to take the field. He ordered his me to, "Fire at will!" and leapt to the ground to find a better position to observe the enemy's movement.

The Confederates stood in the open and returned their own volley of death, then continued their assault without stopping to reload their muskets. Their orders had been to fix bayonets and take the hill in one great offensive. But the fierce resistance of the Federal brigade had not been expected, and enemy soldiers were being slaughtered in their futile attempt to storm the Union's flank. Pushing their men forward, the Rebel commanders could see their battle plan was failing and a retreat was finally called.

The men of the 20th stood and cheered their victory. Sergeant Tozier climbed on top of a green moss-covered boulder and waved the United States colors for all to see. Chamberlain knew it wouldn't be the last attack by the enemy and called the men back to order.

The K company commander, Lieutenant James H. Nichols, appeared before Chamberlain. His company was positioned on the right flank and had been one of the first to engage with the enemy. "Colonel, sir, I think they're trying to move around us! We saw about five hundred of them break off the main group and head behind the line toward our left flank."

Chamberlain scrambled back up the hill a few yards and climbed on top of one of the boulders there. Nichols was right. An enemy column was moving to the left behind the Confederate regiments that had just advanced on the 20th Maine. Chamberlain recognized that when the Rebels renewed their frontal assault there would be no way his regiment could also fend off an attack on their left flank. And if his left flank folded, the back of the entire brigade would be exposed. Chamberlain's mind raced for a plan.

He hurried through the strategy lessons Ames had given him a year before. *I must find a way to give us the advantage?* The resolve came quickly to him. The regiment simply had to adjust its line to cover its left side. The easiest thing to do would be swing the left of the line back, forming a new perpendicular front at the end of the rest of the brigade formation. But the 20th Maine wasn't at the top of the hill, and moving back would mean surrendering ground to the enemy. Chamberlain knew that if that ground was taken and reinforced by Confederate artillery, not only would the brigade fall, but the entire Army would be exposed to indefensible Confederate shelling. Chamberlain calculated the risks. At the same time the enemy renewed its assault. And once again the Rebel yell filled the woods, accompanied with the crackling pops of musket fire raining from both sides of the line.

"Company commanders front and center!" Chamberlain yelled.

Nine officers, their sabers in hand, faces covered with black smoke residue and sweat, ran to their commander's side.

"Gentleman, we have a problem," Chamberlain told them. "The enemy is trying to move around our left flank. If we don't get some men over there this brigade is doomed." Chamberlain brushed the dead leaves and twigs away from a small area of dirt and knelt down over it. "This is the hill and this is our line." Chamberlain drew a circle and a long line next to it with a stick. "The bottom part of this line is the Twentieth Maine. I want to split the regiment in half and move the five companies left of our center back, forming an L shape." Chamberlain etched the new configuration in the dirt. "I'm going to move Sergeant Tozier with the colors to the end of our current line, so use him as a guide. While the left flank takes their new positions, I want the right half of the line to continue supporting fire throughout this maneuver, and slowly spread down to the colors at the same time. The enemy cannot know that we are thinning our front. Do you understand?"

The men all nodded that they did.

"Good,' Chamberlain said in a rush. "Now quickly tell your men what we're going to do first to avoid confusion and then let's get it done." For an instant, Chamberlain's head cleared of his dilemma and he realized he had just uttered the words his father always had when giving directions to him on the farm. *"Now get it done."*

The young officer's saluted their regiment commander and hurried back to their own commands.

Chamberlain stepped behind a thick tree trunk and looked up toward the sky. He prayed for God to make his plan work and then stepped back into the now raging hillside.

Several of the Mainers had moved forward to take advantage of rocks and trees that provided better protection. Their independent action caused the line to become uneven, and word of the unorthodox realignment didn't reach all of those who had sought concealment even further down the face of the hill.

As Rebel lead cut into them, the 20th Maine slowly shuffled into its new position while carrying on its fight with the bloodthirsty mass that had renewed its attack. The barrels of their muskets burned with the heat of the rapid firing, and the accumulation of black powder residue caused the minié balls to jam while being loaded into the long steel-rifled tubes. Now, the warriors had to violently shove their ramrods into their clogging muskets to get their rounds into the bottom of their barrels.

Once the men of the 20th were in their new positions, there fire became more concentrated and accurate, and the Rebel attack stalled. When it was clear their renewed offensive had been repelled, the Rebels were again called to retreat.

Chamberlain and his officers ordered their men to cease firing- an attempt to save some of the sixty rounds each man had been issued. But calls for more ammunition were already coming, and the reserve cartridge supply was quickly depleted. Some of the men ran forward and looted the cartridge pouches of their own fallen comrades.

The gentle rocky slope was now covered with squirming and soulless casualties. Most of the 20th infantrymen who had independently moved forward had been killed. Their bodies lay ripped and torn against the very landmark they believed would protect them.

"Charge!" was the sudden call from a Rebel officer poised below the newly-formed left flank of Maine defenders. Just as soon as the

Alabamans stepped from their cover, a crisp synchronized Federal volley raked through them. Those still standing bolted forward past their dead and wounded, fiercely determined to finally take the Federal position.

A thick stagnant fog of gun smoke lingered beneath the tree tops, unable to escape into the breeze outside of the Little Round Top forest cover. The men coughed and gasped for clean air as they swore wildly between each tug at their triggers. The new offensive was more heated and the determined Confederates smashed into the Union line.

Muskets banged together as men fought toe-to-toe for their own lives, as well as their cause. Some dropped their heavy rifles and clashed with knives and fists. Two men from the 2nd Maine, who were still being detained by their sister regiment, grabbed rifles from the ground and joined the brawl in defense of their brothers.

Chamberlain also went into the bloody fray, firing his side-arm at point blank range and thrusting his sword into gray-coated Alabamans. Enemy soldiers were all around him and he quickly emptied the Colt Navy model revolver into five different enemy chests. Then, with his saber as his only weapon, he went slashing further into the tangling mob.

The entire Little Round Top hillside was engulfed in the sounds of battle- the murderous thuds of skulls being crushed by rifle butts, the ripping of uniform coats as men were torn open by bayonets, and the violent screams of agony. The battle raged until the Confederates again faltered and retreated to the bottom of the bloody hill.

Chamberlain suddenly felt a sharp pain in his right foot. When he found the chance to safely examine the source of the pain, he saw that blood was dripping from a hole on the side of his boot. He wasn't sure if he had been shot, stabbed, or had possibly been simply cut by debris during the furious exchange. But he knew as long as he could walk and stand there was no time to dwell on a minor wound.

"Ammunition!" Ammunition!" The men began calling out. But the reserves were gone.

Chamberlain limped back up behind his men to check the condition of his line. His regiment was slowly being eaten away, only a few more than one hundred men were braced for the next charge. He was aghast at the carnage the two armies had inflicted upon each other. The field below was so littered with bodies, only sparse patches of earth were clear from human debris and strewn gear. Some of the dead were even piled on top of one another.

Chamberlain could also see the remaining Rebel force and they were very much alive. Though battered and exhausted, they were still four times the number Chamberlain had left in his diminishing regiment. Another attack would mean certain disaster.

There was but one last effort the 20th Maine could possibly survive. It would mean the greatest sacrifice his regiment could offer its country- an endeavor so death-defying, the result could mean the annihilation of every man remaining on the line. Attack!

Chamberlain again called for his company commanders. Two had been killed during the last Confederate drive and he immediately replaced them. The first to respond was F Company commander, Lieutenant Holman S. Melcher.

"Sir," Melcher said, huffing to catch his breath. "May I go forward and retrieve some of my wounded?"

"Yes, sir," Chamberlain responded. "In a moment I am ordering a right wheel forward."

Melcher's jaw dropped. The other officers finished assembling.

"Men," Chamberlain began, "we cannot sustain another enemy advance. They greatly outnumber us and we seem to have run out of ammunition. I believe the only way to defend the hill at this point is our own advance. If we take the fight to them, maybe they'll blink."

"But, Colonel, they have a full regiment down there," one of his officers pointed out. "Isn't this what they'd want us to do? Come out of our high ground?"

"That's what they would have liked two advances ago," Chamberlain answered. "Now, they have to believe we're going to sit here and keep taking this beating. We will not. We cannot. If we can surprise them with an offensive move, they might believe we've been reinforced."

"I'm with you," Lieutenant Melcher exclaimed. The other officers were not so convinced and their faces showed it. Still, Chamberlain had been a great commander to them and it was no time to question his authority or leadership.

"The order will be *Left Wheel Forward,* and then *Attack!*" Chamberlain explained. "I want those Rebels to know we're coming. Have your men fire and then sound off a battle cry so vicious we'll scare the hell out of those devils. The objective is to have our left flank swing into them. When that wheel gets parallel with the rest of the regiment, I'll move the whole line down on them. Colonel Gilmore will begin the assault. Are there any questions?"

The officers were silent.

Chamberlain removed his cap and wiped the sweat from his brow with his sleeve. "Hurry back to your companies men," he told them. "We need to take advantage of this lull."

The pain in his foot throbbed with every heartbeat. The sensation of blood filling his boot reminded him of the pile of limbs being stacked outside the surgeon's operating room at Antietam. Chamberlain vowed to himself- if this was the last day he had the limb to stand on, it would be while was proudly leading the men of the 20th Maine.

The Mainers rammed home their last cartridges and placed their final primer cap into position on the nipple just below the musket hammer. Many were covered with blood, much of it their own, some of it their enemy's.

Chamberlain offered one last prayer to God, not for his soul to be saved, but for this his final stand to succeed. He then limped out to the front of his courageous line.

"Bayonets!" he yelled with all the strength he had left inside him.

The rattle and scraping of long steel spikes locking into place signaled only one thing to the Rebel force below. The regiment on the hill was not about to give up. The Confederate officers answered by ordering their men forward one last time.

The Alabamans stalked slowly forward through the broken trees and smoke, and over their dying brothers. In every mind it was clear- this would be the final assault. The Rebels quickly surrounded the angle of the 20th Maine with little resistance. Musket fire from the Confederate line resumed, but the Federals kept their guns quiet. Chamberlain patiently waited for the gap to close between his men and the approaching enemy. When the ranks were so close they could continue the fight by throwing stones at each other, Chamberlain raised his sword straight up in the air. "Right Wheel Forward...!"

Lieutenant Melcher stepped in front of the left flank, waving his saber in the air. "Let's go get'em boys!"

What was left of five Union companies stepped from behind their cover and began to yell at the top of their lungs. The advancing Confederate line stopped in amazement.

"Attack!" Chamberlain roared to his left.

"Charge!" Melcher and the rest of the officers guiding the wheel yelled in response. The Union left fired their last volley and charged through their own muzzle flashes down the hill and sweeping to the right. Shocked enemy soldiers panicked and fired without aiming into the rabid Yankee mob. The woods turned to a sea of chaos as frightened Confederates ran to the safety of the center of their line.

Chamberlain watched the execution of the maneuver patiently as the main body of the Rebel offensive appeared before him. "Prepare the advance!" he yelled to be heard through the ranks.

The rest of the line stepped forward, their jaws flexing with determination. Chamberlain turned to face the enemy and again slowly raised the tip of his sword into the air, waiting for the perfect moment to give the order. Bits of splintering wood and shrapnel fell around him as he watched the enemy bearing down on his line. His regiment's left flank continued moving forward. The two lines were almost even. Chamberlain's men began to yell and taunt the Rebels. It was now Chamberlain, not Ames, grasping the leash of this ravenous pack of Maine wolves.

"Steady!" he called out, trying to hold the men in their ranks. "Steady...!"

The two Union lines suddenly came together.

Chamberlain threw his arm forward, his saber thrusting the Mainers into their enemy. "Attack!"

The rest of the regiment poured down into the Rebels, firing their last round into one Confederate torso, and shoving their bayonet into another. Astounded enemy soldiers turned and ran for their lives as Chamberlain waved his men after them. The few who tried to stay and fight were quickly overtaken, either surrendering or being run through.

Chamberlain ran hobbling into the chaos and found himself facing a trembling Alabama officer who had his pistol leveled on him. The officer fired the last shot in his revolver- the deadly round sailing over Chamberlain's shoulder. Without so much as flinching, the brave college professor stepped up to the frozen enemy officer and placed the tip of his sword at his throat. His opponent's next move would determine whether he lived or had his neck slashed. The Confederate elected to survive the day and handed his empty sidearm and sword to Chamberlain.

The route continued down the hill. When the gray swarm reached the narrow run between the Big and Little Round Top, a fresh Union line raised up from behind a stonewall. It was Captain Morrill and B Company. A blaze of fire burst from their muskets as they raked the helpless enemy with lead ball. The Confederates were now being attacked from two different fronts.

The frenzied advance splintered the 20th's line even as officers tried desperately to reorganize their ranks. Hundreds of Rebel soldiers were surrendering to only a handful of Union soldiers who were armed with empty rifles and had run out of ammunition. Most of the regiment, however, was still chasing those who had not given up.

Chamberlain could see he was losing control and feared the regiment was moving too far away from the ground they were assigned to cover. His frantic commands to return to the hill were only heard when the gunfire ceased and the men slowed to catch their breath. With their return came over 400 Confederate prisoners, more than the number of men left in the entire 20th Maine.

The day had been won and the Little Round Top secured. More significant though, the left flank of the entire Army of the Potomac had been saved by the 20th Maine Volunteer Infantry and its ingenious commander, Joshua Lawrence Chamberlain.

The assault on the hill ended just as dusk settled over the woods. After scouts confirmed that the battered Rebels had retreated back to their main force, the 3rd Brigade began the solemn task of treating their wounded and recovering their dead. Vincent had been mortally wounded during the fight and the commander of the 44th New York, Colonel James C. Rice, took command. He ordered the 20th to take a position on the Big Round Top hill and act as a picket line for the rest of the brigade. Chamberlain moved his men out and they spent the rest of the evening having no idea the weight of their day's accomplishment.

The regiment was replaced and sent back to the middle of the Union line early the next morning. There, the men ate and prepared their equipment for another fight. Chamberlain's foot was examined and it was confirmed he had been cut by either a spent bullet or a piece of shrapnel. Luckily, whatever it was, it was no longer in his foot and he only needed the wound cleaned and bandaged.

Early in the afternoon the two armies began shelling each other again, the bombardment lasting nearly two hours. When the cannons stopped, Robert E. Lee sent 12,000 of his men across an open wheat field, straight into the middle of the Union line. Chamberlain and the 20th Maine were kept in reserve and listened to the final assault from a low area well behind the Union front. In less than an hour, the infamous Pickett's Charge was successfully repulsed and the Battle of Gettysburg was over.

It was a clear Union victory and the men of the Army of the Potomac celebrated with jubilant cheers of self-congratulation. But when the smoke and dust cleared from the battlefield, the revelation of tens of thousands of dead and dying men ripped at their hearts. Hay wagons were quickly commandeered from local farmers and were used as ambulance litters. Every cart that had two wheels still attached to it was stacked with the injured. Still, the two armies stood poised and unyielding-Robert E. Lee waiting for a counterattack, George Meade preparing for another assault.

A gentleman's truce was eventually honored on the field. Then all through the night of July 3, 1863, moans and shrieks were answered by compassionate but inadequate care. By midnight both commanders had their reports in hand. The three day battle had cost the Federal Army 23,000 casualties, the Confederates, 28,000 casualties.

Chamberlain walked among the injured and offered water and words of courage and strength in the darkness. Men died as he held their hands. The magnitude of the suffering eventually consumed him, and several times he had to gather himself and wipe the tears from his eyes before he moved on to the next dying soldier.

The moon slowly disappeared behind a blanket of ominous dark clouds. Then flashes of lightening, followed by an earthshaking crash of thunder, released a torrential rain shower. The drops were thick and heavy, and landed as if being angrily hurled down from the heavens upon the men. Most of the wounded were lying in the open without cover and were quickly drenched. The awful circumstance made the night even more miserable.

Chamberlain couldn't help but think of the story of Calvary, when Christ was crucified and God unleashed a mighty storm on the people who betrayed him. It was clear to Chamberlain that this tempest was another sign of God's disgust with mankind. With that in mind, Chamberlain spread out his rubber blanket and laid himself down facing the stinging cold drops. There, he submitted to the pelting and prayed for God to forgive him and re-baptize him in the holy water being poured down upon the two great armies.

CHAPTER 7

SPOTSYLVANIA TO NORTH ANA

The 20th Maine returned to the Little Round Top on July 4, and buried their dead in a clearing at the bottom of the hill. The storm from the night before lightened, but a steady rain continued throughout the day. The men were horrified to see the condition of their friend's bodies. Some had limbs ripped from their sockets, others had exposed intestines and other organs protruding from long open gashes in their bellies. Fond remembrances of each fallen infantryman were spoken as the bodies were lowered into their shallow muddy graves. None would be forgotten. Chamberlain would spend his evenings throughout the rest of the month writing a personal note of condolence to each deceased man's loved ones back in Maine.

On July 5, the regiment moved out of its encampment and headed southwest. The Army of Northern Virginia was limping back home and Meade wanted to catch them before they crossed back over the rain swollen Potomac. Movement was sluggish, the storm having continued into a third straight day. Wagons got stuck in the quagmire, and artillery pieces had to be dug out from the mud on constant occasions.

A few days later the regiment finally crossed back into Maryland, though many were now sick from nearly a week of marching and sleeping in the rain. But just as circumstances appeared their most dismal, the weather cleared and the sludge of rain-soaked country roads began to dry. With the sunlight also came improved morale and a renewed determination to catch up to the Confederate Army. Scouts had informed the Union command staff that the Rebels were camped near Williamsport, Maryland, waiting for the river's water level to subside. The Federal Army rushed to the west in a feeble attempt to trap the enemy against the Potomac. But when they arrived, the Confederate force was gone.

Meade, believing there was still a chance to outflank the Rebels, sent his army down the Maryland side of the river in a mad dash, and had them cross on pontoons near Berlin. The Army of the Potomac was again on Southern soil. Forced marches of twenty miles a day resumed as the hunt to catch Robert E. Lee continued. Even with increased confidence the men were unable to fight through the fatigue and illness. Days were hot and muggy. The more the men sweat in their dirty uniforms, the more mosquitoes and flies fed on them. Malaria and dysentery again began killing men faster than they could be replaced.

Chamberlain was one of those fighting a fever and chills. By the end of July, he recognized he couldn't continue and confided his illness to the regiment's doctor. The diagnosis was simple exhaustion, nothing contagious, and Chamberlain was immediately relieved and sent to a hospital in Washington to recover. The hospitals in the capital were crowded with men who had been seriously wounded in battle, and Chamberlain's illness was, again, promptly dismissed as stress-related. He was subsequently ordered to take a fifteen day leave and clear out of the bed space he was wasting. Chamberlain gladly obliged and boarded a train to recuperate back home in Brunswick.

The visit home was much different from his first. This time he was ill, and he was often pre-occupied with the nightmarish visions of Gettysburg and the dead laying in long rows waiting to be buried. He continued writing letters to the families of his fallen men, and when he caught himself repeating the same tired phrases of sympathy in those letters, he became angry and even more depressed. Chamberlain was also unsure of his illness and didn't want to infect his two young children. This was a particular concern, having already lost two babies before the war to some other unknown illness.

Daisy and Wyllys couldn't understand the need to be isolated from Chamberlain. To ease their naive concern that their father had lost his great love for them, Chamberlain spent much of his waking hours in a rocking chair next to his bedroom door. Wyllys and Daisy could then playfully pass drawings back and forth to him under the door, and he could read the children fairy tales as they sat patiently in their own little chairs on the other side. Gradually, the time with his children distracted his thoughts of the horrors at Gettysburg, and his soul began to heal.

Chamberlain's physical recovery did not go as expected and he decided to apply for an extension of his sick leave. Instead of granting his request, a dispatch soon returned from Colonel Rice saying he needed Chamberlain back so that he could take temporary command of the brigade. It seemed Rice wanted some time to visit his own family. Chamberlain reluctantly returned, believing it was his duty to assist the colonel after having been entrusted with the temporary command of the entire 3rd Brigade.

Chamberlain arrived a few days later at brigade headquarter near Beverly Ford, Virginia, still feverish but rested. He was met with the news that Colonel Rice would not be coming back. He had been promoted to brigadier general and given the command of the 1st Division. Chamberlain assumed the duties of 3rd Brigade Commander, believing he would probably be given the command formally in the near future. On August 26, General Griffin made it official. In one year of volunteer service, Joshua Lawrence Chamberlain, having no prior military experience, was now leading three regiments of the Army of the Potomac.

Chamberlain regretted leaving the 20th Maine, even though he would still be near them as their brigade commander. The Mainers were sorry to see him go, but glad that he was climbing the ranks as he well deserved. His promotion also meant the regiment's officers would have to be shuffled and several spots needed to be filled. As the brigade commander, those promotions were mostly left up to his own discretion. Chamberlain promoted Major Gilmore to regiment commander and moved Ellis Spears to second-in-command. With Ellis moved from his position as G. Company Commander, Chamberlain decided to fill that spot with his little brother, Thomas.

On August 28, Chamberlain and the rest of the 5th Corps brigade staff were called to General Sykes headquarters. They were informed that they would be conducting an execution of deserters the next day. General Griffin would be in charge of providing a firing squad from his 1st Division. The officers were unsure how to react to such news, but were careful not to voice their apprehension in the formal setting. Some disagreed with the sentence of death to deserters, while others believed it was a just sentence, but not something to be carried out in front of an entire division. It was understood though, that someone much higher in rank than they were wanted to set an example.

Lincoln had begun drafting men into the Army, and the result had been rioting in New York and Philadelphia. Many believed that the Constitution had no provision for being forced into military service. Still, Congress had approved the draft bill and thousands of new regiments were being formed all over the North. What was once an army of men fighting for what they believed in, the Army of the Potomac was now being reinforced by men who could not only care less, but also had absolutely no loyalty to the Union cause whatsoever. Five of those men had been drafted into the 118th Pennsylvania and then promptly deserted. They would pay for their transgression with their lives.

The next day the regiments of the 1st Division were assembled in parade formation. Chamberlain sat on his new horse, Charlemagne, in front of the 3rd Brigade, and watched the ceremony with no control of its outcome. He wondered to himself if the idea of shooting one's own troops for not wanting to fight was cause for execution. *If a man didn't want to fight, better to be rid of him than to discover his cowardice in the heat of battle. What was the point in killing him? Why not send him back to the bosom of his mother, and leave the business of war to the brave and honorable? Was the Army so desperate now that they were ready to march their own men into battle at rifle point?*

The five Pennsylvanians were marched onto the parade grounds. Following them were soldiers carrying their wooden caskets on their shoulders. The surreal procession moved onto an open square in front of the silent division. Five holes had been dug for the coffins, and the pine boxes were each placed adjacent to a separate burial pit. A rabbi, a priest, and a protestant minister followed the men and spoke to them in mumbled whispers.

A captain ordered the men to sit on the edge of their designated coffin and face the ranks. Then a column of fifty armed infantrymen, marching to the solemn beat of a single drummer, filed onto the grounds between the condemned men and the lines of blue behind them. The prisoners were read the final order of their execution and provided a few moments with their religious representative. General Griffin sat impatiently atop his mount and rubbed his eyes with boiling anger. The pomp of the formal ceremony was wearing on all of the men.

"Shoot those men, or after ten minutes it will be murder!" Griffin suddenly shouted from his horse. "Shoot them at once!"

The clergymen were immediately ordered to retreat to safety. The captain charged with leading the execution detail ordered the men to prepare to fire.

Chamberlain was hypnotized by the unimaginable event unfolding before him. The blast of muskets jolted his nerves, but his mind was too numb to react. His eyes never blinked.

Each body fell, some to their backs, some slumping forward. All were dead. Ten musket balls each had ripped though them, sending chunks of flesh into the grass behind the graves.

Even the most hardened men stood at attention with tears rolling down their cheeks. Others stood dazed, alone with their thoughts. None could have ever prepared themselves for this.

Griffin immediately ordered the division back to its camp. Though the fife corps played a surreally lively tune, the spellbound men marched in a daze back to their tents. Chamberlain swore to himself he would never have part in something so horrible again.

Two months later he found his opinion on the matter had changed. While ordered to attend another execution, this time with General Meade in attendance, Chamberlain resigned himself to accept that capital punishment was a reality of war. He still didn't believe in the executions, but it was beyond him to feel sorry for any man who continued to desert after having the example of the repercussions being carried out in front of him.

∾

August passed and then September with little action. Chamberlain was still fighting bouts of fever and body aches. The rest of the men busied themselves with routine duties and socializing. Chamberlain was now a senior officer and he was rarely invited to join the enlisted men in anything other than refereeing disputes. He was well known as an excellent chess player, and was often called upon to clarify the rules of the game. When it came to card game arguments, which were almost always associated with forbidden gambling, the men knew better than to call on Chamberlain.

A new game called baseball was also growing popular with the men, and Chamberlain often sat on the side of their playing field, watching the games and writing letters to Fanny and his children.

The Army had been up-rooted several times, but the enemy was rarely engaged. Then on November 7, General Meade sent the 5th and 6th Corps across the Rappahannock River to attack a railway crossing near Kelly's Ford. Robert E. Lee had been destroying railroad lines as he passed them, causing the Union delays in shipping reinforcements and supplies into the South. The Rappahannock Station crossing had been one of the few the Confederates decided to defend. Meade learned a fort had been built and a long line of trenches had been constructed on high ground surrounding the station and lining the river.

Skirmishers from the 5th Corps engaged an entrenched Rebel picket line near the river in the late afternoon and quickly overran the enemy's position. Chamberlain had his horse Charlemagne shot out from under him during the fight. As he recovered from the spill his brigade rushed forward, reeking death and destruction to everything in its path. It was nightfall before the regiment could be reassembled. To his surprise, the men returned from the woods with 70 Confederate prisoners, 5 of which were officers. Charlemagne would also survive.

Later that evening the 6th Corps, with several 20th Maine soldiers who wanted to join another Maine regiment with the assault, stormed the remaining Rebel fortifications. The Confederates initially put up a strong fight, but after moments of fierce hand-to-hand combat they surrendered. Another 1700 prisoners were taken. But another fortress remained across the river and it was full of fresh enemy troops.

That night the men were ordered to sleep in the cold without fires so the enemy couldn't gather intelligence on their numbers and position. Chamberlain was still sick, and sleeping exposed to the cold misty autumn air only made his chills worse. He decided to get up and walk among the sleeping troops to get his blood circulating and to warm his aching bones.

"Hey, Colonel," a voice whispered from a clump of trees.

"Yes," Chamberlain answered quietly, careful not to arouse any of the other men.

"I got hot coffee. Want some?"

Chamberlain gingerly stepped toward the figure whose face slowly came into focus. It was Private Oliver W. Norton, the brigade bugler.

"Where did you get hot coffee?" Chamberlain asked. He had personally ordered no fires and he certainly didn't see one.

"Come on over and take a peek at what I got here," Norton said.

Chamberlain joined him and Norton led his commander around the back of a thick cottonwood tree. On the ground next to the trunk was the bright orange glow of a ring of hot coals. In the center was a boiling tin coffee pot.

"I couldn't help it, Colonel Chamberlain," Norton said. "If I don't get something warm in me, I'm gonna freeze to death."

Chamberlain looked around to see if anyone was awake and watching. The only stirring was the bellows of snores.

"The orders were no fires, Private," Chamberlain whispered. He wasn't mad. He simply had to play his role as commander.

"This ain't a fire, Colonel. These here are just hot coals. Hell, you can't even see'em unless you look right down on'em."

Chamberlain grinned and shook his head. It was hard to discipline a man under such circumstances. Plus, the idea of joining him in a warm cup of coffee wasn't such a bad idea.

"I suppose you need to keep your mouth warm," Chamberlain said and sat down behind the tree.

"That's certainly the truth, Colonel," Norton answered and lifted the kettle out of the hole. "You know last winter in Fredericksburg I got my lip froze to my bugle 'cause it was so cold. Colonel Vincent thought that was the grandest thing he ever saw." Norton poured the dark steaming liquid into a dented tin cup and handed it to Chamberlain.

"When Colonel Vincent took over the brigade last summer, he'd call me up to his side and says, 'Private, sound the assembly, but don't blow so hard you get that damned bugle stuck to your face again'."

The two men chuckled quietly like old friends swapping stories of their childhood. Both formed mental pictures of Vincent as they warmed their hands to the side of their cups. Vincent was gone now, and the reality of his eternal absence was sobering. Chamberlain rehashed the last words he ever heard from Vincent while they stood together on Little Round Top. *Hold this ground at all costs.*

"A toast to Colonel Vincent," Norton said and held his cup up in the air.

"Yes. God rest his soul," Chamberlain answered.

The two men tapped their cups together cautiously so as not to awaken any of the men around them, and then sipped at the bitter hot coffee.

They finished their drink over small talk of their families back home. Chamberlain enjoyed the opportunity to talk to someone socially for a change. But the night was growing even colder and both men needed to retire. Chamberlain thanked his subordinate and Norton swore to keep their late night discretion confidential. Chamberlain then wandered back to his rubber blanket and lay down on the cold damp ground. When he fell asleep he dreamed of Fanny playing the organ as he watched from the balcony of their church back home.

The two corps assembled early the next morning to continue the attack on the remaining Confederate positions. With the dawn also came the discovery that the Rebels had abandoned their artillery posts and rifle pits. The railroad crossing was back in Union hands.

The men were then redirected to guard the railroad tracks while they were being repaired. All the while there was constant sniper fire from the hills and the threat of an enemy counterattack. The weather also interfered with the reconstruction of the railroad lines. Rain showers during the day turned to sleet at night, and Chamberlain's health progressively got worse.

On November 8, he woke beneath an inch of freshly fallen snow. Several officers he spoke to that morning told him he looked as if he were near death. They couldn't have been more correct. The illness Chamberlain had been fighting for several months had actually been malaria, not exhaustion. His insistence to remain in the field and sleep among the brigade in the wind and freezing drizzle had now given him pneumonia. Two days later, Chamberlain collapsed.

The brigade surgeons tried to reduce his fever, but nothing worked. Chamberlain drifted in and out of a coma for two more days before they put him on a cattle car and shipped him, unconscious, back to a Washington area hospital.

He remained at the Seminary General Hospital in Georgetown through December. Fanny visited him there several times and brought him handmade gifts the children made for their father. He felt well enough to make the train ride back to Brunswick for Christmas, and remained there for another week to bring in the New Year. A disease that would eventually kill thousands of other soldiers was eventually beaten by Chamberlain.

In February of 1864, he was assigned to court martial duty in Washington, and then to Trenton, New Jersey, for the same thing. Fanny was able to join him, but had to assume the role of nurse as Chamberlain had several repeated but less severe bouts of his illness.

Winter dragged on and Chamberlain came to despise his new role in the Army. He was a field infantry commander, not a constable. He wrote several letters to General Meade's headquarters stating he was ready to return to the brigade. He never got a response. Believing he had been forgotten, or was being saved for the summer campaign that would inevitably begin in a few months, Chamberlain and Fanny began enjoying the perks of being a colonel in Washington.

There were luncheons and fancy dinners to attend and even visits to the theater. Fanny discovered it wasn't so bad being the wife of a senior Army officer, and she indulged herself in the benefits the title bestowed.

Winter turned to spring and changes were all around the nation's capital. President Lincoln replaced Meade with Ulysses S. Grant in March. The predominant rumor was that Grant had gotten the job on a promise that he would push the Army forward every day until Jefferson Davis saw the Army of the Potomac at his doorstep. There were telltale signs of a coming offensive to support the rumor.

The city turned into a giant stockyard of men and supplies. Crates of new equipment were piled everywhere, and a flood of new troops and those returning from winter furlough crowded into the city. Spirits were high and the talk around town was that General Grant would have the Confederates whipped by the end of summer.

On May 5, the local papers reported that Grant had attached himself to the Army of the Potomac and had crossed the Rapidan River with Meade. The new campaign had begun. All of Washington waited impatiently for the news of the first encounter with the Rebels. When it came only a few days later, the news of the tragic Battle of the Wilderness in Virginia sent all of the high hopes of a swift end to the war spiraling to the ground. For the third time in two years a Confederate Army half the size of its adversary had soundly defeated the Union Army. That same day Chamberlain's new orders arrived. He was to report back to the 5ᵗʰ Corps and resume command of the 20ᵗʰ Maine.

The 3ʳᵈ Brigade was now commanded by Brigadier General Joseph J. Bartlett, and Chamberlain understood he would not be returning to his prior command of the brigade unless Bartlett promoted. He was just happy he was getting back out into the fight. Chamberlain boarded a train and joined the 5ᵗʰ Corps a few days later. His elation to be back at the front was short lived, though. He learned that several of the men he admired had been killed, including Captain Morrell and Lieutenant Melcher.

The new field of battle was only a few miles south of the Wilderness, near a courthouse in Spotsylvania. Grant had promised the President he would be relentless in hunting down the Confederate Army. This was his opportunity to prove he would be unyielding, even though he had just been soundly defeated a few days earlier. Now Spotsylvania stood in the middle of Lee's escape route to Richmond and both armies scrambled to get there first. By the time Chamberlain arrived to rejoin his old regiment, a battle at Spotsylvania had been raging for several days.

On May 12, the 2ⁿᵈ Corps was called to attack the center of the Confederate line, while the 9ᵗʰ Corps, back under the command of Burnside, attacked its right. The advance began before dawn as the 5ᵗʰ Corps stood poised in front of the left of the Confederate line. What followed was nearly twenty-three hours of two great armies clashing over a long winding Confederate entrenchment, the middle of which twisted back into a U-shape. That curve in the enemy defense eventually became a vacuum, sucking in wave after wave of advancing Union troops. Grant repeatedly poured reinforcements into the battle, but kept the 5th Corps in its position in front of the Rebel left. Lee also sent in reinforcements as the bloody brawl continued into the afternoon and night.

By midnight the fight over the angle in the Confederate line became so piled with the dead, men fought while balancing on human bodies. Two hours later the Confederate line finally broke. The ravaged Union infantry swarmed into the earthworks as the fleeing Rebels took positions behind a second line of trenches. The 5th Corps was never called to join the fight, having acted as a decoy to keep the Confederate left from reinforcing the center and right of its line.

When the sun began to rise the next morning the reality of the nightlong battle could be clearly evaluated. Thousands of dead Union troops were scattered in the open field. The dead Confederates that had fought so desperately to defend their position were stacked in heaping mounds in the trenches they had constructed a few days before. The worst fighting had taken place at the sharp curve in the Rebel line. Corpses from both armies lay on top of each other in a mass grave. The place would be remembered as The Bloody Angle.

Grant had again been unsuccessful in breaking the Army of Northern Virginia. He had only pushed them back to a new line of defense. For the next seven days he tried to move around the flanks of Lee's position, but each encounter was met with fierce opposition. Chamberlain and the 20th Maine were sent out on picket duty several times and engaged with small Confederate skirmishers on every occasion. When they weren't in a forward position, the regiment was ordered to construct breastworks and their own trenches to defend the always looming possibility of a Rebel counter offensive. Finally on May 20, after having thrown his army into a well-fortified enemy line for nearly two weeks, Grant gave up the field. The month of May in 1864 had at that point already cost him 36,000 casualties. It was a Butcher's Bill even the Union couldn't pay. Grant would now have to change his strategy.

On May 21, the 5th Corps moved out and headed south. General Bartlett had become ill and Chamberlain was again reassigned as the temporary 3rd Brigade Commander. The next day, while marching through a dense wooded forest, enemy cannons began to fire on another Union column. The smoke from the artillery barrage gave away their concealed position and Chamberlain sprang into action.

He separated the brigade into two separate groups, sending two regiments to continue forward while the other four moved into the woods to capture the Rebel battery. Chamberlain had become an aggressive commander, and any feelings of apprehension to take action before orders were given him were long gone. He ordered the men to first shoot the Rebel battery's horses when they came into range. This would prevent the enemy from fleeing with their cannons. It was a good plan and Chamberlain was anxious to get his men into position. But the lead 16th Michigan came upon an obstacle, known as the Pole Cat Creek.

The muddy water appeared to be deep, and with its steady flow the men feared it might be a hazard to cross. Chamberlain trotted up to the front of his column to see what was causing the delay. When he saw that it was only a narrow stream, he ordered the men to begin crossing. Had the men at the front been from the 20th Maine, there would have been no apprehension. But the men in the lead were from a Michigan regiment and they stood staring into the water.

Chamberlain's blood boiled. "Into the water, now!" He repeated his order in anger.

A few of the men slowly walked into the edge of the stream as if they were frightened children being taught their first swimming lesson. Chamberlain was disgusted at the continued delay. He looked up and down the creek for a narrower crossing, but there was none. He spotted a wide wooden fence however, that was being used to mark the border of a property line.

"Dismantle that fence and throw it across!" he ordered.

The men stared at him, not able to grasp the point of his order.

Chamberlain slid off of his horse and stormed over to the fence. "Pull this fence from its posts and throw it across! If you need a bridge, here it is!"

Now the men understood and quickly dismantled the wooden structure. But when they slid it across the creek they discovered the water was only waist high, and abandoned the makeshift bridge construction. The lost time had been pivotal and the splashing of four regiments hurrying through the water was heard by the enemy position. By the time Chamberlain had a force big enough assembled across the creek to initiate an attack, the enemy battery was gone.

Chamberlain was beside himself with absolute humiliation. He had never had his orders so blatantly questioned and disregarded. There was no time to chastise the shameful performance, though. If Confederate artillery was somewhere out in the woods, there was certainly infantry also near. He turned his regiments around and marched them back to meet the rest of the brigade.

That night Chamberlain called the men of the 16th Michigan regiment to assemble, and then had them sit among the trees separated from the rest of the brigade. The men knew they were in trouble, and suspected they were about to get a tongue-lashing or worse from their new commander. Chamberlain stood before them in his characteristic pose- hands clasped together behind his back.

"I suppose you all know why you're here," Chamberlain started calmly. "Today, members of this regiment disobeyed my orders and the result was the failure of this brigade to capture enemy cannons. I have only two things to point out to you and then a suggestion. Number one- the next time you face a wall of canister, recognize that the cannon hurling it down upon you may have been one of those we should have captured today. Number two- understand that disobeying an order during the course of battle is punishable by death. If it happens again, the guilty parties shall not be afforded the same manner of council in which I bestow on you this evening." Chamberlain paused and made sure the men understood exactly what he meant. Then he continued. "Now I have a suggestion. I began with the 20th Maine, and understand how a few men can destroy the reputation of a great regiment. May I suggest to you," Chamberlain paused and looked directly at the regiment's young commander, Major Robert T. Elliott. "That you speak directly to those responsible for this day's blunder, and you do everything within your power to assure this does not happen again." Chamberlain paused again and made eye contact with the rest of the officers of the 16th Michigan. When he was convinced that the message was clear, he nodded that he believed his point had been made. "That is all."

"Regiment!" Major Elliott sounded. "Attention!"

The men jumped to their feet and stood erect.

Chamberlain drew his arms to his side and saluted them. He then turned away and walked back to his tent.

It was good that Chamberlain had handled the situation as he did. He could have punished the entire regiment, the result being certain discord and contempt for him. He recognized only a handful had actually caused the delay, and his impatience at the creek had prevented him from even recognizing who the culprits were. He rightfully concluded that the best way to handle the situation was to inform them of his concerns, admonish them of the repercussions of it happening again, and then allowing them to resolve the matter as men among themselves.

The next day the 5th Corps crossed the North Anna River on foot and deployed in the woods to guard the rest of the Army as it crossed on pontoon bridges. Late in the afternoon a Confederate corps attacked their position and a violent battle ensued. The Confederates made several attempts to outflank three Union brigades of the 1st Division that had become separated during the continuous fighting.

Chamberlain ordered his men down into a prone firing line, but stood in front of them so he could watch for the approaching Confederates. When the enemy crept into range, Chamberlain ordered volley after volley while standing over his ranks.

"You've got to get down, Colonel!" one of his staff aides yelled as minié balls whizzed past them.

"I'm in no more danger here than anyone else," Chamberlain retorted. "I have to see what's going on!"

And there he remained, walking back and forth down his line, coaching his men to steady their aim and continue firing.

At nightfall the Confederates retreated, having been soundly defeated by the Union 5th Corps. Some of the bravest fighting came from the men of the recently admonished 16th Michigan, who ran to the support of a 2nd Brigade regiment that was being overrun. News of the brave action of the men of the 16th, and their having taken the initiative to support another regiment without waiting for orders to do so, greatly impressed Chamberlain. He made sure to write the regiment's young commander of his gratitude for their performance.

Grant's army continued southward for the remainder of May and into early June. The 5th Corps was now encroaching on Richmond, and each day Confederate batteries fired into the engulfing Union lines. Orders were given to Chamberlain while at Bethesda Church to dig in and prepare for a Rebel attack. Chamberlain himself helped in the labor of constructing breastworks of dirt and fallen tree trunks. The new fortifications were quickly completed, even though a constant barrage of artillery fire had pounded them throughout the day. At the completion of the new defenses, Chamberlain climbed up on top of the fortress and scanned the horizon through his field glasses, while the rest of the brigade huddled behind the shelter they had just constructed.

"What the hell is he doin' up there?" a sergeant from the 83rd Pennsylvania asked another sergeant standing next to him.

"Well, I believe that's Colonel Chamberlain givin' Bobby Lee the evil eye," the other sergeant answered.

An explosion and resulting shower of dirt and shrapnel rained down on the men.

"Colonel, you better get down from there!" one of the sergeants yelled.

Chamberlain didn't answer. Another mortar round crashed into the fortification, filling the air with flying earth. Most of it rained back down on the brigade commander, who simply ignored it.

The two sergeants dusted the dirt from their jackets and shook their heads at the careless colonel.

"Come on down from there, sir! You're gonna get killed!"

Chamberlain was studying the enemy position with such great concentrating he had no idea he was being addressed.

"That's it," one of the men declared to the other. "I've watched him do this too many times already. Before he just thought he was bulletproof, but now he thinks he's cannon ball-proof. I can't sit here and watch that man kill his self."

"I'm with yuh," the other sergeant said. "Wanna go get'em?"

"Suppose we should."

"He's liable to get real upset with us," one of the men warned.

"Yep."

"Yep."

"You ready?"

"Yep."

The two men carefully climbed to the top of the earthworks, each grabbing one of their brigade commander's arms. Chamberlain lowered his field glasses and looked at the two subordinates as if they were crazy.

"What are you doing?" he exclaimed as they guided him back into the shelter of the entrenchment.

The men didn't answer until they got to the bottom of the fortification.

Then one of the sergeants said, "Sir, I say this with all the respect I'm supposed to have for a colonel, and especially because I like you. You keep standing out there in front of Johnny Reb like that, next time we'll be dragging you back with a big hole in yuh head."

Chamberlain was still stunned at being manhandled by the two sergeants. He straightened his coat and grew embarrassed. "I appreciate your concern, gentlemen," was all he could think to say. He then clasped his hands behind his back and walked away.

General Bartlett took back the reigns of the 3rd Brigade the next day. Chamberlain returned to the 20th Maine and prepared them for an assault on the massive enemy entrenchments before them. On June 3, Grant called for an early morning attack on Lee's main force at Cold Harbor, only a few miles south of the 20th Maine's position. There, Chamberlain and the rest of the 5th Corps could only listen as three other Union corps thrust themselves into nearly impenetrable Confederate fortifications. Shortly after noon, Grant conceded his assault had failed. Nearly 7000 Federal casualties lay scattered before the stalwart enemy line.

On June 5, the new 5th Corps commander, Major General Gouverneur K. Warren, re-shuffled his brigades and appointed Chamberlain commander of his 1st Brigade. The new brigade consisted of five veteran regiments and one new regiment, all from Pennsylvania. Chamberlain was aware that several of his old commanders had been campaigning for his new position, which was normally reserved for a brigadier general. He hoped his promotion wouldn't result in any animosity toward him. He cared much less about the fact that he would continue to serve as a colonel. What did matter was that he was back to where he felt most comfortable. He returned to the 20th Maine camp and personally informed them of his new assignment. The men pretended to be glad for their favored leader, but they knew they were losing a great commander once again.

Chamberlain was at first cautious with how he spoke among his new peers. They were all generals, and regardless of how they felt about Chamberlain, there was always military protocol to follow. Chamberlain decided to simply handle his command as he best saw fit, and to allow the politics of rank to take whatever course it may. This proved another wise career choice. Chamberlain's confidence had not only impressed the men who served under him, but his command-style in the presence of senior officers was also well-received.

Two days after his promotion, Chamberlain formally welcomed himself into his new brigade by calling his officers to a meeting. He had introduced himself to most of his staff personally sometime during the prior two days, but he wanted to meet with them all together and share his expectations. The men sat on a group of fence rails that had been fashioned into a long bench. Chamberlain exchanged salutes and shook hands with each of them as they arrived. When he could see all of his new staff was present, he stood in front of them and folded his hands behind his back.

Chamberlain began, "I wanted to bring you all together tonight to inform you of the manner in which I would like this new brigade to operate. You men from the One Hundred Twenty-First, One Hundred Forty-Second, One Forty-Third, One Forty-Ninth, and One Fiftieth, have all proven yourselves on the field of battle, let there be no question of that. You may never have heard of me, but I have certainly heard of your great achievements. Those of you in the One Eighty-Seventh, well, your day will come. And on that day, I have confidence you will also prevail with bravery and honor.

"My expectations are these, gentlemen. Obey my orders. If you do not understand them, have them promptly clarified. If you disagree with them, assume I know something you don't. I also expect each and every one of you to lead from the front. Any officer who sends an enlisted man into a fight should be willing to stand beside him and also fight. If any of you think your life is a greater commodity than one of those brave knights of the Union, tell me now and I shall have you reassigned to another brigade."

Chamberlain studied the officers' faces to see what their reactions were. They all appeared to be attentive and nodding that they understood and agreed with him.

Chamberlain then promised, "I will never carelessly march this brigade into an enemy line, knowing that it will bring unreasonable casualties. But I will move this brigade in the support of another that has made that unfortunate error. I expect the men to be up and ready when ordered. I expect them to be eager to take the front when they have been reasonably rested. I do not want to be bothered by the mundane complaints of the day. It is your responsibility to keep your men supplied with rations and functioning equipment."

Chamberlain paused. All of the points he wanted to address had been, except for one. "As you know," he began carefully, "I am from Maine and not Pennsylvania. It may be awkward for some of the men or even you to accept that an outsider is your brigade commander. In any other arena this would be a reasonable subject of debate, but unfortunately we are at war and there is no time for it. Assure the men who question my being here that I will do absolutely everything in my power to bring glory to this brigade. And from this moment forward we will refer to ourselves as the Keystone Brigade, in honor of your home. Are there any questions?"

The men shrugged and looked at each other. Chamberlain's message had been understood and well received. There were no questions.

"Alright then, I have orders from General Griffin. We will break camp at dawn tomorrow morning. Get the men ready for at least two long marches. It appears General Grant wants us in Petersburg."

CHAPTER 8

PETERSBURG

The Petersburg, Virginia, of early 1864 was a railway hub and extremely important location to the Confederate capital in Richmond. Just 25 miles to the south, Petersburg not only had a valuable iron works, but was also nestled against the Appomattox River. Connecting to the Appomattox was the James River, which in turn opened into the Chesapeake Bay. The overwhelming bulk of Confederate supplies being sent to Virginia either by railroad or boat had to go through Petersburg first. Grant decided that he could take Petersburg while Lee stood in defense of Richmond. Then it would only be time before the Army of North Virginia either starved itself into submission, or surrendered altogether.

On June 12, the 5th Corps began a long wet march south through the middle of a summer thunderstorm. The rain didn't last, but the mud it created did. Four days of treading through red Virginia sludge was finally ended when the Federals reached the James River on June 16th. The 5th Corps crossed the river on a nearly half mile long pontoon bridge that had already been constructed by the engineers. When the 1st Brigade of the 1st Division reached the opposite shore, Chamberlain ordered them back in for a bath.

The six regiments gladly obeyed the command. Thousands of filthy men secured their letters from home and pictures of loved ones in their shoes, and ran into the cold brown water fully clothed. Chamberlain stood on the bank and playfully tossed chunks of soap bars at his men. The rain had broken the day before and the weather turned muggy and hot. Chamberlain gave the men time to rest and eat after they climbed back out of the river. Within an hour the sun had baked their uniforms dry again, and the brigade was ready to move out.

The columns continued southward through the night, arriving on the northern edge of Petersburg to the sounds of battle being waged in town. The 2nd and 9th Corps had already arrived and were attempting to break a heavily fortified Confederate outpost. The 5th Corps was held in reserve and most of the men slept through the attack that proved fruitless to the other two Union corps.

On June 18, the rest of the Union Army arrived, but their advance on Petersburg had been discovered by Lee. He'd answered by sending over 18,000 Confederate infantrymen toward town to reinforce the earthworks that had already been prepared there. Grant knew the enemy reinforcements were coming and ordered a massive assault on the Confederate line at dawn. If the offensive was successful, the city would be taken before the new troops could affect the battle's outcome.

At 4:30 a.m., the entire Army of the Potomac advanced on the Confederate line. It was still dark when the assault began and the men were being thrown blindly into battle. Closer and closer they marched toward the enemy trenches and salients, but not a single shot was fired their way. The men at the front braced themselves just before climbing over the steep dirt embankments, believing the concealed Rebels were about to pop up and unleash a fiery volley of lead into them. But much to their relief the trenches were empty, and the men waved their caps and cheered. The Confederates had apparently fled from their advance. The celebration only lasted long enough for the light of morning to reveal that the Confederate line had only moved back closer to the city and they were now on higher ground.

Grant called his staff together and the terrain and conditions were reevaluated. An attack had to be made before the Confederate reinforcements arrived, and a sense of rush and panic was in the air. Now that daylight had arrived, the Rebels could see their enemy's positions, and they began firing from several different artillery batteries.

One of those batteries was a few hundred yards south of the rest of the Rebel line and was lobbing shells directly into the 5th Corps. Chamberlain and his commander, General Warren, rode out to a clearing and examined the enemy outpost. The Rebel cannons were strategically positioned to provide a cross fire into a Union force advancing on its main line. If that battery wasn't taken out, the men would be slaughtered before they even got near the main Confederate works.

The Rebel officer responsible for placing the battery there was also smart enough to know how valuable the position was. It was evidenced by the large infantry detachment that was waiting nearby.

Warren lowered his field glasses and looked at Chamberlain. "That artillery fire is very annoying, Colonel," he said casually. "Do you think you can do something about it?"

"Yes, sir, I'd be glad to," Chamberlain answered.

Both men turned their horses and rode back to the formation.

Chamberlain called his regiment commanders and told them that they were going to attack the enemy position at once. As the ranks assembled, Chamberlain devised a plan to march through the cover of some nearby woods and then attack the rear of the offending battery.

At mid-morning, he moved his brigade into the trees and around the left flank of the enemy position. Confederate pickets saw the large Federal movement toward them and alerted their command. By the time Chamberlain and the 1st Brigade emerged from the forest, there was a long line of Rebel infantrymen poised between them and the Confederate cannons. Chamberlain ordered the advance and the Rebels immediately answered with a blast from their muskets.

Waving his men forward from the back of Charlemagne, Chamberlain could see that several of the Confederate artillery pieces had been turned around and were now targeting his men. Chamberlain yelled for his officers to speed up the advance, fearing a slow assault would expose them to too much fire.

Low thunderous booms and ear-piercing explosions rocked the open field. Men were falling all around him, yet the Confederate line began to break. Chamberlain ordered his reserve regiment forward and they entered the battle with a lethal volley of smoke and flames.

Just as the attack was turning to a rout, a final cannon shell tore into the gathering of field commanders surrounding Chamberlain. Several of the officer's horses reared and collapsed with mortal wounds. Charlemagne had also been hit, and he stammered a few feet before he and his rider fell to the ground. Chamberlain picked himself up and saw that the color bearer, who had also been standing near him, was lying dead in the tall yellow grass. Chamberlain grabbed the brigade's flag- a red Maltese cross on a field of white- and ran forward flailing it in the air.

The Rebel infantry was being overrun, and the few still on the field were sprinting away toward their main line, with them, the cannons that had been placed on the hill. Chamberlain ordered the regiments back into a defensive line and prepared for a counterattack. Once his new position was established, Chamberlain found himself standing in an open field almost a half a mile in front of the rest of the Union Army. Chamberlain quickly placed his six regiments of Pennsylvanians behind a gentle slope that provided a modest amount of cover. He then ordered the men to dig in. The Pennsylvanians knew how dangerous a position they had gotten themselves into, and dug frantically to create some kind of defenses.

While the men shoveled and scraped together new fortifications, Chamberlain watched a Confederate force growing across an open meadow in front of them. Chamberlain sent a messenger back to 5th Corps headquarters, advising of his new position and requesting reinforcements. Two hours passed, and the only support Chamberlain could see was a Union artillery battery taking a position far to his right and well behind his line.

Meanwhile, what appeared to be an entire division of Confederate infantry, had now entrenched themselves across the field directly in front of Chamberlain's brigade. The delay in continuing the assault by the rest of the Army provided the Rebels time to build a force significantly greater than Chamberlain's. If they attacked now, the 1st Brigade would have to give up the ground they had just taken.

"He's over there," a private said to a lieutenant colonel standing next to him. He was pointing at Chamberlain.

The officer was a stranger to Chamberlain, and he assumed he was from headquarters delivering orders.

"Sir," the officer said and saluted. "I have been sent here by General Meade to instruct you to attack the enemy position in front of your brigade."

"When?" Chamberlain asked.

"Immediately," was the answer.

"Is this not a coordinated assault?" Chamberlain questioned. He thought it absurd to order an attack "immediately." It sometimes took hours to get every regiment prepared for an advance. Was he to blindly go forward without even knowing the location of his reinforcements?

"I understand you are to attack alone," the officer replied.

"Show me the orders," Chamberlain demanded in disbelief.

"These are verbal orders, Colonel. I have no papers."

Chamberlain studied the man. *Was he a spy trying to lead his brigade into a death trap?*

"You are dismissed, Colonel," Chamberlain said, half expecting the man to turn and walk toward the Rebel lines where he belonged.

Chamberlain raised his field glasses back to his eyes and scanned the enemy horde building in front of him. At least 3000 Rebel infantrymen stared back from behind mounds of dirt and logs. He knew the brigade could never survive this attack alone. Chamberlain called for a messenger and wrote a note to General Meade.

General Meade:

I have just received a verbal order not through the usual channels, but by a staff officer unknown to me, purporting to come from the General commanding the Army, directing me to assault the main works of the enemy in my front.

Circumstances lead me to believe the General cannot be perfectly aware of my situation, which has greatly changed within the last hour. I have just carried a crest, an advanced post occupied by the enemy's artillery, supported by infantry. I am advanced a mile beyond our own lines, and in an isolated position. On my right a deep railroad cut, my left flank in the air, with no support whatever. In my front at close range is a strongly entrenched line of infantry and artillery with projecting salients right and left, such that my advance would be swept by a cross fire, while a large fort to my left enfilades my entire advance, as I experienced in carrying this position. In the hollow along my front, close up to the enemy's works, appears to be bad ground, swampy, boggy, where my men would be held at a great disadvantage under the destructive fire. I have brought up three batteries and am placing them on the reverse slope of this crest, to enable me to hold against expected attack. To leave these guns behind me unsupported, their retreat cut off by the railroad cut, would expose them to loss in case of repulse. Fully aware of the responsibility that I take, I beg to be assured that the order to attack with my single brigade is with the General's full understanding. I have here a veteran bri- gade of six regiments, and my responsibility for these men warrants me in wishing assurances that no mistake in communicating orders compels me to sacrifice them. From what I can see of the enemy's lines, it is my opinion that if an assault is to be made, it should be by nothing less than the whole army.

> *Very respectfully,*
> *Joshua L. Chamberlain*
> *Colonel Commanding 1st Brigade,*
> *1st Div. 5th Corps*

Chamberlain sent the note with his aide, and expected that he would probably be relieved of his command by the end of the day for insubordination. He could live with that. He could never live with the responsibility of murdering his own men.

Ten minutes later the same lieutenant colonel returned to Chamberlain's position. After exchanging salutes, he told Chamberlain, "Sir, I am to inform you that the entire Army is going to attack, but because of your forward line you will lead."

Now the orders made sense. Chamberlain dismissed the messenger and assembled his regiment commanders. He reviewed with them the hazards that they faced with the uneven terrain and swampy ground in front of the Confederate trenches. Chamberlain decided that the distance between the two lines was too dangerous to cross in slow disciplined formation. To reduce casualties, he instructed his officers to advance on the enemy at the double quick, and to not stop to fire until the marshy area just before the enemy barricades was reached. This would limit the number of Confederate volleys being fired on them and provide a better chance at breaching the trenches on the first wave of attack. While the plan was being discussed, another messenger arrived and informed Chamberlain that his open left flank would be supported by the 4th Division, under the command of Brigadier General Lysander Cutler. Once Chamberlain was confident that his officers were ready, he borrowed a horse and rode to General Cutler's command post.

Cutler was a seasoned general who had the reputation of being self-centered and extremely difficult to get along with. He often tested his younger officers on military tactics and replaced them if they did poorly. It was also common for men in his division to be harshly disciplined for very minor violations of military protocol.

Stories of those instances permeated the ranks. Chamberlain knew well the general's reputation and prepared himself for their encounter. Cutler wasn't hard to find. He stood alone, smoking a pipe beneath a canvass canopy. Chamberlain slid off of his horse and walked over to him.

"Sir," Chamberlain began and saluted. "Colonel Chamberlain, First Brigade, First Division, Fifth Corps."

Cutler returned the salute with the pipe still in his right hand.

"What is it, Colonel?" he asked as if he was being rudely interrupted.

"Sir, I have been ordered to attack the Rebel line in front of me and I understand your division will be supporting my left."

Cutler responded by drawing from his pipe and releasing a cloud of smoke into the air. He didn't answer.

Chamberlain continued, "I don't know if you're aware of my position, sir, but my brigade is almost a mile beyond the rest of the Army, and we'll be the first ones taking fire." Chamberlain waited for some kind of reaction, but the salty old general simply stood and waited for him to get to his point.

"I believe I'll be putting in all of my regiments at once," Chamberlain added. "If I hold anyone back in reserve, my first line won't make it."

Cutler took another puff from his pipe. His lack of response was already annoying Chamberlain. This wasn't the type of mind game-playing Chamberlain had expected. He was prepared for some rudeness, but not being ignored. On another day, there might be time for it. But there was no time for it now.

Chamberlain swallowed his temper and said, "Sir, I propose that we move our men out into the field at the same time. This will certainly divert some of the enemy guns away from my brigade, and allow me to get my men into position much closer to the enemy trenches. If I advance on my own, the artillery fire will plow my men down before their infantry fires a single shot."

Cutler pulled his pipe out of his mouth and pointed it at Chamberlain angrily. "I don't take orders from you!" he growled. "I am your senior! You had rather take orders from me!"

Had the confrontation occurred a year earlier, Chamberlain would not have dared continue the discussion. But he was now responsible for the lives of over 2000 men that were about to advance across an open field toward a well-entrenched enemy line. He was not going to sacrifice a single soldier because a general had his feelings hurt and wouldn't support his attack.

"I have my orders, General," Chamberlain insisted adamantly. "And I suppose you have yours. We are to work together and I think it well that we have an understanding."

"You will not address me in such tone, Colonel Chamberlain!"

"Sir, if it is going to save the lives of my men, I shall address you in any manner I see fit!"

"Your conduct will be reported to General Warren."

"I am sure the general will understand," Chamberlain responded confidently, "and I am sure he will be most interested in what I have to say on the matter."

Cutler clenched his jaws in frustration. This was the first time a subordinate had so flagrantly challenged his authority, and Cutler knew that if he reported the incident, Chamberlain's explanation would call the general's actions into question. That would be a particular problem because their corps commander, Major General Warren, was already unhappy with Cutler's recent performance. Cutler wisely decided to end their conversation.

"I shall know what to do when the time comes, Colonel. You are dismissed."

"Then you will be on my left, sir?"

"You are dismissed, Colonel Chamberlain!"

Chamberlain and Cutler locked eyes, the brigade commander from Maine making it clear to the general from Wisconsin that if he did not come to the support of the 1st Brigade, their next meeting would not end civilly.

Chamberlain waited just long enough to break Cutler's stare and then saluted the general before walking back to his horse. On the ride back to the front, Chamberlain vowed to himself that if Cutler did not support him, he would do everything in his power to have the general brought before a court marshal.

It was early in the afternoon now and the sky filled with gloomy gray clouds. The day was smoldering and humid, even with the shielded sun. Chamberlain returned to his staff and learned that his brigade had received orders during his short absence that the attack would begin at 3 o'clock. Chamberlain then promptly called all of his regiment commanders together and reminded them how important it was going to be to keep the men moving forward. As he reviewed his battle plan with his officers, he realized how even more deadly their approach actually was. His throat grew dry and Chamberlain called for a cup of water.

"Here you go, Colonel." A sergeant that was standing nearby held his canteen out to Chamberlain.

"Thank you, Sergeant, but you keep it," Chamberlain replied. "I would not take a drink from an enlisted man going into battle. You may need it. My officers can get me a drink."

A tin cup of water was placed in Chamberlain's hand. He held it up and toasted the man silently for his kind gesture, then turned back to his staff.

At 2:45 p.m., the 1st Brigade was assembled into three battle lines and ordered to prepare for the assault. Each regiment moved up to the small earthworks the forward regiments had been constructing throughout the day. As the men lay against the wall of dirt, Chamberlain stood on top of the trench and paced back and forth. He could sense the anxiety in the men, who could clearly see the heavy defenses they were about to attack.

Chamberlain made one last effort to encourage them before the battle. "Comrades! We have now before us a great duty for our country to perform, and who knows but the way in which we acquit ourselves in this perilous undertaking may depend the ultimate success of the preservation of our grand republic! We know that some must fall, it may be any of you or I, but I feel that you will all go in manfully and make such a record as will make all our loyal American people grateful! I can but feel that our action in this crisis is momentous, and who can know, but in the providence of God, our action today may be the one thing needful to break and destroy this unholy rebellion!"

His words went unanswered by the men. They knew this advance would cause many to fall. It was a time for solemn final thoughts of family and duty to their cause.

Chamberlain removed his pocket watch from his jacket. He calmly checked the time and returned it to the inside of his dirty coat. Then, reaching across his waist, he ripped his saber from its scabbard and turned to face the enemy line. "Attention!"

Echoed commands followed as the three lines, a quarter of a mile in length, suddenly rose up from behind the dirt mound.

"Bayonets!" Chamberlain roared.

The rattling of metal followed down the line.

Chamberlain paused a moment to absorb the glorious sight of his massive command. He then wheeled around to face the Confederates across the field. "Trail Arms! Double-quick... March!"

The brigade's lines jolted forward as the men broke into a ravenous call for Rebel blood. Buglers from the entire Union Army of the Potomac echoed across the battlefield, calling for the great offensive to begin. Chamberlain dashed forward, leading the Keystone Brigade into the waiting jaws of Confederate guns. Rebel cannons immediately opened with a pounding barrage of shells and canister. Deafening explosions began to tear into the advancing regiments.

Chamberlain led the men down into the wetlands where they were met by the first hail of Confederate musket fire. The Rebels knew the Union line would bog down there, and poured volley after volley of deadly minié balls into the Federal infantrymen as they struggled through the marsh.

Chamberlain trudged through the willow reeds and mud to the solid ground on the other side. Men were falling all around him and the advance was being stalled. He turned back to his brigade, waving his sword and ordering the men forward. Slowly, enough men for a forward line passed through the swampy field and reformed on dry grass. Chamberlain circled his sword around his head twice and then pointed it toward the enemy position, now concealed behind a haze of smoke.

"Charge!"

The first line poured past him, having yet to fire a single shot in their defense.

Chamberlain realized the men still passing through the marsh were forming on him and he needed to spread the next line out. He turned his back to the enemy position again and signaled with his saber for the advancing men to move to the left. As he yelled orders for the men to "Spread the line!" he heard the *zip* of a minié ball, and then the *thap* of it striking below him. At the same instant, his hips were suddenly thrown out from under him, and a sharp pain stung in his lower back. The mysterious blow had nearly knocked him off of his feet and only the support of stumbling onto his sword had prevented him from falling.

Chamberlain assumed he'd just been shot, and was angry that he'd been struck in the back. His first thought was the idea that people might think he had been injured while running from the enemy like a coward. Chamberlain reached around to feel the wound, hoping it wasn't serious and could somehow be overlooked or even disguised. To his initial relief, he discovered that blood was gushing from his right hip, not from the back of his coat.

His next thought was to see if any of his staff members were near to assist him in bandaging his wound. He could then resume command of the assault. But all of his officers were scattered in the muddled chaos, shouting commands or running forward. Chamberlain would have to treat his own injury if he wanted to get back in the fight.

He tried to take a step, but his legs wouldn't move. A sudden rush of panic gripped at his chest. He was paralyzed from his waist down, yet he could still feel his legs. Chamberlain desperately looked around the field for help, but only saw that his assault was turning into a disorganized rampage.

"Forward!" Chamberlain yelled and twisted his shoulders around to face the enemy. The maneuver only caused him to lose balance, and he again plunged the tip of his saber into the dirt, leaning desperately onto the hilt to keep from falling. "Go on boys!" He yelled. "Show them what Pennsylvanian's can do!"

The field was now fully enveloped in smoke. Men were gasping and coughing for air as they ran into the incessant fire of the enemy. Chamberlain continued to wave the men onward with his cap. As he struggled to remain standing, he could feel the warmth of his own blood running down his right leg into his boot. Within minutes he grew dizzy, and the field began to slowly spin around him. His hearing began to fade, and Chamberlain found himself strangely separated from the raging battle. Then the percussion of a sudden mortar blast hurled Chamberlain onto his left knee. He tried desperately to lift himself back up, but his legs offered no support. Now he could feel his strength draining from him with each heartbeat. He dropped onto his other knee and then slumped to the ground.

Chamberlain lay helplessly on his side, watching the feet of the men around him still scrambling forward. His head filled with the muffled sounds of voices yelling and men screaming, and bombs bursting around him. Two boots suddenly stopped in front of his head and then a face appeared in front of his. It was Lieutenant West Funk of the 121st Pennsylvania.

"Hold on, Colonel!" he yelled over the blasts of gunfire and artillery. "We'll get you out of here and to a surgeon!"

Chamberlain felt his feet being picked up by another soldier. It was Lieutenant Benjamin Walters from the 143rd Pennsylvania. Funk scooped Chamberlain up by the shoulders and the two men carried him back across the marsh. Chamberlain believed he was bleeding to death, and wanted to make sure someone else was commanding the assault in his absence.

"Put me down," Chamberlain mumbled.

"But, sir," Funk answered, "you need a surgeon bad."

Both of the young lieutenants cowered and flinched as enemy minié balls sailed past them.

"Put me down, Lieutenant!" Chamberlain growled.

The two men gently laid their colonel on the grass and knelt over him.

"Go find Colonel Irwin," Chamberlain ordered. "He commands the One Forty-Ninth. Tell him I am shot and cannot proceed. Inform him that he is now in command of the First Brigade."

"Should I stay with you, sir?" Walters asked.

"No, Lieutenant,' Chamberlain answered. "Both of you go. It is imperative my orders reach Colonel Irwin."

The two Lieutenants could tell from the amount of blood on Chamberlain's coat and pants that he was seriously injured, and the thought of leaving their brigade commander on the field trouble them both.

Chamberlain grew impatient with their reluctance to leave. "Go, damn you!" he shouted.

The two men sprung to their feet and ran back toward the fighting to locate Colonel Irwin.

Chamberlain, his strength completely diminished, rolled his head from side-to-side, watching what was becoming the slaughter of his men all around him. When the carnage became too much to bear, he stared up into the gray Virginia clouds and prepared to die.

His first thoughts were of his family. He found comfort in knowing Fanny's parents, who still lived in Brunswick, could help raise their children. As for Fanny, she would take his death badly, but she was still young and could remarry. Chamberlain then thought of his own mother and knew how his death in battle would break her heart. For over an hour he lay bleeding on the battlefield, hallucinating memories of his childhood as lead and dirt rained in all around. His delirium was only interrupted when four Union artillerymen from the 9th Massachusetts surrounded him and began brushing the dirt from Chamberlain's coat.

"What are you doing?" Chamberlain asked- his words thick and lethargic.

"We come to get you out of here, Colonel!" one of them yelled over the bedlam on the field.

Each of the four enlisted men grabbed one of Chamberlain's limbs and prepared to lift him.

"No!" Chamberlain demanded with his last reserve of strength. "Leave me here. I am finished boys. Take someone who can be saved."

"Sorry Colonel, but we was ordered by our captain to bring you back!"

"I am giving you new orders," Chamberlain slurred like a tired drunk. "I'm your colonel and I said go rescue someone who can be saved."

"Sir, we are from the 9th Massachusetts," another of the men said, "and we don't give a damn if you're a colonel. You sure ain't our colonel. Captain Bigelow says we got to bring you back, so that's what we's goin' to do!"

Chamberlain began to mumble another protest, but it was too late. The four artillerymen lifted him up and placed him back down on a stretcher. He was then lifted again and rushed back to the 9th Massachusetts Battery position.

Chamberlain drifted to unconsciousness even as continual cannon fire burst from a few yards away. He awoke momentarily as his body was being rocked back-and-forth, and discovered he was now alone in the back of a wagon of some kind. He fought to keep his eyes open. He wanted his last vision to be that of the clouds in the sky, not the inside of a filthy canvass wagon cover. But to no avail, the life was too far gone from him and he slipped back to sleep and closer to his death.

The next thing he heard was voices talking quietly nearby. Chamberlain struggled to open his eyes and concentrate on hearing the conversation.

"He's lost too much blood, gentlemen," one of the voices said. "That ball went in on his right and looks like it stopped just below the skin on his left side. There are pelvic bone fragments all over the inside of that wound. I'm sure the ball has run right through his bladder. He's already nearly bled out. I can't do anything else here. I'm sorry."

"Doctor, with all due respect, our regiment was held in reserve today and we don't have any casualties," another voice said. "We'd like to stay with him and see if there's anything we can do."

Chamberlain recognized that voice. It was one of his surgeons from the 20th Maine, Dr. Abner Shaw.

"I don't mind," the first voice answered. "But if you save this man, it will be a miracle."

"If anyone deserves one, sir, it's my brother," a third voice interjected.

Chamberlain also recognized that youthful voice. It was Thomas. His eyes slowly focused on the four blurry figures standing a few feet away next to an oil lamp. He was in a tent somewhere. Outside, there were men screaming and groaning.

"He's awake!" Thomas said.

The four figures quickly moved to Chamberlain's side.

Chamberlain recognized his brother and Dr. Shaw, and one of the other men, Dr. Morris Townsend from the 44th New York. The other man was a stranger, but his blood-soaked apron made his profession clear.

"Can you hear me, Lawrence?" Thomas asked as he grabbed his brother's limp hand.

"Yes," Chamberlain answered softly and nodded.

Thomas smiled and looked at the other men.

"You've been shot in the hip, Colonel Chamberlain," Dr. Shaw said. "The bullet is just under the skin on your left. There won't be a problem getting it out of you, but I think we're going to have to do some extra work on the path it left behind."

Chamberlain began to feel a sharp throbbing cramp in his lower stomach and right side. The more his head cleared, the stronger the pain grew.

"I'll get some morphine in you, Colonel," Dr. Townsend said.

"You're going to be okay, brother," Thomas reassured him.

Chamberlain smiled warmly at the naive attempt to cheer him.

The tent flap flew open and General Warren and General Griffin walked in. Thomas jumped up and saluted.

"How is he?" Warren asked.

Dr. Townsend signaled for the two generals to meet him outside of the tent. They then stepped away together to discuss the grim diagnosis confidentially.

Chamberlain knew what was being said. He was slowly dying, but they wanted him to believe there was still hope. By the sounds of the agony outside, he wished the doctors would turn their attention to those who still stood a chance at surviving.

A few moments later the two generals and the doctor returned. Warren and Griffin knelt down next to Chamberlain's cot. Chamberlain forced a smile through the pain. "I know I am done," he said softly.

The two generals had both grown very fond of the professor from Maine, and watching him die filled them with grief. Death was understood by the three officers though, and it was more appropriate to bestow a final honor on Chamberlain, than to patronize him with unrealistic words of encouragement.

"I will see to it that our recommendations of your promotion to brigadier general are forwarded immediately to General Grant," Warren said.

"Thank you, sir," Chamberlain answered. "I'm sure my family will be most honored."

"Would you like me to write to your wife?" Griffin asked.

"She would only find more sorrow in it," Chamberlain answered. "But I have a young son named Wyllys, sir, and it would mean a great deal to me if you could tell him that I perished having fought with honor."

"Consider it done," Griffin answered.

"How did the men do?" Chamberlain asked.

"They did fine, Colonel," Warren lied.

The assault had been a disaster for the Army of the Potomac.

The two generals assured Chamberlain that his brigade would be kept together and the men would be taken care of. They then stood and ordered the surgeons to keep them apprised of Chamberlain's condition and progress. Warren and Griffin then replaced their caps and gave Chamberlain a salute before stepping back out into the night.

With his consciousness the pain in his side and abdomen quickly became excruciating. Chamberlain had accepted the fact that he was about to die, but the word that he was going to be posthumously promoted changed everything. If he was going to be a brigadier general, he wanted to live to see the stars on his shoulders, and not pass away and have them buried with his body.

"When are you going to take it out?" Chamberlain asked the two surgeons.

"We need to get set up first," Townsend answered.

"Well, let's get on with it," Chamberlain ordered. "It looks like I'm going to be a general, and I'll be damned if I don't get to live at least one day just to be addressed as such."

The two doctors prepared for the surgery. Both had arrived with their medical bags and an additional wooden box of medicines and bandages. Thomas remained at his brother's side to help guide him through the torture of being operated on without an adequate supply of chloroform or ether for anesthesia. Dr. Shaw warned Chamberlain that the pain may become unbearable, and suggested he bite into a knotted wet rag to help him endure it. The small amount of morphine they had would need to be regulated. It would be of little service during the surgery, but would be most beneficial to help Chamberlain endure the residual pain of having had surgeons dig through his guts to remove bone fragments.

The men tending to Chamberlain stripped him and rolled him onto his left side. The hole in his hip was covered with caked dry blood and had to be cleaned before they could cut into it. Chamberlain winced with each gentle swipe of the bruised skin around his wound. When it was sufficiently cleaned, Dr. Shaw gave Chamberlain a warning that he was about to open the hole and it would be painful. Chamberlain put a wet towel in his mouth and grasped onto the rails of his cot. Thomas nodded to the surgeon that his brother was ready, and the two doctors began to cut into his hip.

The path of the minié ball was devastating. White shards of shattered bone lined the narrow tunnel of mutilated muscle and organ tissue. Shaw gently entered the enlarged bullet hole with a cloth swab to clear some of the blood inside. The instant he made contact with the ravaged tissue, Chamberlain's body convulsed uncontrollably. His scream of agony was barely muffled by the rag in his mouth. Thomas embraced his brother and pinned him back to the bed.

The two surgeons continued repairing Chamberlain's hip and severed blood vessels throughout the night. The operation proved to be extremely painful, but Chamberlain demanded the doctors continue, even when they tried to give him a rest. Early in the morning, Shaw and Townsend agreed they could do no more and sutured the wound closed. Chamberlain was given a final dose of morphine and sunk back into unconsciousness before he could thank the men who were trying so desperately to save his life.

During those same early morning hours, a message was delivered to Grant and Meade's headquarters.

Major General Meade,

Colonel J.L. Chamberlain of the 20th Maine Regiment Commanding the 1st Brigade of the 1st Division was mortally wounded it is thought in the assault on the enemy yesterday, the ball having passed through the pelvis and bladder. He has been recommended for promotion for gallant and efficient conduct on previous occasion, and yesterday led his brigade against the enemy under most destructive fire. He expresses the wish that he may receive the recognition of his services by promotion before he dies for the gratification of his family and friends, and I beg that it may be done.

G. K. Warren Maj. Gen.
Commanding 5th Corps

Late in the afternoon, Chamberlain woke to find Thomas still at his side. He was encouraged to be alive, but had an ominous feeling that death was still hovering over him. He asked his brother to get him a pencil and paper so he could write a letter to Fanny. Thomas volunteered to take the dictation, but Chamberlain insisted he write it himself.

My darling wife I am laying mortally wounded the doctors think, but my mind and heart are at peace, Jesus Christ is my all sufficient savior. I go to him. God bless and keep and comfort you, precious one, you have been a precious wife to me. To know and love you makes life and death beautiful. Cherish the darlings and give my love to all the dear ones. Do not grieve too much for me. We shall all soon meet. Live for the children. Give my dearest love to Father, Mother, and Sallie, and John. Oh how happy to feel yourself forgiven. God bless you ever more precious, precious one.

Ever yours,
Lawrence

Chamberlain then kissed the note and instructed Thomas to deliver it upon his death.

The two surgeons knew that Chamberlain would not survive if he was left in a field hospital. They sent word to General Warren that his brigade commander had lived through the night, but needed transfer to a regular hospital as soon as possible. Warren ordered Chamberlain be immediately carried to City Point on the James River, where he could be transported by ship to the nearest hospital. Three days after receiving his wound, Chamberlain found himself lying in the Officer's Ward at the Naval Hospital in Annapolis, Maryland.

The day before, Ulysses S. Grant had sent a dispatch to the Senate in Washington, notifying them that he had promoted Colonel Joshua

Lawrence Chamberlain to the rank of brigadier general. His reason stated, "For meritorious and efficient service on the field of battle, and especially for gallant conduct in leading his brigade against the enemy at Petersburg, Virginia."

Grant then wrote a short letter to Chamberlain announcing his formal promotion, and thanking him for his outstanding service to the country. The Commander of the Federal Army then ordered that the letter be dispatched immediately, for fear a delay may result in Chamberlain passing before he knew of his promotion. It was the only promotion of its kind Grant ever made during the war.

Chamberlain was no sooner being introduced to his new doctors when the letter from Grant arrived in Annapolis. A captain from Grant's staff handed the letter to Chamberlain, and stood by at attention as Chamberlain read it to himself. Chamberlain read it twice and then placed it between some pages in a bible left on his bedside table.

"Is that all, General, sir?" the captain asked.

"Yes, Captain," Chamberlain answered. "Thank you."

The young officer saluted and about-faced.

Before he could walk away, one of the doctors leaned over and whispered to him, "This man is only a Colonel, Captain."

"Not anymore," the officer said. "General Grant just promoted him without even waiting for the Senate to approve it. I've never served for General Chamberlain, but I've sure heard of him. If there's such a thing as a hero in this war, Doctor, you got one laying in that bed right in front of you."

The captain marched out of the ward as the doctor informed his colleagues of Chamberlain's new rank. A flurry of adjustments then followed to compensate Chamberlain for his elevated status.

He was first moved to his own room and then assigned a full time nurse to monitor his condition. Doctors checked him on the hour and made every effort to ease his constant pain. But Chamberlain was unable to enjoy the first class treatment. He couldn't walk, stand, or even sit up for that matter. The constant pain was made even more excruciating when he had to relieve himself. Both his bladder and urethra had been nicked by the near fatal round. Urine leaking into his abdomen stung as if a dagger was being thrust into his belly.

On the morning of his third day at the hospital, Fanny arrived and replaced the nurse at his side. Fanny had received a wired message of his "mortal" injury two days after the battle at Petersburg, and had to wait a third day before she was notified of the hospital he was being transported to. The newspapers were all reporting that the Federal Army had been soundly defeated, and lists of casualties from the battle were being posted in town halls and courthouses throughout the North. Chamberlain's name was mistakenly placed on several of those lists, causing even his own brigade to question whether he was still alive or dead.

John also arrive a few days later and joined Fanny in trying to nurse Chamberlain back to health. John admired his older brother's attempt to fight his impending death, but Chamberlain's pale skin and gaunt eyes reflected a man who was losing his personal battle. The bleeding had been stopped, but infection and fever were now draining his body. Fanny and John had to hold him down during the frequent episodes of convulsions and uncontrollable shivering. Morphine helped reduce his pain but also made him delirious. The following weeks passed slowly, and it often seemed they were only prolonging the miserable slow death of their loved one.

On July 24th, a little over a month after Chamberlain was shot, Fanny walked into the hospital after having slept in a nearby hotel. She had no reason to expect anything other than a day of sponging her husband's forehead, reading to him, and feeding him his meals. But when she walked into his room she was startled and nearly fainted.

"Come on in, darling," Chamberlain said. He was sitting up in his bed, cheerily cutting a piece of pork sausage that was on a plate in his lap. "I feel wonderful today. Would you like some breakfast?"

Fanny stood frozen and speechless in the doorway, covering her opened mouth with her hand.

"Nurse!" Chamberlain shouted toward the opened door. A young woman wearing a brown dress with a plain white apron stuck her head in the threshold. She couldn't very well enter. Fanny was in the way and unable to move.

"Can I get something for you, sir?" the young volunteer asked.

"Yes," Chamberlain answered. "I believe my wife would like some breakfast and a cup of coffee. Wouldn't you like some coffee, dear?"

Fanny came to her senses and ran to him. She swatted the plate off of Chamberlain's lap with a crash and wrapped her arms around him in a frantic embrace. Hospital staff rushed to the room when they heard the commotion, only to find a hysterically exuberant wife cradling her beloved husband.

Chamberlain's fever had broken during the night and a healthy pink hue had returned to the new brigadier general's skin. Both Chamberlain and his wife knew the worst was over.

Chamberlain continued to recover at a remarkable pace throughout the rest of July and into August. The muscles in his hips had been ripped and torn by the initial wound, and then even further aggravated by the operations that followed. When he got back onto his feet, simply raising his legs to take a step was, at first, impossible. But daily rehabilitation soon restored the strength needed to walk, and by September he was able to discard his cane.

When he wasn't trying to mend his body, Chamberlain wrote responses to those who had sent him letters while he was in the hospital. Fanny particularly enjoyed sharing the letters she had received of condolence at his supposed death. Chamberlain wrote those friends also, thanking them for their sympathy, but assuring them that he was still quite alive.

Though much of his recovery remained painful, Chamberlain eagerly struggled through it. Remarkably, though he had been separated from his brigade for over two months, they were still at Petersburg where he left them. Chamberlain thought it clear, from what he read in the newspapers, that Grant was going to stay in the besieged city, and take the supply junction no matter what his army had to do to get it. That was made obvious to Chamberlain when he read of Grant's attempt to tunnel under the Confederate line, and blow a hole in their defenses with an underground bomb. The unorthodox attempt had failed, but it was a definite sign that Grant would stop at nothing to take Petersburg away from the Confederates.

Chamberlain was inspired by Grant's persistence. He decided he wanted to be a part of the war's finish and he would do whatever it took to get back in a uniform. And if he could manage it, he was going to go back to Petersburg, and finish what he and the rest of the 1st Brigade of the 1st Division of the 5th Corps had started. The only question was; would the Army of the Potomac wait for him?

CHAPTER 9

"SOUL OF THE LION"

C hamberlain was released from the hospital on September 20, though he was still very weak. Fanny took him back to their home in Brunswick where he could continue to heal. Wyllys and Daisy were ecstatic that their father was returning to them. They spent the days before his return eagerly crafting gifts and drawing pictures to celebrate his much anticipated arrival.

The last time their father had been sent home from the Army, he had quarantined himself from his children for most of the duration of his short visit. Though he hadn't been specifically diagnosed with a contagious disease, Chamberlain had been rightfully cautious not to expose his children to the mystery illness that was later discovered to be malaria. This trip home would be different. The only thing the children knew about their father's injury was that he'd been hurt- nothing specific- but he was going to be alright and just needed a little time away from being a soldier until he felt better. When Chamberlain and his wife arrived at the Brunswick train depot, he was greatly amused by his young children's total lack of understanding of the severity of his injury.

"Does it hurt, Daddy?" Chamberlain's daughter asked.

"Just a little," her father answered modestly.

"Good, because we have to play a lot more than we did the last time you came home."

Wyllys was more intuitive. "If it doesn't hurt, why do you walk like a duck?"

Chamberlain smiled at Fanny and winked before responding. "Because, I'm getting old, son, and old men are supposed to walk this way."

Wyllys accepted the answer without a second thought and the subject was never addressed again.

The presence of his two energetic young children, coupled with Chamberlain's new appreciation for life, continued to accelerate his recovery. He was also overjoyed to learn from Fanny that she was pregnant again and they could expect a child sometime in January. She had kept the news from her husband while he was in the hospital, fearing it would distract him from his rehabilitation. Now that Chamberlain was home and getting better, the news of a baby in their future was a blessing, and there would be no more concerns of Fanny having to raise a fatherless child.

Friends and college colleagues frequently stopped by the house to visit. All were surprised at Chamberlain's change in demeanor. He was no longer the reserved little professor they once knew. In just over two years Chamberlain had grown into a confident military leader, and a brigadier general at that!

On November 18th, 1864, after having been pronounced dead by the press the previous June, and having been promoted by U.S. Grant to the rank of brigadier general, even though Grant believed the rank would go no further than his gravestone, Chamberlain returned by carriage for duty at Union Headquarters, Petersburg, Virginia.

He was still unable to climb onto a horse or walk any great distance, but Chamberlain believed he could find some way to contribute to the giant operation that had turned into a bitter siege of the city. Chamberlain discovered that the Union position outside of Petersburg had grown into its own small city. A railroad had been built to supply the Army from the east, and the open ground had been reformed into great earthworks and trenches. There was plenty of food, winter had yet to arrive, and Abraham Lincoln had just been reelected.

Grant's new plan was to bombard Petersburg from a distance and cut all of its supply lines. The average Yankee infantryman had done little more than stand by and watch for months. But while the Federal's rested comfortably, the Confederates and civilians inside the city were starving to death.

On December 7th, the 5th Corps moved out on a mission to destroy railroad lines supplying the Confederates from the south. The Weldon Railroad was still functioning beyond the Union line south of the Nottoway River. The Confederates had been unloading cargo at the Stoney Creek Station and were smuggling it forward by wagon to their men in Petersburg. If the Federals could cut this last supply line before winter set in, it might be the final straw in breaking Lee's defensive hold on the town.

Chamberlain led the 1st Brigade during the six day excursion. He had to be helped into his saddle, and after a few hours of riding, the pain in his lower back and bowels grew intolerable. To prevent collapsing in agony, Chamberlain would stop several times a day and watch the men proceed while he leaned against a tree and caught his breath. He wouldn't give up though, believing his physical limitations needed to be broken, not rested.

Most of the six day mission was spent prying railroad rails from their tracks, heating the steel in huge bonfires, and then bending them in irreparable triangle shapes. At night the men pilfered every house, farm, and country market they could find. Apple and peach brandy barrels were discovered the third day of the operation and became especially popular with the men. That night, cantankerous singing and horseplay became uncontrollable. Even those sent to quiet the unruly drunkards found it difficult to avoid the lure of the sweet tasting Apple Jack. The barrels were eventually destroyed, but not before hundreds of hardtack biscuits had been marinated in the intoxicating elixir.

The corps was moved further south the next day, and many of the men who had over-indulged in the previous night's festivities fell behind. On December 9th, it began to snow and General Warren decided he would march the 5th Corps back to Petersburg the next morning. Their mission completed, the tired soldiers turned around on the 10th and headed back to their winter quarters. Along the way, they discovered the dead bodies of some of their comrades who had straggled behind after the night of drunkenness a few days before. The dead men had their throats cut and their jackets and boots were missing. Word spread through the columns that Rebel sympathizers had murdered the men in cold blood as they slept. Some of the regiment commanders reacted by allowing their angry troops to break from their normal column formation, and fan out from the road as long as they kept pace with the rest of the division. The result was the revengeful torching of nearly every standing structure all the way back to Petersburg.

Chamberlain returned from the agonizing trip exhausted and ill. He could feel a grinding sensation in his pelvic bone, and feared he had dislocated a section that hadn't completely healed. He finally had to accept the fact that he was unfit to continue.

On January 15, 1865, Chamberlain and his aid, Lieutenant Benjamin Walters, left Petersburg for a hospital in Philadelphia. There, his wound was reopened and another surgery was performed. The repairs to his pelvis and urinary tract were successful and Chamberlain returned again to Brunswick to recuperate. When he arrived home for the second time, after having only been gone a few months, he was introduced to his new baby daughter, Gertrude Loraine.

Chamberlain's unexpected return to Brunswick gave everyone the impression his military career was finished. The Bowdoin College president even visited Chamberlain and reminded him that his position was still open. He was also offered a variety of other reputable jobs in the community, including that of Collector of Customs for the District of Bath. None of the offers even raised an eyebrow of interest in Chamberlain. As long as there was a war on, he had to be a part of it.

Chamberlain felt he had recovered enough to return to the field much sooner than anyone had expected. In late February he said goodbye to his family once again and reported back to Petersburg.

Chamberlain returned to the 1st Brigade, which now only consisted of the 185th New York and the 198th Pennsylvania. He quickly settled back into the command by convincing his staff that he was much more battle ready than his last attempt at returning to the field. It was apparent to everyone he was in a healthier state- his walk was now steady and deliberate. Charlemagne had been located in a stable of recovering injured horses and was returned to Chamberlain. From the minute the two were reunited, Chamberlain felt much more comfortable returning to horseback. The warmer March weather was also helping Chamberlain with his health, as the previous cold had often caused his mending bones to ache.

Grant had been waiting for the spring weather, and was now ready to put the final plans together for his advance on the Army of Northern Virginia. Major General William Tecumseh Sherman was poised in North Carolina with another army of Union troops, and if Grant could get Lee to spread out his line, it could finally be crushed.

On March 29, the 5th Corps broke away from the rest of the Army at Petersburg and moved south. With them came the 2nd Corps and General Philip Sheridan's two divisions of cavalry. Their objective was to move around Lee's right flank and force him to draw reinforcements from the stronghold still facing Grant outside of Petersburg.

The 5th Corps crossed the Rowanty Creek, and then changed its direction northbound up several country roads toward another creek called the Gravelly Run. Griffin's 1st Division was in the lead and Chamberlain's brigade was at the front of it. Just before reaching what they expected to be a bridge, several scouts rode back to Griffin and reported that the crossing point had been destroyed. It was also apparent that a small enemy force had entrenched itself on the other side of the creek and they were waiting for them.

Chamberlain and Griffin reviewed a hand drawn map that had been provided to them by General Warren. There was clearly no way to avoid the Rebel defense.

"Let's take them here," Chamberlain suggested.

"I believe we'll have to," Griffin answered. "But how do we do it?" he thought out loud.

"Give me a battalion of the One Ninety-Eighth to put up front in a skirmish line," Chamberlain answered. "We can put the One Eighty-Fifth on the left of the road, and the rest of the One Ninety-Eighth on the right. If we initiate the advance with fire from the right side of the line, I will cross with the left. We'll be on them before they can fire three volleys."

"We certainly must do something quickly," Griffin conceded. "They know we're here and it will be a turkey shoot if they get reinforcements. Proceed General. I'll order the One Eighty-Seventh from the Second Brigade up to your reserve."

Chamberlain called to his side Colonel Gustov Sniper of the 185th, Lt. Colonel Daniel Myers of the 187th, and Brigadier General Horatio Sickel of the 198th, and relayed his plan to the three regiment commanders. A few minutes later, a long battle line of Union infantry marched toward the bank of the Gravelly Run.

As soon as they faced the small Confederate line across the creek, the Pennsylvanians opened with a fusillade of musket fire. When the Rebels answered with their own salvo of minié balls, Chamberlain ordered his regiment of New Yorkers into the waist deep water. Many of the Confederates were still reloading when the first of the 185th climbed out of the creek on the other side.

The Southerners had erred in digging their trench too close to the water's edge and were immediately faced with six Union companies that were firing on them, with another twelve companies still advancing rapidly across the creek. Some of the Confederates tried to hold their position, but the Federal force was too overwhelming. Those that remained were quickly overrun after a short period of hand-to-hand fighting. Most that hesitated before fleeing were cut down with bullets in the back.

Chamberlain reassembled his tiny brigade on the north side of Gravelly Run, and sent a staff member back to tell General Griffin that he was going to pursue the Rebel force. Chamberlain then sent his men dashing into the heavily wooded countryside, allowing them to maneuver forward in loose ranks. The chase ended a mile from the creek in an open field. The Rebels had made it to an abandoned farm, where a long mound of sawdust and woodchips from a sawmill that once operated there stretched across the property. The Confederates formed a new line behind the knoll of sawmill waste, but it offered poor cover and they were pushed back again.

The 1st Brigade scattered across the weed-covered field, and again chased the fleeing Rebels into a thicket of trees on the other side of the abandoned farm. The overzealous Union ranks outran their officers, and Chamberlain and his staff tried frantically to rally their men back into a defensive position. Suddenly, a wall of musket fire thundered out of the woods and the forward ranks of the still advancing Union troops were nearly all cut down. A second line of Confederates had been concealed in the dense forest, and they quickly unleashed a second volley into their stunned enemy.

Chamberlain immediately ordered his buglers to sound the retreat. He had no idea how large the opposing force was and wasn't about to challenge it ill-prepared. His well-trained men turned and ran back across the field to the cover of the trees on the opposite side of the farm. The Confederates followed them as far as the long mound of sawdust and stopped. Griffin rode up to Chamberlain and they assessed the situation together.

"There's another line out there, General," Chamberlain told his superior.

"How many is the question," Griffin answered. He peered through his field glasses, but couldn't find an enemy position in the trees. He could see, however, at least two enemy regiments forming a defensive line behind the breastworks of the long mound of sawdust. "We took a few prisoners and one says we're about to meet a whole Rebel division."

"Whose?" Chamberlain asked.

Griffin lowered his glasses. "Does it matter?"

"No, sir," Chamberlain answered.

"What does matter is that whoever they are, they're not on the field yet and that is our advantage. We must take that position before they are reinforced. I'll have the One-Eighteenth from the Third Brigade advance from the south on your left flank. Artillery from B Battery should be available shortly, but there is no time to wait. I need you to take that position now, Chamberlain, while I get the rest of the division up here."

Chamberlain saluted, and called out, "General Sickel! Colonel Sniper!"

The two officers trotted their horses to his side.

"We are going to advance on the enemy at once. General Sickel, you take the right wing, Colonel Sniper, you take the left. The One-Eighteenth will be advancing from our south in support. I'll keep the men moving from the center. We will make the attack at the double quick, so advise your men no stopping to fire and reload. We must breach their position as quickly as possible. Remind the men that the enemy has taken cover behind loose wood shavings. A ball should pass easily through the top portion. Any questions?"

"No, sir," the two men answered in unison.

"Good. Let's get the men forward and break those damned Rebels."

A flurry of shouted commands and rattling equipment followed as the small Federal force was assembled to move again. There was no time for speeches or last minute prayers. The 1st Brigade was rushed into a battle line and marched out onto the field. When all the men were clear of the trees, Chamberlain ordered them to fix bayonets.

There was psychology in performing this order in front of the enemy and Chamberlain used it wisely. For the men behind him, it meant that their commander was confident his men were going to reach the enemy position. For the Confederates before them, it meant the opposing force was not going to stop until they stared each other in the eye. When the clatter of steel shanks being twisted onto musket barrels silenced, Chamberlain turned his warhorse and faced the enemy. Then with his saber waving overhead, Chamberlain ordered the attack.

The men let out a chilling roar and began their sprint across the open field toward the Rebel breastwork. The Confederates answered with an almost immediate barrage of fire. Their impatience to wait until the Federals were within range resulted in an almost completely wasted volley.

Chamberlain made sure the last of the brigade had joined the mad dash toward the enemy position, and then dug his spurs into Charlemagne's sides to join them. In only a few moments, Chamberlain's horse galloped wildly ahead of the rest of the men as if he too was eager to return to battle. But his overzealousness quickly put his rider at the foot of the enemy defenses alone. Chamberlain yanked at Charlemagne's reins to regain control of him, and the horse reared his head up to slow down. In that instant, a Rebel minié ball sliced through Charlemagne's neck, traveled up Chamberlain's left arm, and then smashed into the brass-mounted hand mirror Chamberlain kept in a breast pocket over his heart. The bullet then deflected around his side exiting his jacket, finally striking the holstered sidearm of a lieutenant who was riding next to him.

Chamberlain fell forward onto his horse's neck, momentarily knocked unconscious from the nonlethal blow to his chest. The blood from Charlemagne's wound oozed onto Chamberlain's coat and smeared the side of his face. His cap had fallen to the ground, and his stringy blond hair absorbed the crimson goo like a sponge. With the added blood from the superficial cuts from the bullet's trail up Chamberlain's arm, he appeared to be, once again, mortally wounded.

Griffin was monitoring the attack with the 187th Pennsylvania that was being held in reserve, and saw Chamberlain's horse trotting back toward the Union line. Chamberlain was slumped over and teetering in the saddle, his saber dangled from the lanyard wrapped around his wrist. Griffin galloped out to his fallen comrade to offer him aide. When he lifted Chamberlain up from Charlemagne's neck, he could see it was too late.

"My dear, General," Griffin said quietly. "You are gone."

Chamberlain heard the words and shot up in his saddle. He looked around the field and saw that his right wing was faltering under a Rebel counterattack and Union soldiers were starting to flee.

"Yes, General, I am!" he answered. The bloodied brigadier general then dug his heels once again into the ribs of his faithful Charlemagne and galloped away.

Chamberlain sped into the retreating Pennsylvanians and caught sight of General Sickel and one of his majors, Charles Maceuen. The two officers were desperately trying to turn their men around. Before Chamberlain could reach them, a shell exploded at the hooves of the two officer's mounts, causing them both to be blown from their saddles. Sickel grabbed his shattered right arm and began struggling with the reigns of his frightened horse. Maceuen was not so lucky. His chest had been ripped open by the blast and he had perished instantly.

Chamberlain assumed command and dashed into the confused mob, pushing the men together like a rancher herding cattle. When their loose lines were reestablished, Chamberlain then ordered them forward with their own counterattack.

With the strength of his right side restored, Chamberlain rode back to the center of his line waving his sword in the air and yelling commands of encouragement. The glorious scene of their blood-soaked general, desperately leading them on in his last living moments, inspired the men to continue pounding their way into the enemy position. But Charlemagne was finished. He stopped and lowered his head long enough for Chamberlain to dismount. When he saw that his general was safely on the ground, the beautiful brown Morgan lowered himself to the grass and rolled over onto his side. Chamberlain was accustomed to having horses shot out from under him, and paid little attention to the severity of Charlemagne's wound. Instead, he fearlessly tramped up to the front of the enemy barricade and began waving men forward to join him.

The Rebels had spilled over the hill of sawdust during a counter-attack, and had successfully taken the fight to the open field before it. Chamberlain had no idea he'd actually walked through the Rebel front and was now standing behind their offensive line.

"Drop your sword and surrender!" a voice demanded of him.

Chamberlain turned around slowly. Three tattered Rebel soldiers had their musket barrels lowered on his chest. Chamberlain looked down at his filthy uniform and realized how dusty and bloody he had become.

"Surrender?!" he shot back. What's the matter with you? What do you take me for? Don't you see these Yanks right onto us? Come along with me boys and let's break'em!"

Chamberlain then darted back into the middle of the chaotic field. The three Confederates were right behind him. Chamberlain led them into the heart of the 185th New York, and then, when they were obviously surrounded by blue uniformed soldiers, he turned and suggested they all surrender. The confused Rebels dropped their weapons, expecting their officer to do the same. Instead, Chamberlain put his hand on the senior man's shoulder and assured them that they would be treated fairly. Before the reality of what had just happened could sink into the Confederates, the imposter general was handed a fresh horse and headed back to the front.

Chamberlain could see that his left wing was now under a concentrated attack and needed to be reinforced. He shouted for an aide who could carry a message for him. Before he could complete the orders, General Griffin appeared through the smoke.

"I need some support here for Colonel Sniper!" Chamberlain yelled over the noise of the battlefield.

"I can have a battery up in ten minutes!" Griffin answered. "Can you get them to hold!"

"Yes, sir!"

Chamberlain yanked his horse toward his weakening left flank and galloped out to find the leader of the 185th. It wasn't difficult to find the regiment's commander. Sniper was standing in the middle of his men with the colors in his hand, directing his soldiers to keep up a steady fire. The brave commander was glad to see Chamberlain riding toward him, even in his ghoulish state.

"I can't hold this position much longer!" Sniper yelled up to his brigade commander.

"General Griffin is bringing up the artillery, Colonel!" Chamberlain answered.

"Can we get some infantry support, General?!"

"I am here, Colonel Sniper!" Chamberlain answered. Then, raising his voice to all the men around him, Chamberlain shouted, "Give it to them, boys! Try the steel! Hell for ten more minutes and then we are out of it!"

The New Yorkers answered by lunging forward with renewed vigor, repelling the Rebels back into the woods. Chamberlain and Sniper then formed a new line at the edge of the trees so the arriving battery could use it as a mark. The Confederates quickly regrouped and countered, but after a few minutes of vicious hand-to-hand fighting, they were pushed back again.

Chamberlain looked over his shoulder and could see the artillery wagons of Battery B of the 4th U.S. Artillery were assembling a few hundred yards behind him. He ordered Sniper to keep his men in place and expect an artillery barrage at any moment. Chamberlain then sped back to the line of Napoleon cannons to direct their fire.

The battery's commander, Lieutenant John Mitchell, was shocked and a little frightened of the blood-caked general when he rode up to him. He didn't recognize Chamberlain, though he knew him well.

"Mitchell," Chamberlain started gruffly. "Do you think you can put solid shot or percussion into those woods close over the Rebel's heads without hurting my men?"

The lieutenant recognized the voice. "Yes, sir, if they'll keep where they are."

"Well then, give it to them." Chamberlain ordered. "But stop quick at my signal, and fire clear of my men when they charge."

Mitchell spun around and ordered his men to set fuses for overhead detonation and to sight in the enemy position in the trees. Within minutes the cannons exploded with deadly flames and smoke. Chamberlain rode back out to Sniper's position and realigned his regiment to defend a Confederate attack on the battery. Just as the men were placed behind the left flank of the battery, a crowd of enemy infantrymen stormed out of the woods.

Mitchell was waiting and swung his guns around to face the suicide attack. Case shot and canister swept the Rebel advance in a murderous swath, but not before Mitchell was shot in his right arm. It would not be enough to stop him from commanding his battery throughout the rest of the fight.

With his weakened left wing secured, Chamberlain now rode out to the center of his line to check their condition. He quickly discovered his Pennsylvania regiment was falling back, surrendering valuable ground to the enemy. He sent a request to the 2nd Brigade for an extra regiment to come to his aide. Soon afterward, Lieutenant Colonel Isaac Doolittle and his 188th New York Infantry appeared on the field in support. Behind them was a regiment from Pennsylvania dressed in French blue pantaloons and colorful red sashes- the 155th Zouaves.

Chamberlain ordered the New Yorkers to attack from the left, and the Pennsylvanians to advance from the center where the weakened defenses of the sawdust pile stood. Without hesitation or question, the two regiments formed in battle lines and moved onto the field. Chamberlain stood in the foreground and watched the Zouave colonel, Alfred L. Pearson, take his regimental colors in hand and lead his men victoriously over the enemy's breastwork. At the sight of the two fresh Union regiments, the weary Confederates gave little fight and retreated even further into the woods.

The defeat of the Rebels had been a sound one. Chamberlain's persistence to lead from the front provided him the ability to compensate for his brigade's weaknesses, and overcome their enemy's repeated attempts at retaking the field. As the smoke cleared and the men reassembled, 5th Corps Commander General Warren rode out to Chamberlain's side.

"My God, man! Are you shot again?!" Warren exclaimed.

"I've just a scratch, sir," Chamberlain answered, having yet to examine the cause of the sharp pain in his arm and chest. "I believe I've been mostly bled upon by my Charlemagne."

Warren was greatly relieved to hear it.

"General, you have done splendid work," Warren told him. "Absolutely splendid."

The senior officer handed Chamberlain a fresh canteen.

"Thank you, sir," Chamberlain answered. He poured the cold water onto his hands and used it to rinse his face.

"I am telegraphing the President directly," Warren added. "You will hear from it."

"That is not necessary, sir," Chamberlain answered. "Our success here is reward enough. The thought is well appreciated though, sir."

"It is as well already done, General. Your humble manner will not dissuade me."

The two men parted and began directing the men into defensive positions. Chamberlain then rode to a hospital wagon to treat his wounds. Much to his own relief, the sharp pain in his chest and ribs would only mean bruising, and the bullet's trail up his arm only required a heavy bandage.

After having the gash on his arm wrapped, Chamberlain rode back out to the line and ordered his brigade to an advanced position at the junction of the Quaker and Boydton Plank Roads. There, they began the daunting task of digging defensive trenches. Once the men were sufficiently started, Chamberlain rode off to the secured farm buildings where the injured were being cared for. The cloudy afternoon turned to night and a frigid rain began to fall.

Chamberlain discovered Charlemagne lying in a barn with other wounded horses. Someone had led him from the field and had bandaged his neck wound. Chamberlain was beginning to feel the pain of his bruised ribs, and decided to sit for a while in the calm stable with his horse. The tired warrior eased his sore body down to the straw bed like a brittle old man, and gently stroked the forehead of his fearless partner.

Chamberlain remained with his horse for a half hour while he procrastinated over whether he should wait out the storm in the dry barn, or if he should go back out and make himself somehow useful.

He decided he could at least help with the care of his injured men, so he left Charlemagne's side and walked back out into the night. During his rounds, he discovered General Sickel lying in the rain outside of a farmhouse.

"Dear Lord," Chamberlain declared in amazement when he recognized the general. "Let me get you in some shelter."

"No no, General," Sickel answered. My arm is only wounded and I will live. Better to get these other men inside for treatment first."

"Poppy cock!" Chamberlain said and scooped up his sopping wet 198th Pennsylvania Regiment Commander, even though his own right arm was in a sling.

Chamberlain staggered through the crowd inside the makeshift hospital, ordering those loitering about to get out of his way. He found a long wooden table that was littered with household wares the men had piled there to make more space for the wounded. Chamberlain pushed the clutter off of the table and laid Sickel on the hardwood surface.

"Shall I summon the surgeon?" Chamberlain asked.

"I will wait my turn," Sickel answered. "I am in no hurry to have my limb separated from me."

Chamberlain looked sympathetically down at his once superior officer who was now his subordinate. Amputation was the most likely resolve to any serious arm wound and both men knew it.

Sickel could see the compassion in Chamberlain's eyes. "General," he said. "You have the soul of the lion, and the heart of a woman."

"You are too gracious, sir," Chamberlain answered.

Sickel thanked Chamberlain for bringing him out of the rain but told him that he should go.

Chamberlain squeezed Sickel's hand and walked out of the room, having first alerted one of the doctors inside the house that a general officer was there with a serious wound.

Chamberlain made his way to the kitchen where he sat down and wrote a letter to Major Maceuen's father, advising him of his son's heroism while facing death. When he finished the letter, he folded it neatly and placed it in his breast pocket.

The 5th Corps spent the rest of the night constructing breastworks and fortifications in the rain. The Confederate line was less than a mile away and the day's battle would certainly bring Rebel reinforcements to their front. The corps objective had been met, and it was assumed that when Grant initiated the more massive attack on Petersburg from the northeast, the enemy would have to thin its line to support the defenses there. The rain continued through the next day as both armies made final preparations for the ominous battle that lay ahead.

Shortly before noon, Confederate Major General George E. Pickett was spotted marching a division of infantry down the White Oaks Road toward an intersection appropriately named Five Forks. Warren sent a wire to Grant's headquarters, advising of a plan to intercept Pickett's advance with the assistance of the 2nd Corps. Meade and Grant agreed with the idea and Warren moved his 5th Corps forward to prepare for an attack. The continuous rain turned the roads to mush and the trampled open fields to swamps, making the massive troop realignment sluggish at best.

Just before the planned assault on Picket's division on March 31st, Grant and Meade canceled Warren's plan of attack, fearing poor road conditions were bogging down troop movement. Pickett, on the other hand, took advantage of his adversary's delay and attacked Philip

Sheridan's cavalry that was now alone with no infantry support. The overwhelmed Union force was pushed back across the Boydton Plank Road into Dinwiddie Court House to the south.

Several miles to the northeast, Grant had ordered Warren to proceed with his attack after the rain slackened shortly before noon. Warren and 2nd Corps Commander Brigadier General Romeyn B. Ayres marched their men into an open field having no idea what was in front of them. Suddenly, three regiments of Confederate Major General Bushrod Johnson's infantry screamed out of the woods and fired into the surprised Union ranks. The Yankees scattered before their officers could even form them into battle lines.

Chamberlain and most of the 1st Division were being held in reserve next to an artillery battery across the Gravelly Run Creek when the fighting began. The men had been positioned in a staggered line, and were drying their cloths and heating coffee when the Rebel yell and musket fire broke out in the distance in front of them. Chamberlain called his brigade into formation and moved them out to the edge of the wide swollen creek side, then waited for the order to advance. The spectacle unfolding before him was unimaginable. Both the 2nd and 5th Corps were running for their lives while being pursued by a force only one-quarter their strength. Warren and Griffin were desperately trying to turn their men, but it was useless.

As retreating men splashed back through the muddy water of the creek, Chamberlain ordered the battery next to him to fire into the approaching Confederate infantry. The Rebel attack stalled, yet retreating terrified Union soldiers continued to pour past the steady 1st Brigade. Warren and Griffin galloped back to their stalwart General Chamberlain.

"General, the Fifth Corps is eternally damned!" Griffin raged with humiliation.

"Not until you are in heaven," Chamberlain responded like a good subordinate.

"I told General Warren you will wipe out this disgrace and that's what we're here for."

"Sir, I am honored, but my brigade is too small," Chamberlain countered. "Why not the 3rd Brigade? They are rested and have six more regiments than I do."

"We have come to you, sir," Warren said. "You know what that means."

It was not a question.

"I'll try it," Chamberlain responded cautiously. "Only don't let anyone stop me except the enemy."

"I will get a bridge constructed in the hour," Warren assured him. "You can't get men through this swamp in any kind of order."

"We cannot wait, sir," Chamberlain said. "The enemy will be entrenched before I can get my men across. Your bridge may do to come back on, General, but it will not do to stop and wait for its construction now. My men will go straight through."

Chamberlain immediately ordered half of his brigade into the chest-deep water, holding their muskets and cartridge boxes above their heads while the remaining regiment provided cover fire. When the first group formed their battle line on the other side, the second regiment crossed. Soaking wet, with only dry heads, rifles and cartridge boxes, Chamberlain advanced his force toward the Rebel attackers.

General Ayres' 2nd Corps had reassembled and they followed Chamberlain's brigade from the left rear, while Brigadier General

Edgar M. Gregory's 2nd Brigade from the 5th Corps followed from the right.

Chamberlain wisely ordered the advance to be carried out in loose ranks to avoid excessive casualties. The plan worked and he forced the Confederates all the way back to their original breastworks in the woods beyond the open field. Chamberlain then slowed his advance until Gregory's brigade came up on his right wing. With the two brigades now forming a single line, Chamberlain ordered a joint attack on the enemy defenses.

Bugles echoed and a stifling synchronized curtain of lead smashed into the outnumbered Rebels. Gregory's brigade then rushed the breastworks and swarmed over the Virginian's desperately trying to defend their position. The counterattack was a complete success and Chamberlain continued to drive the Confederates back across the White Oak Road.

While Chamberlain was securing his new line, Sheridan's cavalry continued to move backward in the face of Pickett's advance far to the south. Sheridan's request for support from the 6th Corps was denied by Grant, who offered him the 5th Corps, which was much closer. Sheridan had worked successfully with the 6th before and asked for them again, stating his preference was for a more familiar corps. Grant repeated his offering of the 5th Corps, and sent a message for Warren to move south in Sheridan's support.

Before the orders arrived, Warren sat with his commanders listening to the distant booms of artillery and crackles of musket fire near Dinwiddie Court House. Warren decided to send General Bartlett's 3rd Brigade to Sheridan's aide, even though he had not yet received orders to do so.

In the late afternoon and early evening, a series of contradictory orders arrived by messenger and wire. Grant initially wanted the entire 5th Corps to move south, but then later altered his request to only a single brigade move to Sheridan's support. Warren had already sent Bartlett's 3rd Brigade, but Grant's new order was to have them approach from the Boydton Plank Road, a different route than the one Bartlett was using. Just to cover himself, Warren sent three regiments on the path indicated in the orders, and sent a message to Bartlett to return to the 5th Corps. No sooner than those directions were put into effect another dispatch came, this one summoning an entire division to respond to Sheridan on the road Bartlett was returning on. Warren decided to send his 1st Division, in hopes the experienced officers of the unit could determine the reason for such confusion.

In the early evening General Meade began sending dispatches that even further aggravated the situation. Grant was specific in his last order to have the remaining two divisions of the 5th Corps prepare for an offensive the next morning. Now Meade was ordering Warren to abandon the field and split his 2nd and 3rd Divisions on separate roads toward Dinwiddie Court House. Warren, now exasperated, confirmed the last order and moved his entire 5th Corps south to the aide of Sheridan.

CHAPTER 10

FIVE FORKS

The night march to Dinwiddie Court House was miserable and slow. The Boydton Plank Road was still muddy, and had deep ruts and holes cut into it from the wear of being trampled through the days before. Wagon and artillery wheels repeatedly sank into the sludge and had to be pulled out by teams of already exhausted men. When the 5th Corps reached the Gravelly Run Bridge they found it had been destroyed, which causes an even further delay in their rendezvous with Sheridan's cavalry. The engineers dismantled a nearby house and quickly constructed their own bridge with the framework and planks that made up the home's wood siding. But the obstacle had been unexpected and its address time consuming.

Grant's last message to Sheridan was that he could expect Warren's corps by midnight, but it was already 2 a.m. when the first of the long columns began crossing the rain swollen creek. The 1st Division finally reached Sheridan's headquarters at dawn, and Chamberlain's brigade was the first to enter the camp. Sheridan was standing outside his tent with a scowl on his face when they arrived.

Chamberlain rode up to the angry general and saluted. " Brigadier General Chamberlain, sir. I report to you, General, with the head of Griffin's Division."

"Why did you not come before?" Sheridan asked angrily.

"The road was in terrible condition, sir, and the bridge over that flooded creek was nothing but rubble. Our boys had to make a new one out of the side boards of an old house. With all due respect, General, I'm amazed we got here at the speed we did."

"Then you are easily amazed, General," Sheridan responded unsympathetically. "Where is Warren?"

"He's at the rear of the column, sir."

"I should have expected that. What is he doing there?"

Chamberlain was loyal to his corps commander and wanted Sheridan to know Warren was leading from the end of his line for a reason. "General, we are withdrawing from the White Oaks Road where we fought all day. General Warren is riding with his last division, expecting an attack from the rear."

Sheridan's attention was distracted by another officer trotting up to him. It was Griffin. He saluted Sheridan and climbed off of his horse.

"Major General Charles Griffin, sir. My deepest apologies for our delay."

Sheridan snidely looked back to Chamberlain. "That's how it's done, Mr. Chamberlain." He looked back at Griffin. "You should share with your brigade commander the finer points of how to address a superior officer after a poor performance."

"Yes, sir," Griffin answered. "Do you have orders for my division, General?"

"Get them off their feet and fed. We will have a great battle today and General Grant expects a decisive victory. The success of the invasion of Petersburg is dependent on us."

"Understood, sir."

The three generals exchanged salutes as the 12,000 strong 5th Corps continued to march into camp.

Griffin climbed back onto his horse and ordered Chamberlain to follow him. When they were a safe distance away from Sheridan's tent, Griffin broke into a smile. "So, what was that all about?"

"The general asked my why we were late," Chamberlain answered. "I explained the poor road conditions and the bridge. He didn't seem to care."

"Ah ha," Griffin answered. "What General Sheridan meant to ask was, 'what is your excuse?' The correct answer being, 'there is no excuse, sir.'"

"My apologies, General," Chamberlain replied.

"We will make a military man out of you yet, Professor."

"I believe this dilly dallying with nonsensical protocol will never come to me, sir."

"Rest easy, my student. It is only the standard of a few who are best described as the hind-quarters of the beasts we now ride upon."

Chamberlain grinned. "My only response is that I must agree with my division commander."

"We will leave it at that then," Griffin said. "Class dismissed."

"Would you like me to send a man back to get General Warren," Chamberlain asked.

"No, I'll do it. In case you haven't heard, Grant gave Sheridan the power to relieve General Warren if he doesn't perform to his satisfaction. I need to prepare our general for his first meeting with our new commander."

"Yes, sir," Chamberlain answered. Then I'll get the men down and fed."

"Good."

The two men saluted each other and parted.

Chamberlain ordered his brigade to a wooded area where the trees would offer them shade from the new morning's sunlight. The tired men then slept until noon, just as the last of the 5th Corps finally arrived.

Sheridan refused to postpone his advance another day, and called Warren and his division and brigade commanders to his headquarters to go over his battle plan. Sheridan introduced his young protégé, Brigadier General George Armstrong Custer, to the 5th Corps men and informed them that Custer would lead his cavalry into a diversionary assault on the Confederate's right. His other brigadier general, Thomas C. Devins, would advance on the center of the enemy line. When the two armies engaged, Warren's infantry was to attack on the Confederate's left and swing around his flank to continue the assault from the rear. Ayres' 2nd Division would begin the infantry attack by hitting the Rebels on their far left. Then, Griffin's 1st Division and Crawford's 3rd Division would complete the sweep around the back of the enemy line. The plan was clear and appeared to be well-thought-out. Sheridan ordered the advance to begin at 4 p.m. The generals then returned to their commands, confident they would carry the day.

Griffin decided to give Chamberlain the three regiments of his 2nd Brigade in order to strengthen the 1st Brigade's weakened ranks. Just as Chamberlain began to move his men forward, he received a diagram of the battle plan and a written copy of the orders. Both had come from General Warren's command post. Chamberlain stopped his horse and studied the map with confusion.

According to Warren's sketch, Ayres' division was now attacking the center of the Confederate line and Crawford was attacking the left. But when Chamberlain read over the written orders that accompanied the drawing, they corresponded with Sheridan's original plan, not the movement indicated on the drawing.

Chamberlain galloped off to find Griffin to clarify the discrepancy. When Chamberlain caught up to his division commander, he could tell by the look on his face that something was concerning him.

"Sir," Chamberlain began with a salute. "I have received a diagram of our attack that does not coincide with my orders."

"We will not worry ourselves about diagrams," Griffin replied. "We are to follow General Crawford. Circumstances will soon determine our duty."

Chamberlain was smart enough to read between the lines. Griffin was also aware of their corps commander's mistake and was noticeably concerned about it. Chamberlain decided not to question his direct superior and returned to his brigade.

A few hours later the 5th Corps reached the White Oak Road and the Confederate trenches adjacent to it. They had mistakenly marched an extra half mile east of their target, and were still oblivious to the error. Ayres' division formed battle lines and took the enemy position with little resistance, believing they were attacking their designated position of the greater Rebel line. In fact, they were only fighting a small band of skirmishers.

At the same time, Crawford had stumbled onto a small force of dismounted Confederate cavalry and the two were locked in a heated exchange. The fight in the Rebels convinced Crawford that he had actually struck the objective of his orders, and he sent his entire division forward. The Confederates broke and fled north with Crawford's 3rd Division giving chase. Griffin's orders had been to follow Crawford, so the 1st Division blindly trailed from the rear. By the time Crawford slowed his advance to forge through some woods, he and the 3rd Brigade were well north of where they were supposed to be and were chasing ghosts. Warren was advised of the deviation from the formal battle plan and personally rode out to bring his two divisions back to their originally ordered positions.

Meanwhile, Ayres soon realized that he was too far east of the Rebels left flank and he could hear the Union cavalry now engaged to the west. He decided to swing his battle line around at a ninety-degree angle and attack the Rebels from the flank of their entrenchments. When he sent his 2nd Division forward, they soon came under fire from a now reinforced Confederate line.

Chamberlain heard the sudden eruption of battle from Ayres' advance, and also recognized his division had been led away from the fight. He told 3rd Brigade Commander Joseph Bartlett that he was breaking off from the rest of the division and taking the 1st and 2nd Brigades to support Ayres' division. Griffin was nearby and Chamberlain signaled that he wanted to take his two brigades west. Griffin nodded and waved his approval. Chamberlain then reformed his men and marched them toward the sound of the guns.

The woods were dense, but the underbrush had not yet thickened with the warming season. Chamberlain and his staff rushed the men forward in a scattered mass formation. As the front of the Federal line came upon a steep gully, they spotted the Confederate position.

Chamberlain reformed the men into several columns of loose battle lines and had the first line fire a volley into the Rebel fortification. He then moved the second line forward and ordered them to fire a second volley into the enemy earthworks. As the Confederates scrambled to reposition themselves, Chamberlain ordered a resounding, "Advance!"

Chamberlain followed his order by leading the swarm of blue-clad Yankees into the attack. When he was confident his officers were keeping the line moving, Chamberlain broke away to find General Ayres. As he crossed through the middle of his men, he spotted a group of staff officers formed behind his line. Believing it was possibly Ayres, or a cavalry unit's command staff, Chamberlain directed his horse toward them. As he grew nearer to the group, much to his surprise, he discovered it was Sheridan and several of his officers.

"By God that's what I want to see!" Sheridan yelled to the approaching Chamberlain. "General officers at the front. Good job Chamberlain. Now where are *your* generals?"

"The First and Third Divisions are north of here, sir," Chamberlain replied. "General Warren is leading them back. It appears they temporarily lost their bearing and are out of position. General Griffin ordered me to bring two of his brigades back to support General Ayres."

"Then you take command of all the infantry around here and break this damn line!"

"Yes, sir!" Chamberlain answered, and galloped off to continue his search for Ayres.

Chamberlain soon came upon a forest that was filled with disoriented Union soldiers who had become separated from their regiments. He found one man in particular who was cowering alone behind a shattered tree stump.

"What are you doing?" Chamberlain asked the soldier.

"I'm lost," he timidly replied.

"Look here, my good fellow. Don't you know you'll be killed here in less than two minutes? This is no place for you. Go forward."

"But what can I do, General? I can't stand up against all this alone."

"I'm forming a new line here," Chamberlain improvised. "I want you for guide center. Up and forward."

The private sprang to his feet.

"Wait here. I'm sending men your way," Chamberlain advised him.

"Yes, sir."

Chamberlain galloped through the woods gathering stragglers and sending them to the private, who quickly formed them into a line. Chamberlain then ordered one of his staff officers to lead the new company of over 200 men back into the Confederate position.

Another large Union column appeared in the woods and Chamberlain rode out to see who they were. It was the 3rd Brigade of Ayres' Division under Brevet Brigadier General James Gwyn. Chamberlain asked Gwyn what his orders were.

"That is my problem, General," Gwyn answered, visibly frustrated. "I have no orders. I'm trying to get back to my division and I assumed you were part of it. I don't know what to do."

"Then come with me," Chamberlain told him. "I will take the responsibility. You shall have all credit. Let me take your brigade for a moment."

"What are your plans, General?" Gwyn asked.

"I have two brigades in the fight now. With your regiments, we can renew the advance and take the enemy's left flank."

"We are at your service then, sir," Gwyn answered. He turned to his staff officers who were close behind him. "We're going in with General Chamberlain!"

Gwyn's men cheered, rejoicing that they were finally going to get their chance to fight.

Chamberlain directed them to the edge of a clearing and began pulling his still engaged regiments over to form a single solid Union line.

Suddenly, Sheridan appeared behind him in a fit of infuriation. "You are firing into my cavalry!"

"Then the cavalry have got into the Rebel's place!" Chamberlain answered sarcastically. He would play the games of rank when he had to, but there was no time for humbling oneself to the general's bad attitude in the course of battle. "One of us will have to get out of the way," Chamberlain continued. "What will you have us do, General?"

"Don't you fire into my cavalry, I tell you!" Sheridan insisted.

Chamberlain momentarily dismissed the arrogant little commander, and wondered how it was that his infantry had come so close to the Union cavalry position in the first place. Ayres then rode up and was greeted with the same accusation from Sheridan.

"Why are you firing into my cavalry?!"

Ayres wasn't going to put up with the attitude either. He replied, "We are firing at the people who are firing at us, General. Those are not carbine shot. They are minié balls. I ought to know, sir."

"You will redirect your fire at once!" Sheridan ordered, and trotted away a few yards to examine the field.

Griffin soon appeared and reported to Sheridan's side.

"We flanked them gloriously!" Sheridan said as he scanned the line through field glasses.

Chamberlain was amazed at how quickly his demeanor had changed. One second a raving dictator, the next a spirited leader. Sheridan wheeled his horse around and sprinted through the men. "Smash'em boys!" He yelled. "Smash'em!"

Chamberlain rode back into the fighting and saw that his old 20th Maine regiment and the rest of the 3rd Brigade were caught in a fierce battle at the foot of a Rebel salient. Chamberlain called for his 2nd Brigade to move forward and the two Union forces joined together. With the added support, the 1st Brigade stormed the enemy fortification and took the position after a brief period of hand-to-hand fighting.

Chamberlain then moved back across his left wing. Though the Confederate defenses at Five Folks were clearly beginning to disintegrate, he found his own 198th Pennsylvania pinned down in a desperate fight over a Rebel breastwork. He rode up to the 198th regiment's commander, Major Edwin A. Glenn, and asked him their status.

"Well, sir," Glenn replied, "I've got plenty of men, but I'm having trouble getting them out from behind these trees."

"Do you have enough to take that fortress?" Chamberlain asked.

"I believe I do, yes, sir."

Then do it, Major," Chamberlain ordered. I will make a wager with you, sir. If you take that position, I'll have you a colonelcy. Agreed?"

Glenn smiled. He put his pistol in his left hand and shook the General's hand with his right. The gentleman's agreement was sealed.

Chamberlain stepped back and watched the brave major call out to his men to prepare for an advance. The promise of promotion breathed new confidence in the young officer. He formed a new battle line, paying little attention to the bullets whizzing about him. Chamberlain saw himself in the performance and was proud the major belonged to one of his regiments.

Once Glenn's men were in place, he pulled his cap off and placed it on the tip of his sword, then shouted for his Pennsylvanian's to follow him. The men answered with a glorious yell of certain victory and ran toward the Rebel breastworks in a death-defying frenzy. Their commander reached the dirt mound first and turned to wave his men onward. It was a gallant display of leadership, and Chamberlain thought to himself that he would make a note of it in his subordinate's promotion request to General Grant.

When the Pennsylvanians began to breach the fortification, Glenn turned back to the front and climbed up to the crest of the salient himself. As he stood waving his sword and encouraging his men onward, his body suddenly convulsed.

Chamberlain watched in horror as Glenn staggered to gain his balance and then tumbled back to the bottom of the hill. Chamberlain bolted from his comfortable position behind the line and ran to the major's aide. When he knelt beside the fallen officer, he could see that a musket ball had cut through the center of his chest. The young officer's lifeless eyes stared back at his commander. Chamberlain's body began to tremble and his heart wrenched as if it were being squeezed in a blacksmith's vice. It had been his promise of promotion that delivered young Edwin Glenn to his doom.

Chamberlain yanked his head up and glared into the sky- tears streaming down his face. He wanted to damn his God for allowing such senseless slaughter, but all that escaped from his lungs was a violent crying out. His spirit had finally been broken.

Even as the furry of battle continued around him, Chamberlain cradled and rocked the young man whose death he had sealed with a handshake only a few moments before.

When the enemy position was taken and the Pennsylvanians regrouped, they found Chamberlain still holding their dead regiment commander. Captain John Stanton stepped forward and leaned into Chamberlain's ear.

"It's done, sir," he whispered. We've taken the trenches."

Chamberlain looked up at him, his eyes those of a helplessly lost child.

Stanton took him by the arm and slowly lifted the general to his feet. Chamberlain wiped his face and gazed stoically at the brave men of the 198th Pennsylvania. Each man brought himself to attention without the command, and saluted him.

"You go on now, General," Stanton told him. "I'll take over here."

Chamberlain cleared his head and wandered back to his horse alone. While riding back to find new orders, one of Griffin's staff officers rode up to Chamberlain and informed him that Sheridan had relieved Warren of his command of the 5th Corps. Sheridan had become upset that Warren couldn't be found during the battle, even though it was explained to him that Warren was with his displaced 1st and 3rd Divisions. Griffin was now the 5th Corps commander.

Chamberlain found his way back to Sheridan's command post and met with Griffin, who was redirecting troop movements. Sheridan was also there barking orders in his desperate attempt to finish off the Confederates before nightfall. Griffin ordered Chamberlain to take the 1st Division command and attack the last remaining stronghold of Confederates assembling on the right of their line.

Chamberlain, both physically and emotionally drained, obeyed the command without even thinking about it. He called the division into battle formation, and to his surprise, General Warren appeared at the front with the 5th Corps flag in his hand. Chamberlain marched the brave legion forward into an open wheat field so the Confederates could get a good look at the huge mass that was about to destroy them.

Chamberlain then stopped his lines and gave the Rebels plenty of time to absorb the display in front of their trenches. As he stood atop his horse glaring at the enemy, Chamberlain boiled with a festering hatred for the men of the Confederacy who were responsible for the war. Before, he had been able to distance himself from those feelings with his pledge to remember the enemy fighters were still fellow countrymen. Yet, in what would be Chamberlain's final significant battle during the Great Rebellion, he was suddenly unable to quell the anger simmering inside his heart. He had seen too much senseless killing. He had too many friends that were now dead. Now the responsibility of gallant young Major Glenn's death was more burden than his soul could carry. It was time for the Rebels to pay. It was time for a final reckoning.

Chamberlain ordered, "Bayonets!" with a violent roar, letting it be clear- any Rebel that stayed to fight would be his army's prey.

When the bugles and drums sounded, disgraced Major General Warren led the final attack from the center. Union artillery opened fire over their own infantrymen, blowing huge holes in the enemy breastworks. By the time the division reached the Rebel's point of final stand, most of the waiting Confederates knew any attempt to defend their position would be futile. They were starving, tired, and nearly out of ammunition. Some of the Rebels put up a brief token fight, but most chose to surrender before their numbers could be decimated.

Chamberlain returned to Sheridan less than an hour later with 5000 Confederate prisoners. When the general from Maine rode among the surrendered Confederates, his hate and anger toward them subsided. Many were weeping, and their poor physical condition changed his emotions to those of sympathy. These weren't the same stalwart men he'd once faced at the foot of Marye's Heights, or in the woods on Little Round Top hill. These men looked more like poor neglected derelicts.

As darkness fell on the battlefield, Chamberlain sat among the other officers of the 5th Corps discussing the mistreatment of General Warren. They had learned that Warren approached Sheridan after the battle and asked that he reconsider his decision to replace him. Sheridan had disrespectfully refused and had already put the demotion in writing. What should have been a night of celebration was instead shrouded by anger and discontent.

Chamberlain was alone with his thoughts when one of the men called them to attention. He slowly rose to his feet and saw that Sheridan had come to join them with a riding crop in his hand.

"At ease," Sheridan told them and motioned that they could remain seated. He stepped in front of the group and cleared his throat. "Gentlemen, I have come over to speak with you. I may have spoken harshly to some of you today, but I would not have done it to hurt you. You know how it is," he continued, taking a few steps to the side. "We had to carry this place, and I fretted all day until it was done. You must forgive me. I know it is hard for the men, too, but we must push. There is more for us to do together. I appreciate and thank you all. It was a fine victory."

Sheridan didn't wait for a response or questions. He casually saluted the men with the small leather horse whip in his hand and walked away.

Chamberlain's mind was numb and he wasn't sure how to interpret the speech. It sounded sincere, but having personally watched Sheridan's vindictive behavior on the field, it was easy to believe he might have an ulterior motive for his humble presentation. Still, Chamberlain couldn't help but empathize with him. The responsibility placed on Sheridan had been enormous and his battle plan had not been followed as he ordered. Maybe his behavior had been reasonable under the circumstances. His persistence had kept the men moving forward. That was certainly not an attribute of the earlier commanders in the war. Chamberlain decided he would wait to pass judgment on the matter another day. For now, his body ached too much from his old wounds and his recently bruised ribs to worry about a rude commander.

He wrote a letter to Major Glenn's parents, praising the young officer's heroic last efforts. Chamberlain shared with them that he felt responsible, but didn't say why. He also included in the letter that their son would be posthumously promoted to Lieutenant Colonel, and his bravery during the battle at Five Forks would be documented and sent to Congress for citation consideration. After he finished the letter, Chamberlain gave it to one of his staff members and ordered that it be delivered post haste.

He then went out among the men, congratulating them on a job well done and making sure the wounded were being cared for. Into the early morning hours, even though he was in pain and tired, Chamberlain comforted the dying by writing one last letter home for them. Some passed before the short messages of love and reassurances could even be completed.

Finally, Chamberlain laid himself down. His head again filled with visions of his children and Fanny, as was usual just before he slept. His heart ached to see them again. As he thought of his family, there was no way the college professor from Maine could have possibly known that the next morning would begin the final march toward the steps of Appomattox Court House, and the end of the American Civil War.

CHAPTER 11

APPOMATTOX

The humiliating defeat at Five Forks spoiled any chances of Lee successfully defending Petersburg, much less Richmond to the north. His only chance at survival was to withdraw his Army of Northern Virginia westward to Appomattox Station, where he could resupply and feed his men at a supply depot there. He would then have to find a way to join General Joseph E. Johnston's Army of Tennessee. Johnston had a force of about 20,000 men in North Carolina, and Lee's army was still almost 60,000 strong. But the Confederate commander knew he still faced overwhelming odds at Petersburg, and his army would suffer devastating casualties if he stayed to fight there.

Grant began his final assault on Petersburg before dawn on April 2nd. Sheridan's orders were to cut off Lee's escape and make sure he didn't reach Johnston. Sheridan was given General Edward O.C. Ord's Army of the James and the 6th Corps of the Army of the Potomac to perform his mission.

Sheridan and his cavalry shot out ahead of the infantry, and spent several days capturing Rebel soldiers who had fallen behind their units. When not taking prisoners, his men destroyed everything they found that the Confederates could use as food or shelter.

Chamberlain took his two brigades of the 1st Division across the Southside Railroad on the 2nd, and captured the last Rebel train fleeing Richmond. A small Confederate force tried to defend the railroad later in the afternoon, but they were easily defeated by Chamberlain and General Edgar Gregory's brigade.

On April 3rd, the wire dispatches reported that Grant and Meade had moved into Petersburg and Lee was on the run to the west. Rumors that Richmond was also being evacuated were especially motivating to the men. Chamberlain and the rest of the corps marched over sixty miles during the next two days, fueled by the realistic idea the war might soon be over.

Early in the evening of April 4th, the men were placed in a defensive line across the Danville Railroad at Jetersville, Virginia. Believing they had outrun Lee and were about to intercept him if he turned south, the Federals prepared for one final stand. The next day the 2nd and 6th Corps arrived, and the Army of the Potomac was again assembled together. With the massive gathering of troops, Chamberlain was ordered to leave his division with his brigade commanders, and spend the day assisting Sheridan's cavalry with escorting prisoners back to the main Union line.

Lee was spotted marching across the Federal's left flank the next morning. Sheridan sent his cavalry and the 2nd and 6th Corps in pursuit. Chamberlain and the 5th Corps were to follow the movement of the other two corps from the south, and intercept a possible escape by the Confederates. The armies met at Saylor's Creek and, once again, the Rebels were crushed. By the end of the day over 5000 prisoners had been taken, and over 200 supply wagons had been captured by the Federal Army. Lee's army was left barely alive and was fleeing desperately toward Appomattox Station, where a supply train was scheduled to be waiting for them.

The Great Rebellion was coming down to a foot race and everyone knew it. Sheridan dashed ahead again with his cavalry as the infantry followed slowly behind. The two huge Union armies marched all day the 7th and 8th, finally stopping at midnight. Chamberlain was just drifting off to sleep when a staff officer holding a lantern shook his arm gently and handed him a message. Chamberlain sat up and read the note to himself. It was from Sheridan to all infantry commanders.

I have cut across the enemy at Appomattox Station, and captured three of his trains. If you can possibly push your infantry up here tonight, we will have a great result in the morning.

Sheridan

Chamberlain scrambled to his feet amid the sudden commotion of officers shouting orders and bugles trumpeting. The men were slow to rise, so Chamberlain ran among them saying, "Sheridan has them trapped a few miles from here! Let's go finish it boys!"

That explanation for the interruption of their slumber was enough to bring them to their feet. Within minutes the blue mass had fallen into columns and was again on the march. Chamberlain's two brigades were near the middle of the column, wearily staggering toward the sound of distant cannon and small arms fire. As the sky began to turn orange with morning, the men could hear the distinct pitch difference in the rifle fire being exchanged. One side was firing carbines, the other infantry muskets. The carbines had to belong to Sheridan's cavalrymen.

As the infantry continued forward, a cavalry officer suddenly darted out of the woods. He rode up to Chamberlain, in search of the nearest commanding officer.

"General, do you command this column?" he asked.

"Two brigades of it, sir," Chamberlain answered. "We are the First Division of the Fifth Corps."

"Sir, General Sheridan wishes you to break off from this column and come to his support. The Rebel infantry is pressing him hard and our men are falling back. Don't wait for orders through the regular channels, but act on this at once."

"Where does he need us?" Chamberlain asked.

"Straight north of here, sir."

"Good. Now go back to Sheridan and tell him General Chamberlain is on his way."

The two men separated and Chamberlain ordered his men to fall out on the side of the road. He quickly advised his officers that they were leaving the larger formation to assist a cavalry unit in need of support. He then rushed his men northward through the trees at the double quick.

About a quarter mile later the woods gave way to a wide open field. Chamberlain pulled his men up to the edge of the tree line and rode out to meet Sheridan, who was watching the battle from the top of a gentle slope. Before Chamberlain could reach the general, Sheridan turned around and spotted him. Sheridan pointed toward a thinning line of blue cavalrymen who were facing an enemy force much greater than theirs. Chamberlain nodded that he understood and returned to his brigades.

He called the men up into two battle lines and positioned his artillery to their right. Chamberlain's battery then began hurling shells into the Confederates. The Rebels pulled back from the Union cavalry position and turned to face Chamberlain's two brigades that stood ominously along the crest of a grass covered hill.

Griffin rode up to Chamberlain as he directed artillery fire on horseback.

"General Chamberlain," Griffin began with a smirk on his face. "Would you care to explain to me how you managed to bypass half the entire Army of the Potomac and find yourself already in a fight?"

"I received special orders, sir, and the order specifically stated I was to act immediately. I apologize if our action has caused a problem." Chamberlain grinned, as did his commander.

Griffin knew that he had been summoned by Sheridan, and was glad that Chamberlain had taken the initiative to advance before asking for the orders to be confirmed.

"How many do you think are out there," Chamberlain asked, referring to the enemy line directly in front of him.

"Maybe forty thousand," Griffin answered

"That looks like another battle flag coming around the ridge there," Chamberlain said.

Griffin raised his field glasses to his eyes and grinned. "You're getting old, Professor. That's no Rebel flag. That's a blossoming peach tree."

Chamberlain took the glasses and held them up to his eyes. Sure enough, it was a beautiful lone orange and red tree.

"I'm a bit nearsighted, sir," Chamberlain excused himself. "I'm not much accustomed to this long distance fighting either."

"Whatever you say, my friend."

Chamberlain smiled as Griffin rode away. He then walked back to his battery and pulled his artillery commander to the side.

"Do you see that brightly colored redish thing out there, Captain?" Chamberlain asked and pointed below to the ridge line.

"You mean that peach tree, sir?" the captain responded.

"That is all."

"What?"

"Get back to your business, Captain."

"But..."

"But nothing."

"Yes, sir," the confused officer replied and walked back to his post.

Chamberlain ordered his cannons to continue as more Union divisions formed on the field. Lee's army was indeed trapped, and desperately trying to repositioning itself for one final stand. Custer soon appeared with his cavalry behind him, each horseman with his saber ready in hand. The vision of the dashing young general with his long golden locks flailing in the air from beneath his forage cap mesmerized Chamberlain. He had, himself, reached a point where he hungered to lead men into battle. But the aura Custer radiated as he galloped back-and-forth along the field, showed just how much the twenty-six-year-old absolutely loved it.

Chamberlain surveyed the vast blue legion that continued to grow all around him, and then gazed across the field at the remnants of what was once a great Rebel army. *This will be the end,* he thought to himself.

Chamberlain rode out to his right flank and called his men into formation. Bugle calls and officers shouting orders echoed across the rolling countryside. Chamberlain stood at the front of his battle-ready men, waiting for the command to finish Robert E. Lee's Army of North Virginia. As he sat atop his war-torn Charlemagne, with the 5th Corps colors flapping by his side, he noticed a Confederate soldier on horseback break from the Confederate line.

Chamberlain grabbed his field glasses and focused on the lone gray rider who was galloping toward him. Through his glasses he could see that the man was holding a broken guidon with a torn piece of white sheet tied to the top of it. Chamberlain ordered his men not to shoot and allowed the enemy soldier to ride up to his position. Chamberlain was obviously the officer in command of that part of the line, and the Rebel slowed his horse as he approached him.

The soldier was a young Confederate major who saluted Chamberlain confidently and said, "Sir, I am from General Gordon. General Lee desires a cessation of hostilities until he can hear from General Grant as to the proposed surrender."

The war is over. Chamberlain could feel his heart beating in his chest.

"Sir, that matter exceeds my authority," Chamberlain answered calmly, trying to mask his relief. "I will send your message to my superior. General Lee is right. He can do no more."

Chamberlain dismounted and asked the enemy soldier to join him. As the two men spoke about the condition of the Confederate force, two more riders galloped up to them. One was a Confederate officer, the other a Union cavalry colonel from Custer's staff.

"This is the end, General!" The colonel said, unable to contain his exuberance. "It's unconditional surrender! I just came from Gordon and Longstreet's camp. Gordon says 'For God's sake, stop this infantry or hell will be to pay!' I'll go get Sheridan."

"Go then, immediately," Chamberlain ordered. "I'll hold my brigades here and order my cannons to cease firing."

The colonel sped off with the two Confederate officers to notify General Sheridan of the request for surrender terms. Chamberlain rode over to his artillery battery and promptly ordered them to stop firing into the enemy lines. He wanted to make sure that not one more life was lost, on either side. Unfortunately, just as he left his infantry, a Confederate shell slammed into the ground in front of his line, killing a lieutenant from the 185th New York. He would be the last soldier of the Army of the Potomac to fall during the Civil War.

Chamberlain waited until his cannons were silent and then rode back to his brigades. The men knew that the Rebels wanted to quit, but the question on their minds was what would Grant's terms be. Chamberlain kept his men in formation and calm. He feared that premature celebrations would get out of control. Finally, a staff officer from Grant's headquarters rode up to Chamberlain and announced there was to be a formal cease fire until 1 p.m.

The men in the front ranks heard the verbal order and began to cheer. Their joy spread through the ranks, and soon kepis were flying, men were embracing, and songs of home were being sung. Chamberlain dared not stifle their rejoicing. He only wished he were in less a position of authority so he could join them.

Shortly thereafter Colonel Gregory rode up to Chamberlain with a look of astonishment on his face. "What is the reason for this madness?" he asked.

"Only that Lee wants to surrender," Chamberlain answered matter-of-factly.

"Glory to God!" Gregory bellowed, and grabbed Chamberlain's hand with such force it nearly knocked him off his horse.

"Yes, and on earth peace and goodwill toward men," Chamberlain added.

The morning hours passed with the men seated in the shade of the tree line, talking about their future plans and debating over the future of the South. The men had been on their feet for almost thirty-six hours, but the monumental events of the day prevented them from napping.

One o'clock passed, and Griffin ordered Chamberlain to prepare his brigades for an attack. Chamberlain reluctantly obeyed the order, believing the negotiations had possibly stalled and Grant simply wanted to send the message he was willing to finish the Rebels there at Appomattox. Chamberlain understood the art of posturing, and hoped that his call back to arms was nothing more than just that.

The men formed back into two long battle lines and waited solemnly for orders. Every soldier in the Federal Army had assumed that the war was over, and now they were poised to go right back into a fight. Except this battle would be a one-sided slaughter. The reality of the situation cast a dark and eerie quiet over the great Union force.

Chamberlain closed his eyes and prayed for God to give the leaders of both armies the wisdom to end the killing on this Palm Sunday. At the end of his prayer he opened his eyes and felt a strange presence, as though his request had been received. The sensation gave him goose bumps, and he wheeled around expecting to see that some heavenly manifestation of peace had arrived on the field.

Chamberlain was at first startled by the epiphany he saw slowly moving between his lines. But the sad expression on the ghost's face was peaceful and far from threatening. Chamberlain studied the lone horseman in flawless Confederate officer's dress, superbly mounted on a lightly spotted stallion. His noble posture though, was lost in his heavy eyes and tightened lips. The angelic white-bearded figure, who at first glance appeared to be an angel of God, was none other than Confederate General, Robert E. Lee.

Chamberlain and his men watched the Rebel commander with awe as he passed silently through their line. He somehow appeared unaware, or possibly just unconcerned that he was passing through crowds of gawking enemy soldiers. No words were spoken- no acknowledgments exchanged.

A few moments later, from the left of their line, another lone rider slowly made his way to the rear of the Union position. This horseman was immediately recognized by the Federal troops. His partially unbuttoned blue coat, weathered slouch hat, and muddy knee-high boots would never be recognized by a stranger as the attire of a general. But the row of stars on his shoulders was certain indicators of his power. Lieutenant General Ulysses Grant was himself tired of war, and not at all concerned with his appearance. His thoughts were instead centered on the task at hand; the surrender of the Confederate Army.

The two Commanders met in a modest three-storey brick home at Appomattox Court House. Ironically the home owner, Wilber McClean, had moved to Appomattox to get away from the war after having previously lived in a home that became a command post during the battles at Manassas. The rest of Appomattox was nothing more than a small Virginia village with a county courthouse, jail, general store, and tavern.

At 4 o'clock, the general's conference ended and the two leaders parted once more. Word spread quickly that Lee had signed a formal surrender, and the next few days would mean little more than keeping the peace.

Meade instructed his staff to go out among the different commands and pass the order that boisterous festivities should be kept to a minimum. It was imperative that the beaten Rebels not be subjected to having to listen to their victor's celebrations. The Union men were to show compassion during the volatile few days the two great armies still faced each other. Meade wanted no chance of his Federal Army's behavior being misconceived by the Confederates as rubbing their nose in their defeat.

Chamberlain received the notice and permitted his men to celebrate as long as not a shot was fired into the air, or a harsh word was spoken about the Southerners. His guidelines were adhered to without a single unruly incident. Several of his men even asked if they could go out and meet some of the Rebels. Chamberlain told them they could, but to go with caution as some may not have been so willing to surrender as their leaders had been.

Chamberlain also ordered for a tent to be constructed for a command post, assuming his brigades would be stationary for a few days. He then sat inside and wrote a letter to Fanny while his men entertained themselves outside. Later in the evening he was summoned to the courthouse building where a committee of hand-selected officers was arranging the logistics of the formal surrender.

Chamberlain walked inside and saw Griffin leaning over a large table that had several other generals seated around it, three of whom were Confederate. One of the seated generals cleared his throat when he noticed Chamberlain standing in the doorway, signaling an unauthorized party was in their presence. The room fell silent and Griffin turned to see what had caused it.

"It is Chamberlain," he told the group, and they went back to their meeting as if he had been expected.

Griffin then walked over to his 1st Division commander. Chamberlain tried to salute him, but Griffin impatiently took hold of his arm and escorted him to the hallway.

"Is something the matter, sir?" Chamberlain asked.

Griffin squared off in front of him and studied his eyes. The glare was intimidating, and made the subordinate general very uncomfortable.

"Have I done something wrong, sir?" Chamberlain asked.

"No," Griffin mumbled, and continued his stare as if trying to see into Chamberlain's mind. He had to take one last look into his general's eyes before he could be sure the Maine volunteer was the right man for the assignment he was about to be given.

"Those Confederates in there are Longstreet, Gordon, and Pendleton," Griffin said. "We're making plans to get their men parole papers and some food. Their whole damn army is near starving to death."

Chamberlain nodded that he understood. He assumed he was about to get some mundane chore of supervising ration distribution or something similar.

"Part of the surrender agreement is that their infantry has to formally hand over their flags and arms," Griffin continued. "Grant wants the 5th Corps to receive that part of the surrender."

Chamberlain extended his right hand to congratulate his commander on having been assigned such a glorious honor. Griffin took his hand and firmly held it.

"We want you to do it," Griffin said and released his grasp.

"What exactly is that, sir?" Chamberlain asked with a puzzled frown.

"General Grant and I would like to bestow the honor to you, General Chamberlain. We want you to be the officer who accepts the Confederate infantry surrender."

"But, General," Chamberlain stammered nervously, " I'm uh..." the words wouldn't come to him.

"You deserve to have a page in the history of this war, Lawrence. This is our way to guarantee it."

"And this comes from General Grant?"

"When he gave the assignment to the 5th Corps, I suggested it and he heartily agreed."

"Sir, I would not be comfortable taking this noble task from your hands," Chamberlain submitted graciously.

"Nonsense," Griffin said. "It is I who would think lesser of myself, knowing a man of your caliber was lost in the ranks behind me as I pretended to be worthy of such a gesture. You will do it, and that is that."

Chamberlain looked down at his dirty boots for a moment and thought. If he was to accept such a privilege, he wanted his old regiment, the 20th Maine, a part of it.

"May I transfer back to the 3rd Brigade and have my old regiment at my side?" he asked.

"Consider it done," Griffin answered. He pulled a cigar out of his breast pocket and handed it to Chamberlain. "Go now and enjoy this historic evening."

Chamberlain took the cigar and swept it under his nose. "I wish I had a couple hundred of these to take back to the boys."

"You'd want to see General Grant about that. He might just have them."

"I believe he would," Chamberlain said casually. Grant was reputed to have a cigar in his mouth the second he rose up in the morning, to his last conscious breath at night.

"Really," Griffin answered seriously. "While he was stuck in Petersburg, people up North were sending him cigars by the case.

I've personally seen him throw boxes out by the bushel when they dried up because he wasn't able to smoke them fast enough."

"Do you think I might be able to get into some of those reserves?" Chamberlain asked.

"How many do you want?"

"Whatever you can get me."

"Alright, let me send someone over and see what I can do," Griffin answered.

The two men shook hands and Chamberlain departed after a final salute. He then returned to his tent and finished his letter to his wife, not mentioning the dramatic leading role he had just been given.

Spring showers rained on the field during the next day. Chamberlain discovered a large wooden crate outside his tent when he stepped outside for breakfast, and he dragged it back inside his tent before opening it. His eyes widened at the sight of its contents and he immediately sent for Captain Thomas Chamberlain of the 20th Maine.

When Thomas arrived a short time later, his big brother showed him the crate. Chamberlain then suggested that Thomas find a nice dry spot away from the rest of the 3rd Brigade, and have what was left of the 20th Maine assemble there when it started to get dark.

After a day of meetings and ceremony planning, Chamberlain steered a small supply wagon into a patch of trees where a large group of fellow Mainers were loitering about. The men were surprised to see him, especially steering a wagon without an aide. Chamberlain groaned at the pain in his hip when he hopped down to the ground. Then righting himself, he returned the salutes of the men.

"How have you boys been?" he asked with a carefree smile.

A chorus of answers came back to him.

"Well, I met with General Grant yesterday," Chamberlain said sheepishly, making no effort to conceal the fact that he was making up a story. "He asked me, 'Lawrence', he calls me that by the way. Well he says 'Lawrence, who should I have standing at the front when those Rebel boys come marching down that road to surrender their colors.' I answered that the Twentieth Maine would be my personal choice. He said, 'Why do you say that?' I answered that those Twentieth Maine men were the hardest fighters I'd even seen, and they're a damn fine looking bunch, too."

The men laughed and cheered.

"Then what did he say, General!" one of the men shouted.

"He replied, 'That's just the ingredients I need. So you ride on out and tell them they have the job'."

The men cheered again.

"He also told me to bring these out with me!" Chamberlain yelled over the hollering men and pulled the top off of the wooden case. "Just in case you needed convincing!"

The back of the wagon was swarmed and a crate full of cigars was quickly emptied. Chamberlain only stayed with the men long enough for them to get their smokes lit, knowing that their language and demeanor was controlled with his presence. He wanted to provide them the space to relax and not worry about offending the general, even if he was one of them.

All day the 10th and 11th, both camps welcomed visitors from the other side, as long as their intentions were of fellowship and not animosity. Few of the Union men held any grudge against their beaten foe, but much of the Confederate ranks were still distraught over their loss. The sight of their remaining caissons and artillery pieces being wheeled to the Federal line was especially depressing.

The goodwill of the Federal enlisted men was marred though, by the rumors that Sheridan and his favorite general, Custer, were being rude and condescending to Confederate officers. This apparent breach in etiquette only added to the anxiety of the Confederate soldiers, who wondered what humiliation might have to be endured when they marched into Appomattox and surrendered their guns and flags. Confederate Generals Longstreet and Gordon knew of Chamberlain's reputation on the field as a ruthless fighter, but had no idea of his personality away from battle. They only hoped he didn't share the same cocky arrogance of Sheridan and Custer.

❦

On the morning of April 12, exactly four years after the beginning of the fateful assault on Fort Sumter, Chamberlain assembled his sea of blue-coated men along the Richmond-Lynchburg Stage Road. The long Union line stretched from a white farmhouse east of the village, to the McClean house on the west side of the tiny town. Chamberlain positioned himself at the right of his line, his 3rd Brigade proudly standing behind him.

At 9 a.m., a jagged column of tattered infantrymen slowly wove its way down the country road toward their conquerors. A lone Confederate general riding at the front, swayed glumly with each step of his horse. Behind him were the disheartened and heavy spirited souls of the South. As the reluctant Rebel's grew closer, the battered condition of their regimental flags and the infamous Stars and Bars battle flag was visible. Most of the men were noticeably malnourished and dressed in filthy rags. Few were in uniform-at least half were shoe-less. Their condition proved they were truly a beaten force, even their colors reflected it.

Lee had selected General John B. Gordon to represent his army in the grim ceremony. Gordon and Chamberlain had much in com-mon, but didn't know it. Both were college educated volunteers be-fore the war, who quickly rose to the rank of general. Both had recovered from suspected mortal wounds, Gordon having been shot five times in the Bloody Lane at Antietam. The two men would later become governors of their home states and both even had wives named Fanny.

Chamberlain studied his Confederate counterpart, who slowly directed his horse to the awaiting Union Commander. Chamberlain couldn't help but feel sympathy for the man. *What a terrible assignment he has been given.* Gordon was clearly struggling to maintain his stat-ure. His cold eyes starred almost lifelessly into some distant place. His face was etched with shame and hopelessness.

Chamberlain waited until the Confederate leader was only a few feet from him, then he turned and gave a quiet command.

The 1st Division's bugler broke the silence with a call for the marching salute, and the Union ranks began a long succession of men snapping their muskets to carry arms. The symbolic repositioning of the rifles took almost an entire minute to complete before it reached the final company assembled at the other end of the line.

Gordon raised his head in confusion and then realized the chival-rous gesture being bestowed to his men. He wheeled his horse to the front of Chamberlain and with a kick of his spurs, reared the beast up into the air. When the horse's head came back down in a graceful bow, Gordon swung the tip of his saber down to the toe of his boot. Without a pause, the horse rose up and Gordon turned to his column, ordering them also to the carry arms position.

The significance of that singular moment would never be lost on the men present at Appomattox Court House. They had done everything they could to destroy each other for the past four years, and it was ending with a mutual gesture of respect.

Gordon then proceeded forward with his head held high, leading what remained of the Confederacy into the gauntlet of the Union Army. When his line was in position, he turned them to face the Federal soldiers and ordered his men to stack their muskets.

Men on both sides of the line wept, some with joy, some despair, some not having any idea why. Next came the surrender of the Rebel flags, something Chamberlain personally felt unnecessary, but was ordered to carry out. While the faded and torn banners were being neatly folded, some of the Confederates broke from their ranks to touch their glorious symbols one last time.

Before one of the colors was handed to a group of staff officers standing next to Chamberlain's horse, the Rebel soldier delivering it told them, "Boys, this is not the first time you've seen this flag. I have borne it in the front of battle on many a victorious field, and I would rather die than surrender it to you."

Chamberlain overheard the comment and leaned down to the shoeless warrior. "My brave fellow, I admire your noble spirit and only regret that I have not the authority to bid you keep your flag and carry it home as a precious heirloom."

The soldier's eyes welled with tears. He embraced the folded cloth, touched his lips to it, and then handed the cherished symbol to Chamberlain.

The ceremony was over before the magnitude of it could be understood. There were no cheers, nor were there any violent outbursts on the cloudy Wednesday morning; only a sad and quiet act of submission by a defeated army.

Chamberlain dismissed his men after the last Confederate regiment marched from their line. The Federals then scattered back into the village to drink in the tavern and celebrate. But Chamberlain stayed on the now hallowed ground alone after biding his staff to also leave him. There, he absorbed the moment and watched the ravaged Rebel columns trudge away, every Southern man's shoulders slumped and head bowed to the ground.

Chamberlain wondered what the men would be returning to. Almost the entire war had been fought on their soil. Most of their factories and homes had been burned to the ground, their shops and farms looted and pillaged. Now millions of slaves would be released into their communities, and they would expect the same rights and privileges as a white man. And some would want revenge.

Chamberlain knew the war wasn't over for the South. Even with the support of Northern money and reconstruction efforts, there would still be unbridled hatred toward the Yankees. For Chamberlain though, it was over. He was a volunteer and not a professional soldier. The war had provided him the opportunity to play a role in saving his country, and for that he would be able to carry himself with dignity and self-respect for the rest of his life.

As he watched the last Rebel soldier disappear over the horizon, his heart warmed and he found solace in the idea that not another American would perish in the great American Civil War.

ᗧᖇ

Two days later, on April 14, 1865, another leader of the Union Army was thinking those very same thoughts as he daydreamed in his box seat at the Ford Theater in the nation's capital. That great man would not survive the assassin's bullet about to be fired into him. And he would, tragically, never witness the rebirth of his country as his great volunteer officer from Maine would.

When Chamberlain read the news of President Lincoln's death, he thought of the time just after the battle at Antietam, when the President had visited McClellan's headquarters in the field. Chamberlain remembered how melancholy the President appeared to be, even though they had just won a supposed great victory. He could only hope that Lincoln had experienced at least one day of comfort before his final breath.

That night, Chamberlain lay in his tent and dreamed he was standing on the edge of his father's pasture in Maine, feeding his old horse Prince an apple from his hand. The field was covered with a lush blanket of spring grass, and next to him, the leaves of a towering maple tree lazily danced in the air. As he closed his eyes to smell the season, a gentle gravelly voice called his name. Chamberlain turned to find President Lincoln walking toward him.

"I hope you've been keeping him up, General," Lincoln said as he reached Chamberlain's side. The President smiled and began to stroke Prince's thick muscular shoulder.

"He's good as new," Chamberlain answered.

"I've been waiting a long time for this, Lawrence," the President said warmly. His tone was as if he and Chamberlain were old acquaintances and their meeting had been anticipated.

"I know, sir."

"Is he ready?"

"He's just been waiting for you, sir," Chamberlain answered.

The President removed his stove-top hat and peeled his black suit coat from his shoulders.

"You can keep these old things," he said, finishing with the removal of his tie. "I'm tired of wearing this costume, anyway."

Chamberlain handed Lincoln the leather reigns and took the discarded clothing items from the President. Prince wasn't fitted with a saddle, so Chamberlain carefully folded the President's jacket, placed it on the ground with the tie and hat, and moved forward to offer the Commander in Chief a boost onto his mount. Lincoln nodded his thanks and stepped into Chamberlain's cupped hands. The President then stepped up and swung his right leg over the majestic white stallion's back.

"It's beautiful up here, Lawrence, just beautiful."

Chamberlain sensed that Lincoln was talking more about the freedom he was experiencing, and not so much the beautiful kelly-green landscape.

After a moment of smelling the air and sensing the breeze on his face, Lincoln looked back down at Chamberlain. "I thank you, sir."

"You are welcome, Mr. President," Chamberlain answered humbly.

With that final exchange, Lincoln gingerly nudged at Princes haunches, and the two slowly disappeared into the gently rolling hills of Northern Maine.

EPILOGUE

Joshua Lawrence Chamberlain returned to Bowdoin College soon after the war and resumed his position as Professor of Rhetoric and Oratory. Unfortunately for the school, the retired volunteer general had outgrown his desire to simply teach for the rest of his life and he quickly grew anxious. Much of his anxiety to move on could be attributed to struggles within his family, and a subsequent desire by Chamberlain to preoccupy himself with more work.

His fifth child, Gertrude Loraine, passed away before her first birthday, which was within weeks of Chamberlain's return from the war. Chamberlain had a special place in his heart for Gertrude, partly because she was the result of a passionate visit home during the war, and also because Chamberlain's battle wound had left him unable to father more children. The death of a third child also wore heavily on Mrs. Chamberlain.

Immediately upon his return to Maine, Chamberlain's celebrity status, which was now widely known throughout the state, exposed him to suggestions of running for public office. Chamberlain was at first reluctant, but eventually succumbed to the idea that he would make a good political leader.

Because he was so well-known, and his great reputation was based on his ability to lead, Chamberlain was solicited to run for governor. His support came from the relatively new Republican Party, which needed a strong candidate to replace the current governor, Samuel Coney, who was relinquishing his position at the end of his term.

After winning his own party's nomination, Chamberlain was pitted against a wealthy newspaperman from Augusta named Eben Pillsbury. Pillsbury had been an outspoken critique of Lincoln and the war, and his opinions were widely known due to his splattering them all over his newspaper.

Had the war been lost or was still in progress, Pillsbury might have had a chance. But the war had been won and Lincoln was being hailed throughout the North and some of the South as a martyred hero. Add to that stack of odds an opponent who was a still very much alive war hero, and the writing was on the wall. Chamberlain won the election by the largest majority vote ever polled in the state up to that time. In early January of 1867, Chamberlain became the 12th Governor of the Great State of Maine.

He quickly gained a reputation as being firm in his ideals, yet both fair and patient with his constituents and rivals in the State Legislature. Elections were held annually in those days and Chamberlain was subsequently reelected four times. He left the office at the end of 1871, only after having grown tired of the constant battles over capital punishment, prohibition, and political gamesmanship in general.

Following his career as Governor, Chamberlain returned to Bowdoin College, this time as the school's president. He immediately began instituting radical changes in the curriculum, including the addition of science and engineering classes, and the introduction of mandatory military drill. His idea of drilling the students stemmed from his idea that a great crisis occurred sometime in every generation. Chamberlain's goal with the new program, which was similar to today's Reserve Officer Training Corps or R.O.T.C., was to provide his young men with basic leadership skills so they could step into a volunteer military position if needed, just as he had done. Chamberlain also cut the amount of time the students were required to spend in formal prayer, and changed the foreign language requirements from Greek and Latin, to French and German.

The sweeping changes he made were accepted, some reluctantly at first. But nearly every revolutionary change he made eventually ran into insurmountable conflict. Even with an increase in tuition and financial donations, the new programs were draining the school of money. The students even conducted their own revolt of the military drill requirement, and it was abolished in 1879 after several modifications were attempted.

Chamberlain was also the volunteer major general of the state's militia, and in early January of 1880, he almost single-handedly quelled an attempted takeover of the state's governorship. Chamberlain had been ordered to Augusta when a group of Greenback Party members, angry over questionable election results, appeared in the city heavily armed. During the standoff, Chamberlain placed a division outside of town so as not to escalate the uprising by confronting the vigilant mob with his own armed men. Even as he received repeated death threats and thwarted kidnapping attempts, Chamberlain calmly persisted in defusing daily conflicts by standing his ground.

In the most dramatic incident of the revolt, Chamberlain faced an angry gang of men who appeared at the steps of the state capitol, firearms in hand. They sent a staff member into Chamberlain's office with the message that they were there to kill him.

Chamberlain bravely walked out onto the capitol's veranda and calmly addressed the group, dressed in his navy blue officer's coat. "Men, you wish to kill me I hear," he said calmly. "Killing is no new thing to me. I have offered myself to be killed many times, when I no more deserved it then than I do now. Some of you I think were with me in those days.

Chamberlain continued, "You understand what you want, do you? I am here to preserve and honor the peace of this state until the rightful government is seated, whichever it may be, it is not for me to say. But it is for me to see that the laws of this state are put into effect, without fraud, without force, but with calm thought and purpose. I am here for that and I shall do it. If anybody wants to kill me for it, here I am. Let him kill."

Chamberlain is said to have then torn open his jacket, exposing his chest to an assassin's fatal round. It was never fired. Instead, a voice yelled from the crowd, "By God, General, the first man that dares to lay a hand on you, I'll kill him on the spot!"

The crowd then grumbled for a few minutes and walked away. A few days later the Supreme Court handed down a decision, validating a Republican Legislature in the state. Chamberlain was subsequently relieved of his duties and went back home to Brunswick.

In 1883, Chamberlain's lingering acute pain from his old war injuries got the better of him. After a much needed corrective surgery in Boston, and at the insistence of his doctors, he resigned his position and left Bowdoin College.

Chamberlain decided to leave the world of politics and education, and moved to Florida where he formed a land development company with some other investors. He acted as president of the Homosassa Company until 1892, when, after years of struggling, he decided to redirect his business interests and moved to New York City. He then became the president of a business called the New Jersey Construction Company. The goal of that company was to buy up liens, or remove claims from various railroad companies, and then develop their own railroad. Unfortunately, that business also faltered. In all, Chamberlain served as president of a land development company, a railroad development company, a power company, and a bonding company all between 1883 and 1896. During that time he also presided over a new college in New York City called the Institute for Artists and Artisans.

∾

On a blustery August afternoon in 1893, Chamberlain and his family were called to the hallowed halls of the Federal Capitol building in Washington. Fanny, Wyllys who remained single, and Daisy who was married with three daughters, all stood proudly in the chamber's balcony as Chamberlain was called to the front by the Speaker of the House.

A proclamation was read to the congressmen, in it a description of the war hero's great accomplishments during the war. After the document was read, a congressman from Maine stepped forward and read aloud the words on a proclamation he held ceremoniously in front of him.

"For gallantry beyond the call of duty at Little Round Top, Gettysburg, Pennsylvania.

Gentlemen of the Congress, Mr. Speaker, it is with great privilege that I represent you and the Great State of Maine, in awarding the Congressional Medal of Honor to Brigadier General Joshua Lawrence Chamberlain."

The men in the hall stood and gave an ovation as the blue and white ribbon with a bronze eagle clutching a five-pointed star was placed around Chamberlain's neck.

Chamberlain then bowed his head to each section of the round assembly hall, offering his appreciation. When the appropriate acknowledgment to the statesmen was completed, he looked up into the balcony and raised his hand to his family.

The house speaker adjourned the ceremony shortly after the applause subsided and the formalities were ended. Chamberlain was then personally congratulated by each congressman.

The rest of the Chamberlain family made their way down the Capitol building's second floor steps and waited in the large marble lobby. While they stood together reliving the brief ceremony, a smartly-dressed old woman appeared at Wyllys's side.

"Are you General Chamberlain's son?" she asked.

Wyllys was a little puzzled at the inquiry, but didn't feel at all suspicious of the fragile woman.

"Yes," he answered. "I am Harold Wyllys Chamberlain."

The old woman smiled and asked if she could have a private word with him. Wyllys still questioned what was going on, but complied with her request and stepped away from his family.

"My name is Abigail Griffin. My husband was Charles Griffin. He was your father's commander during the war."

"I am so pleased to meet you, Mrs. Griffin," Wyllys said taking her hand. "My father often spoke of your husband." Wyllys knew Griffin had passed away shortly after the war while stationed in Texas and, therefore, didn't enquire about him.

"Well, Charles also often spoke of your father," she answered. "I am sorry to say the business of fighting wars was an unpleasant topic to me, and I gave little attention to my husband when he spoke of it. But he did mention a General Chamberlain quite often and always fondly."

"I appreciate your kind words ma'am. I shall relay them to my father as soon as he can free himself from his audience. Would you like to meet him?"

"Oh, I'm not here for your father, sir," Mrs. Griffin said. "I am here to see you."

She then reached into a small beaded purse and removed a folded piece of paper. The note was brown with age, but still intact. She handed it to Wyllys and gestured for him to open it.

Wyllys took the paper and slowly unfolded it, careful not to crack its fragile creases. When it was opened he began to read the handwritten message.

His eyes widened as he finished the short letter. They then began to tear as he read it a second time and realized its significance. Wyllys had been raised around constant references to his father's heroism during the war, and the stories had become fairytale legend to him. But now all of his father's almost unimaginable feats of courage had somehow been confirmed with the short message written so many years before.

Mrs. Griffin saw Wylly's reaction and explained how she had come upon the note. "My husband sent that letter to me back in eighteen sixty-four, and I was supposed to forward it to you in Maine. Charles didn't tell me what it was and I didn't open it until a few years ago. I do remember that my husband sent a wire to me the day after I received it, saying I should refrain from forwarding it to you as he had originally instructed. I just put it in a hat box and there it sat for almost twenty-five years. I found it while I was getting rid of some old things and decided to keep it, simply because it was written by my dear Charles. Then I saw in the papers that a man named Joshua Chamberlain was being awarded the Medal of Honor for heroism during the war. I remembered that name Chamberlain, and read the letter again. I just knew the man getting the medal and the man in the note were the same. Well, I did some checking, and discovered that this man Joshua Chamberlain did, in fact, have a son named Wyllys. I knew right then and there that the letter needed to be delivered to whom it was intended, even if it was written all those years ago."

Wyllys had to clear his throat before he could thank Mrs. Griffin. When he did get the words out, his voice cracked with emotion. Mrs. Griffin responded by taking Wyllys' hand.

"I hope you're proud of your father, young man. My husband certainly was."

The old woman then gave Wyllys a warm wrinkled smile and squeezed his hand. The two gazed into each other's eyes as the words from the letter replayed in their heads.

June 18, 1864

Dear Wyllys Chamberlain,

It is with the heaviest burden on my heart that I must inform you of your father's death. I was with him in his last moments, and his final thoughts were that I write you of his actions here in Petersburg, Virginia. Know that your father received his mortal wound while leading his men in a magnificent charge on an enemy position. Know also that his gallant display saved the lives of men, who might have otherwise perished during a lesser officer's retreat. A more brave officer, I shall never meet. A greater man, I shall never know. If there is a measure of valor, let your father be that standard.

Sincerely,

Brig. General Charles Griffin

Commanding 1ˢᵗ Div. 5ᵗʰ Corps U.S.A.

It is true that Joshua Lawrence Chamberlain received his Medal of Honor in August of 1893, thirty years after the incident for which it was awarded. But the truth is; it was mailed to him.

The truth is also that Chamberlain eventually died from the wounds he received while leading an assault in Petersburg, Virginia, in 1864. The year of his death was 1914, at the age of 85. He is buried next to his beloved Fanny, in a small modest graveyard in Brunswick, Maine.

Made in the USA
Coppell, TX
08 July 2020

30374913R00173